D1617332

Dostoevsky and Soloviev

Dostoevsky and Soloviev

The Art of Integral Vision

Marina Kostalevsky

Yale University Press

New Haven and London

Printed in the United States of America by BookCrafters, Inc., Chelsea, Michigan.

Frontispiece: Dostoevsky (left) and Soloviev in the 1870s

A catalogue record for this book is available from the British Library.

The paper in this book meets the guidelines for permanence and durability of the Committee on Production Guidelines for Book Longevity of the Council on Library Resources.

Library of Congress Cataloging-in-Publication Data

Kostalevsky, Marina.
   Dostoevsky and Soloviev : the art of integral vision / Marina Kostalevsky.
      p. cm.
   Includes bibliographical references and index.
   ISBN 0-300-06096-3 (cloth : alk. paper)
   1. Dostoyevsky, Fyodor, 1821-1881—Philosophy. 2. Dostoyevsky, Fyodor, 1821-1881—Influence. 3. Solovyov, Vladimir Sergeyevich, 1853-1900. I. Title.
PG3328.Z7P5454   1997
891.73′3—dc20   96-44164
                                      CIP

10 9 8 7 6 5 4 3 2 1

Father Alexander Men'
In memoriam

Contents

Preface

The theme of this book first crossed my mind in Moscow, toward the end of the years when official Soviet criticism still used the word *reactionary* to describe both Dostoevsky and Soloviev. At the same time, however, there also existed an unofficial or semiofficial critical school, with which I had the good fortune to come into contact. Mikhail Mikhailovich Bakhtin was one of the remarkable members of this school who made this experience unforgettable. The frequency of my meetings with Bakhtin was in a way determined by his reading list. I had connections with an underground network of Moscow bookdealers, a singular group of people who exhibited a fantastic blend of intellectualism, bohemianism, thirst for profit, and generosity. Through them one could buy or borrow (sometimes just for a night) any kind of literature: books published in Russia before or shortly after the Revolution, books published in the West, and certain recent Soviet editions that one never saw in bookshops. Bakhtin was mainly interested in the second category. I remember bringing him books by Berdiaev, Mikhail Chekhov, Evreinov (Bakhtin was then meditating on theater), and Nabokov. He naturally made me stay for tea, and the two of us would talk.

One morning Mikhail Mikhailovich remarked, "I had a curious dream last night." And he told me of how he had dreamed that he had left his apartment and set off down the street toward the subway station. (I should mention that he could do this only in a dream—he was virtually confined to his armchair.) Suddenly he saw Viacheslav Ivanov coming toward him carrying a loaf of fresh bread. The bread was golden brown and airy, with a wonderful aroma. Bakhtin asked, "Viacheslav Ivanovich, wherever did you buy such a marvelous loaf of bread?" And Ivanov replied, "Didn't you know? Vladimir Soloviev opened a bakery on the corner."

Acknowledgments

With great pleasure and grateful appreciation I acknowledge my debt to a number of people. I want to express my particular gratitude to Robert Louis Jackson, my teacher and friend, who, throughout the development of the book, gave me the invaluable benefits of his exemplary scholarship and enthusiastic encouragement. I give my heartfelt thanks to those who graciously devoted their time to reading my manuscript and following its progress. Louis Dupré read an earlier version and made useful comments accompanied by quiet, contemplative observations. Richard F. Gustafson's genuinely expert guidance led to many corrections and improvements in the text. Nikolai Kotrelev read the first draft and provided me with important suggestions, source references, and the photos for the book. Jaroslav Pelikan, with his superb generosity, has been the guardian of this book since his reading of the first draft, and I hope the final version reflects the brilliance of his ideas. Vasily Rudich, my intellectual companion for many years, read my manuscript several times, demonstrating once again his unfailing willingness to discuss my work and to make insightful recommendations. Tomas

Venclova, upon reading the first draft, offered his helpful advice, based, as usual, on his erudition, intuition, and honesty.

I am indebted to Paul Bushkovitch and Caryl Emerson for their comments on certain parts of the book. I am grateful in many ways to Svetlana Evdokimova, Vladimir Golstein, Olga R. Hughes, Rita Lipson and the late Leon Lipson, Gary Saul Morson, Alexander Schenker, and Edward Stankiewicz. My special thanks to my dear friends Roza Gevenman and the late Iosif Kunin, for whom Russian culture was never a concept but a biographical fact; to Anatoly Shchukin and Mikhail Utevsky, indispensable partners of distant dialogues in Moscow; to my selfless mother, Alexandra Blinder; to my son, Joseph, for his philosophical attitude; and to my husband, Igor Frenkel, for his unlimited support, intellectual inspiration, and uncompromising persistence in achieving mathematical precision for my formulations. I am also grateful to Ralph Burr, Jr., and Robert Bird for dealing with the deficiencies of my English; the latter kindly extended his assistance by making useful suggestions. Thanks to Jonathan Brent for being my wonderful editor; to Cynthia Wells and Harry Haskell for their editorial expertise and patience; and to the staff of Yale University Press. Finally, with everlasting gratitude, I wish to remember David Blinder, Iosif Kostalevsky, Yuri Seliverstov, and Mikhail Mikhailovich Bakhtin.

Introduction

In Search of Unity

The mind by its very nature strives for unity, but unfortunately up to now men
still have not truly understood in what the real unity of things consists.
—Peter Chaadaev

Nikolai Berdiaev once said: "So great is the worth of Dostoevsky that to have produced him is by itself sufficient justification for the existence of the Russian nation in the world." In the West Dostoevsky is, in a sense, if not the justification at least the convincing proof of Russia's existence. He is often associated with Russia in much the same way that the kangaroo represents Australia (if you will pardon the comparison). Of course, for the educated reader Dostoevsky is more than a name. Besides the countless editions of his works, there exists a vast literature on him, ranging from scholarly monographs to fictional treatments in which he appears as a character. Somewhere in the middle lies a special literary stratum: essays and utterances on Dostoevsky by practically every major writer of the twentieth century.

Up to now, however, in the West as well as in Russia, certain aspects of his life and art have not been sufficiently clarified. The first goal of this study is to examine one such aspect: the relationship and interaction of Dostoevsky with his younger contemporary, his "follower and teacher," Vladimir Soloviev.[1] Dostoevsky and Soloviev struck up a friendship during the final decade of Dostoevsky's life. Soloviev's thought and personality are directly reflected in *The Brothers Karamazov*. Yet the nature of their affinity for each other cannot be grasped simply by studying the text of Dostoevsky's last novel; it has to be viewed within the context of the entire legacy of both writers and the historical and philosophical ambience of the times.

The second aim of my book is to shorten the distance between the English-speaking reader and the great Russian philosopher Vladimir Soloviev. Soloviev's significance in the history of Russian thought was succinctly stated by his friend, the philosopher Lev Lopatin: "Soloviev was the first truly original Russian philosopher, just as Pushkin was the first national Russian poet."[2] The philosophical and historical issues raised by Soloviev prophetically anticipated the spiritual, intellectual, and political crises that humankind encountered in the twentieth century. Some of his worst fears have been realized, from the rationalization of the modern consciousness and instability of religious and moral values to the present-day events in the Balkans and the alarming state of the environment. What Soloviev was saying on the threshold of the twentieth century remains highly relevant on the threshold of the twenty-first. Moreover, for the Russian intelligentsia of our day the name Soloviev signifies not only one of the giants of Russian culture but also a spiritual and intellectual choice. It is a watchword by which kindred spirits recognize one another. It is impossible to understand the concerns of philosophically oriented minds in today's Russia (and the Russian mind by its very nature tends to philosophize) without examining Soloviev's legacy.

My third task was to offer some revisions regarding the history of the literary critical tradition about Dostoevsky. If most Western literature on Dostoevsky can be broken down into either the scholarly or the essayistic genre, a significant portion of Russian literary criticism followed Soloviev, who arrived at religious and philosophical interpretations of Dostoevsky's work and charted a synthetic method based upon the linkage of literary theories and philological analysis with philosophical arguments and creative speculations. But Soloviev's critical method has itself only recently begun to attract the attention of specialists and requires further study and appraisal.

Any comparative study is fraught with the double danger of overemphasizing either the resemblances or the disparities of what is being compared.

When discussing Soloviev and Dostoevsky, it is perhaps harder to resist the temptation of placing more weight on their affinities than on their differences, since the former evidently transcend the latter. Yet their differences, however small, played a significant role in their mutual understanding during the years of their personal acquaintance and, in particular, in Soloviev's attitude toward Dostoevsky after the latter's death. This aspect must unquestionably be taken into account as we attempt to understand the interaction between Dostoevsky and Soloviev. It is an interaction which requires interpretation on three levels: the universal, probing questions of a metaphysical order; the contextual, tying their writings to the state of Russia in the late nineteenth century; and the particular, reflecting the intellectual and spiritual originality of these two brilliant representatives of Russian culture.

The influence of both Dostoevsky and Soloviev on the subsequent development of Russian creative thought is indisputable. Just as it is impossible to imagine modern Russian (and world) literature without Dostoevsky, so it is impossible to imagine Russian philosophy without Soloviev. Yet for these two men the tasks of literature and philosophy so converged that they gave promise of a synthetic unity, particularly in Dostoevsky. For this reason the juxtaposition of the names of Soloviev and Dostoevsky symbolizes not only "the highest achievements of Russian spiritual culture"[3] but also the path of literary-philosophical synthesis that has been followed by most verbal art in the twentieth century, for all its diversity of ideology and method. At the same time, their friendship testifies to the rapprochement that occurred in Russian culture in the latter half of the nineteenth century between philosophical and artistic representations of the idea of unity. For both Soloviev and Dostoevsky, the very concept of unity could be realized only within the parameters of the Christological universe. Unity, in the elder Zosima's simple definition, is unattainable without Christ.[4] Such an understanding not only reflects the viewpoint of Dostoevsky and Soloviev but also derives organically from the Russia's own historical past, in which the urge toward political unity was traditionally linked to (and at times masked by) the religious and spiritual unity of the nation.

THE RUSSIAN WAY

Unity as an idea has, from time immemorial, held a persistent fascination for minds reared against the geopolitical backdrop of the boundless, scattered lands called Russia. Starting with the acclamation of Moscow as the "Third Rome" at the beginning of the sixteenth century and with the centralization of power under Ivan the Terrible, this idea was personified and embodied—in the respective realms of politics and spirituality—by two forces: autocracy and Orthodoxy. (Not until the mid-nineteenth century would the concept of *narodnost'*[5] appear as the last and theoretically most vulnerable component of the famous motto: "pravoslavie, samoderzhavie, narodnost'" [Orthodoxy, autocracy, nationality].) The foundations of both autocracy and Orthodoxy proved, however, far from unshakable. The French Enlightenment, in the peculiar interpretation of Catherine the Great, challenged the strength of an Orthodox Church that had already been weakened by the Schism and the reforms of Peter the Great, while the French Revolution and the American Constitution sowed doubt in Russian minds with respect to the absoluteness of absolutism. The monarchic and Orthodox conception of unity began, in the eyes of some, to appear limited in comparison to the constitutional and pan-Christian formulations of the same idea. One significant factor contributing to undermining the monopoly of these two traditional forces on the hearts and minds of the nobility was the advent of the Russian Enlightenment and the activities of its leader, the Freemason Nikolai Novikov.

Though Masonic lodges first appeared in Russia by the mid-eighteenth century, it was not until the reign of Catherine the Great that they began to acquire any noticeable influence. Both versions of European Freemasonry took root in Russian soil: the rationalistic and deistic, which combined a secular form of religious life with social liberalism; and the mystical, aimed at the achievement of absolute knowledge and absolute morality with the help of the occult sciences. Nikolai Novikov was a representative and advocate of the former. For him, the key to moral and intellectual progress was education. In his essay "On the Dignity of Man in His Relations to God and to the World," published in his own journal *Morning Light (Utrennii svet)* (the first Russian philosophical periodical), Novikov, in harmony with the paradigm of enlightenment, asserts that man has a right to conquer the world by reason. Why? Because reason, the distinct property of humanity, places man in an exclusive position as an intermediate link between the realms of matter and spirit.[6] This last point, albeit in an entirely different philosophical context, lies at the bottom of Soloviev's teaching about God-manhood: "The connecting link between the divine and the natural world is *man*."[7]

The dramatic events of the last decade of the eighteenth century and the first decade of the nineteenth, spreading outward from their epicenter in France, caused irreversible political and social cataclysms throughout the world. Russia's participation in these events and its triumph over Napoleon resulted not only in the benefits of victory but also in the awakening of a hitherto slumbering public opinion. The officers and soldiers who returned from conquered Paris could not help but compare what they had seen there with what they found at home, could not but question Russia's political and spiritual place in world history. They were not all, by any means, able to generalize their experience and give it a historical and philosophical perspective. Nonetheless, it can be said that if, according to Pushkin's dictum, the reforms of Peter I "cut a window" from Russia into Europe, the victorious march of Alexander I and his army down the Champs Elysées opened the doors of Russian salons to intellectual debates in the European style. The results became evident all too quickly.

The awakening of a national consciousness led eventually to the emergence of two secret societies whose members, after their abortive revolt of 14 December 1825, became known as the Decembrists. Despite the absence of any uniform program of political reform, their disagreement on specific issues did not obscure their common goal—the achievement of constitutional freedoms in Russia. Decembrist ideology reflected a curious mix of influences from both rationalist Enlightenment and Romantic idealism. In this respect, it is interesting to note that the concrete historical significance of the Decembrist movement was relatively modest: as is well known, constitutional liberalism never triumphed in Russia. But the Romantic aura that surrounded the doomed uprising on Senate Square proved sufficiently bright to spawn a legend celebrating "the first Russian revolutionaries."

In the realm of philosophical thought, the most active intellectual forces formed the so-called Society of Wisdom-lovers. In contrast to the Decembrists, whose political philosophy was rooted in French soil, the Wisdom-lovers eagerly embraced the philosophy of German idealism—in particular, that of Schelling, whom Prince Vladimir Odoevskii, the central figure of the group, called the Columbus of the nineteenth century, revealing to man "the unknown part of his world, that is, his soul."[8] Odoevskii was one of the earliest Russian thinkers to assert the need for synthetic cognition of the world. His aspiration to a "magical unity of science, art and religion" anticipates the major postulates of Soloviev's system: integral creativity (free theurgy) and integral knowledge (free theosophy). Likewise close to Soloviev's aesthetics is Odoevskii's belief that there operates in art a force that was once the property of the whole of mankind, but which became obsolescent with the growth of rationalism.

The affinities between the philosophical concepts of the two thinkers reflect the common, if unequal, influence of Schelling. Still, the general impact of German thought on Russian philosophy should not overshadow the significance of similarities or differences among Russian thinkers. An echo of Odoevskii's meditations is discernible not only in the writings of

Soloviev but also in the philosophico-historical constructions of the Slavophiles and in Dostoevsky's moral anthropology. Thus, for instance, Odoevskii
in his philosophical novel *Russian Nights* proclaims Russia's historical mission in a spirit that anticipates Slavophilism: "In the year of fear and death
the Russian sword alone cut the knot that bound trembling Europe. . . .
Europe called the Russian her deliverer! In this name another, even higher
title is concealed—a title whose power must penetrate all spheres of public
life: we must save not only the body, but the soul of Europe! We have been
placed on the border of two worlds—that of the past, and that of the future;
we are new and fresh; we do not pertain to the crimes of the old Europe;
her strange, mysterious drama unravels before our eyes, and its solution,
perhaps, lies hidden in the depths of the Russian spirit."[9]

One might also compare a fragment from Odoevskii's *Psychological Notes*
with the moral dilemma posed by Dostoevsky in *Crime and Punishment:* "I
do not understand the rules of those who permit themselves to commit a
little bit of evil with the aim of thereby bringing about good." Odoevskii goes
on, differing from Dostoevsky only in his reference not to Napoleon but to
another famous Frenchman: "Indeed, there have been those who sought to
excuse Robespierre by saying that he regarded the destruction of thousands
as only a means of achieving the future welfare of his country!"[10]

Both the Decembrists and the Wisdom-lovers were intimately linked with
Freemasonry. Their common genealogy is reflected in the way they divided
among themselves the European philosophical heritage: the Decembrists
were naturally associated with the rationalist Freemasonry of the Enlightenment, the Wisdom-lovers with the mystical branch of Freemasonry, the
German Rosicrucians.

It would not be an exaggeration to state that the philosophical activity of
Peter Chaadaev, while a continuation of existing trends in Russian thought,
at the same time opened up to it decidedly new vistas. On the one hand,
Chaadaev's participation in the war against Napoleon, his intimacy with
Decembrists, and his interest in the Enlightenment had all naturally tied
him in his youth to the liberal movement of the first decades of the nineteenth century. On the other hand, his philosophical and religious convictions, which apparently began to form with his exposure to German idealism
at Moscow University, eventually determined the fundamentally Christian
features of his worldview. It is remarkable that, having absorbed both developments in early nineteenth-century Russian thought—radical liberalism
and religious idealism—Chaadaev's philosophical views generated the passionate polemics from which the main ideas argued by the next generation
of thinkers—the Slavophiles and the Westernizers—were to emerge. Fur-

thermore, one must recognize that the conventional dichotomy which associates liberalism primarily with the Westernizers, and Christian ideology with the Slavophiles, simply does not fit Chaadaev.

Nor does Chaadaev's biography resemble the conventional *vita philosophorum,* being marked by paradox and surprise. Thus in 1821, at the peak of a brilliant military and court career, Chaadaev the officer chose to retire for reasons that remain a mystery. In 1823, Chaadaev "the Decembrist" went abroad for three years, thus escaping the tragic fate of his comrades. Following the publication in 1836 of his first *Philosophical Letter,* which gave some hint of the global intellectual dimension of Chaadaev the religious philosopher, its author was declared officially insane and remained under house arrest for the next year and a half. However, one thread that runs through his life illuminates not only Chaadaev's biography but also that of his greatest contemporary, Alexander Pushkin. Poems, letters, diaries, and reminiscences provide abundant testimony to the intellectual and spiritual significance of this relationship for both men. Although it is not always easy to evaluate the close interaction of prominent individuals, it is clear that Chaadaev's role in the development of the young Pushkin was considerable. According to their common acquaintance Iakov Saburov, Chaadaev's influence on Pushkin was "amazing," "he compelled him to think."[11] In one of his many invocations of Chaadaev, Pushkin wrote: "Your friendship amounted to my happiness."[12]

Even though a detailed inquiry would certainly reveal various disparities, a general juxtaposition of Chaadaev and Pushkin, on the one hand, with Soloviev and Dostoevsky, on the other, still seems not inappropriate. Such a comparison goes beyond the mere fact that in both instances ties of friendship bound together a philosopher and a writer. It is crucial to recognize that both cases represent an intimate kinship between philosophical and artistic vision, and that it is this kinship, for all the multiplicity of its manifestations, that unifies the four men. The same urge toward an integrality of perception and cognition, which lies at the root of Soloviev's and Dostoevsky's philosophical and artistic vision, is clearly evident in both Chaadaev and Pushkin. Naturally, the idea of the unity of the elements of the physical and metaphysical worlds is enunciated primarily on a philosophical plane by Chaadaev and, more comprehensively, by Soloviev. Pushkin and Dostoevsky both embodied the very same principle on an artistic plane—Pushkin perhaps intuitively, Dostoevsky with more philosophical awareness.

The circumstances surrounding the publication of the first *Philosophical Letter* affected not only Chaadaev's life and writings but the fate of his entire philosophical legacy—and, indeed, the subsequent development of Russian thought. The ban on Chaadaev's future publications resulted in his major works remaining unknown to the reading audience until 1905.[13] However, a concurrent factor seems even more significant: Chaadaev's brilliant—and merciless—judgment of Russia's status in history and in the world became the philosopher's lasting trademark, thus limiting his immediate impact on Russian philosophical thought to the philosophy of history. This has created an obstacle to any comprehensive understanding of Chaadaev's Weltanschauung. As V. Zen'kovskii observed, Chaadaev's view of Russia "was a logical inference from his general ideas regarding Christian philosophy,"[14] one of which was Chaadaev's concept of socio-metaphysical unity, the integration of all mankind into one universal, Christian social and cultural system.

According to Chaadaev's doctrine, the hierarchical structure of being consists of four stages: God, who creatively affects the created world; the all-human global consciousness, which receives Him and maintains the unity of being through tradition; the individual consciousness of the separate individual who has lost its connection to the whole; and the world of nature. The idea of an all-human universal consciousness became the central theme of Chaadaev's philosophical constructions. "Just as I conceive of all tangible matter as one whole, so must I also conceive of the sum total of all consciousnesses as a single and sole consciousness." This supreme global consciousness is "the spiritual substance of the Universe."[15] Here Chaadaev's metaphysics both echoes Schelling's doctrine of the World Soul and anticipates Soloviev's teaching of God-manhood.

Establishing the immediate boundaries of Chaadaev's influence on Soloviev demands a special inquiry. Though the latter must certainly have been well acquainted with Chaadaev's philosophical concepts, the extent of his knowledge of the actual texts remains uncertain. In any event, Soloviev never mentions Chaadaev by name in his writings.[16] Be that as it may, the paradigmatic affinity of Chaadaev's and Soloviev's outlooks cannot be doubted: the theurgic interpretation of history; the devotion to the idea of the integration of religion and philosophy; the view of the Church as a theocratic institution capable of uniting all mankind for the realization of the kingdom of God on earth; a recognition of the religious unity of the Christian West and East (Russia)—all this forms a circle of ideas common to both philosophers. In the final analysis, they both demonstrate the faculty that Dostoevsky celebrated in Pushkin and that he himself strove to attain—a universalist "worldwide sensitivity," symbolizing the idea of all-human unity.

For Dostoevsky, Chaadaev was a fascinating figure: he was even inspired to model a character after Chaadaev in his planned novel *The Life of a Great Sinner*. "At that point," he wrote in a letter to Maikov in 1870, "I'll put

Chaadaev in the monastery (under a different name, of course). Why shouldn't Chaadaev spend a year in a monastery? Imagine that Chaadaev, after his first article, for which doctors certified him every week, couldn't resist and published, abroad, for instance, in French, a pamphlet—that could very easily have happened, for which he would have been sent to a monastery for a year. Others can come visit Chaadaev: Belinskii, for instance, Granovskii, Pushkin even."[17] With the early Slavophiles, some of whose theories arose in response to Chaadaev's philosophy of history, the idea of unity found its particular expression in the concepts of "wholeness" and *sobornost'*.[18] The former implies the "living unity" of all the psychophysical powers of man, a unity to be accomplished by the Orthodox believer, who due to his fidelity to true Christianity is capable of restoring "the essential personality in its primordial indivisibility."[19] The latter could be broadly defined as a free unity of Christian individuals based on the Russian Orthodox religion and sealed with the "inner truth" manifested in the common people through their faith, tradition, and custom. According to Aleksei Khomiakov, who along with Ivan Kireevskii was a founder of the Slavophile movement, the notion of sobornost' conveys the specific sense of a harmony between unity and freedom preserved in Orthodoxy since the earliest ages of Christianity, as opposed to the Western European models of unity without freedom, represented by the Catholic Church, and freedom without unity, embodied in Protestantism.[20] Therefore, the Orthodox religion, intrinsically endowed with the unifying spirit of sobornost', is both the principle and the means of bringing together all aspects of human life and thus achieving its wholeness.

For the young Soloviev, the religious philosophy outlined by the classics of Slavophilism was the breeding ground of his own philosophical system. It is not surprising, then, that the Slavophile ideals of wholeness and sobornost' found their development in Soloviev's conception of "integrality" (although in both cases one can trace their common roots to German idealism, especially Schelling's philosophy of identity, as well as to the Eastern Orthodox tradition, wherein the idea of "integral knowledge," attainable not by reason alone but through the activation of all of man's inner assets, has existed from the times of the early Greek Church Fathers).[21] Within the discourse of the idea of unity and its development in Russia, a comparison of Soloviev's early philosophical works with the writings of Kireevskii and Khomiakov provides a number of illustrations of the impact which the elder thinkers exercised on the younger. Thus in his speech *Three Forces,* delivered in St. Petersburg in April 1877, Soloviev comes close to Khomiakov's construction, according to which neither Catholicism nor Protestantism fully corresponds to the needed synthesis of unity and freedom, which can only be achieved under the aegis of the Orthodox Church. Soloviev's triad, however, goes beyond the framework of Christianity: Islam is viewed as a despotic unity that suppresses individual freedom, while Western civilization is characterized by the triumph of individual anarchy. As in Khomiakov, the role of the reconciling principle is assigned to Orthodoxy. Incidentally, Dostoevsky, in the short essay "Three Ideas" (*Diary of a Writer*, January 1877), expresses nationalist sentiments in the same Slavophile vein and with the help of the same logic, opposing Catholicism and Protestantism to Eastern Orthodoxy.[22]

No less significant are the parallels that exist between the early writings of Soloviev and Ivan Kireevskii. In his first major work, his master's dissertation entitled *The Crisis of Western Philosophy (Against the Positivists)* (1874), Soloviev echoes a series of ideas found in Kireevskii's last work, "On the Necessity and Possibility of the New Principles in Philosophy" (1856). Both writers consider one of the causes for the emergence of rationalist philosophy to have been the gap between theoretical thought and religious faith, which disrupted the harmonious integrality of the human being. They are both dissatisfied with the achievements of Western philosophy and express the need to create, in Soloviev's words, "the *universal synthesis* of science, philosophy and religion," or, as Kireevskii put it, "the integral consciousness of reason imbued with faith."[23] Likewise, they resemble one another in their definition of the role of philosophy in the desired process: to Kireevskii, philosophy is the "conductor" of thought between science and faith; to Soloviev, it "stretches a hand" to religion while relying on the positive evidence of science.[24]

Despite such parallels between Kireevskii and the young Soloviev, the independence of the latter's philosophical thought must not be denied.[25] In the first place, Soloviev's defense of his views is founded on a substantial analysis of Western philosophy, while Kireevskii's essay embraces a considerably smaller amount of material.[26] Furthermore, while sharing much of Kireevskii's epistemology and philosophy of history, Soloviev, even in his dissertation, emphatically avoids one of the central ideas of Slavophilism, the necessity of the West's submission to the East. (Thus Kireevskii, for instance, finds the Reformation historically legitimate but claims that Luther's fateful error consisted in his failure to bring the West back to the bosom of the *Christian*, that is, Orthodox Church.[27]) Consequently, Kireevskii and Soloviev differ in their final perspectives on the historical future of philosophy. Kireevskii aspires to Russia's attainment of an "autonomous love of wisdom [*liubomudrie*],[28] which corresponds to the basic principles of the ancient Russian tradition of knowledge [*obrazovannost'*] and will be capable of *subjugating* the divided tradition of knowledge in the West to the integral consciousness of reason imbued with faith."[29] Soloviev, on the other hand, believes that "the newest philosophy strives to *unite* [my emphasis] the logical perfection of the *Western form* with the fullness of the *spiritual contemplations of the East*."[30] These examples allow us to establish a point of divergence that eventually would result in Soloviev's complete break with the later Slavophiles.[31] One assumes that his contemporaries would not have failed to detect the Slavophile influence on Soloviev, yet this did not prevent Leo Tolstoi, after reading Soloviev's dissertation, from emphasizing precisely the independence of his thought: "One more man has joined that small regiment of Russians who allow themselves to think their own mind."[32]

Although some affinities with the early Slavophiles may be traced in Soloviev's subsequent writings, such as *The Philosophical Principles of Integral Knowledge* and *A Critique of Abstract Principles,* his departure from the camp of contemporary Slavophilism became apparent by the end of 1870s. While it may be argued that Soloviev continued to develop the concept of unity in Russian consciousness that he had received through the classics of Slavophilism, the younger Slavophiles took from these same classics the thesis of messianic nationalism. In both cases the consistent development of one idea led to the elimination of the other. Soloviev's vision of unitotality clearly left no room for any nationalist ideology, while the "demolatry" or "nation-worship" (*narodopoklonstvo*), as Soloviev put it, of the later Slavophiles essentially repudiated the Christian universalism that characterized the worldview of Khomiakov and Kireevskii. By the end of the 1880s Soloviev had become so intolerant of any manifestation of nationalist sentiment in Russian life that, in his fight against chauvinists and right-wing conservatives, he did not spare even the founders of Slavophilism.[33] The peripeteias of his relationship with Slavophilism could not help but be reflected in his attitude toward Dostoevsky, in whom the universalism of the earlier Slavophiles was intricately interwoven with the chauvinistic tendencies of their epigones. Soloviev perceived this contradiction in Dostoevsky as tragically insoluble. "Death liberated Dostoevsky from the unbearable inner struggle," he said ten years after the departure of his elder friend.[34] By then Soloviev was no longer inclined to ignore, as he had at one time, Dostoevsky's deviations from the *all*-human Christian principle, although his criticism was intentionally brief and fairly melancholy in tone. Soloviev felt not indignation but rather compassion for Dostoevsky's failure entirely to fit the desired ideal. For this reason it can be said that Dostoevsky's identity as "the forerunner of a new religious art," as portrayed by Soloviev in his first memorial speech, remained an articulation of a higher reality (in Viacheslav

Ivanov's sense) which Dostoevsky could not himself attain but which was nonetheless attained in his artistic works.

The idea of unity, fundamental both to Soloviev's entire philosophy and to his development of individual concepts, is also an organic part of Dostoevsky's work. One could cite numerous illustrations of Dostoevsky's interpretation of the idea of unity. Yet one example of an actual formula of unity will suffice—the famous words of the elder Zosima in *The Brothers Karamazov*: "Everyone is responsible for everyone and everything." The idea of unity is not only one of the fundamental concepts of Dostoevsky's worldview, it characterizes the writer, who, in the words of Mikhail Bakhtin, "understands worldview not as an abstract unity and sequence in a system of thoughts and positions but as an ultimate position in the world in relation to higher values."[35]

Bakhtin's conception of the polyphonic novel offers a positive point of reference for an examination of the principle of unity in Dostoevsky's fiction. Moreover, in many respects Bakhtin's interpretation of unity in Dostoevsky reflects Soloviev's views on the category of unity—a fact that deserves particular attention here.[36]

Bakhtin calls the principle of unity in Dostoevsky's work "a polyphonic unity" or "a unity of a higher order," that is, "unity not as an innate one-and-only, but as a dialogic *concordance* of unmerged twos or multiples."[37] The famous conception of the polyphonic novel was developed by Bakhtin specifically to describe the special artistic nature of Dostoevsky's novels. According to Bakhtin, Dostoevsky was the first "polyphonic" writer, the creator of "a new artistic model of the world"[38] in which the decisive factor is the position of the author in his work.[39] The author, while remaining the creator of his characters, relinquishes unconditional control over his creations and enters into a dialogue with them as equals. Once "slaves," the characters become "free people." Thus the polyphonic novel is distinguished by a "plurality of independent and unmerged voices and consciousnesses, a genuine polyphony of fully valid voices."[40] Accordingly, polyphonic unity is based not on the ultimate monologic authority of the author but on the dialogic concordance of the many or the plurality.

It is not difficult to find an analogy to the idea of "polyphonic unity" in Soloviev.[41] Although Soloviev's treatment of the topic is not specifically applied to literature, his understanding of the nature of unity clearly has something in common with Bakhtin's view of unity as applied to the novels of Dostoevsky. "Unity in the true sense," writes Soloviev, "is realized in the many, not canceling it out, but freeing it from the limits of exclusivity."[42] "The truly united is that which does not exclude plurality but, on the contrary, effects plurality within itself without being divided. It remains both plural and united, thereby demonstrating that it is absolutely united, united in its very essence, and incapable of being canceled or destroyed by any plurality."[43]

Bakhtin continually stresses the special character of "polyphonic unity": "The unity of the whole in Dostoevsky is not a matter of plot nor of mono-logic idea, that is, non-ideational. It is a unity above plot and above idea."[44] Regardless of whether his words are seen as theologically inspired or merely as a philosophical metaphor, Bakhtin's notion of the existence of "a unity of a higher order" corresponds in its very wording to Soloviev's formulation. "Only that life," writes Soloviev, "that culture which excludes nothing, but in its wholeness combines a higher order of unity with an uttermost devel-opment of free plurality—only this can give genuine, lasting satisfaction to the demands of human feeling, thought, and will and thus be a truly panhu-man, or universal, culture; moreover, it is clear that at the same time and precisely as a result of its wholeness this culture will be more than human, leading people into actual contact with the divine world."[45]

Bakhtin saw the central goal of his study of Dostoevsky to be "to reveal the artistic unity of the world he created,"[46] to reveal, as Bakhtin put it, "the unity of the polyphonic novel—a unity standing above the word, above the voice, above the accent."[47] Bakhtin never gave a formulaic definition of polyphonic unity. However, the very semantic construction of the definition just quoted points to the ideal character of this unity. Bakhtin's analysis would seem to allow us to see in the novels of Dostoevsky an artistic em-bodiment of the principle of unity which Soloviev postulated in his philoso-phy. "Love toward one's own self is impossible," Bakhtin asserts with his conception.[48] Just as a dialogue with oneself is impossible. Just as polyphony is impossible within a single voice. "Love is the basis of plurality," Soloviev tells us. "When we say that the absolute primary cause by its very definition is unity as regards both itself and its negation, we are repeating, only in abstract form, the words of the great apostle: God is love."[49] In speaking of the unity of the absolute source, Soloviev is clearly referring "in abstract form" to God. And even if we cannot fully assert the divinity connotation of unity in Bakhtin, in Dostoevsky it goes without saying.[50]

SUM AND SUBSTANCE

It is above all essential to penetrate the spiritual and intellectual ambience of Dostoevsky and Soloviev's creative activities—in other words, to interpret the subjects that occupy them on their own terms. An understanding of what united and what divided Dostoevsky and Soloviev—of where the lines, sometimes parallel, sometimes even coincident, of their proximity pass, and where points of divergence and even of antagonism are found—naturally entails treating the major intellectual preoccupations characteristic of both thinkers.[51] Consequently, their discourse is ultimately inexplicable outside the system of Christian beliefs. This fact conditions the necessity of addressing certain specifically religious and theological issues whose importance might not be so obvious in a study of the work of other Russian writers.

The first problem selected for detailed treatment is the opposition of the God-man and man-god in the writings of Soloviev and Dostoevsky. Fundamentally, this opposition is based on the dogma of the God-manhood of Jesus Christ, and the idea of the "superman," which existed in various forms long before it became the trademark of Nietzsche. The two poles of this antinomy, when projected onto social being, provide for two opposing paths of social development: the idea of the man-god leads to totalitarianism in its various manifestations, while the principle of the God-man inspires the theocratic ideal. This latter, as reflected in the works of Soloviev and Dostoevsky, is the second problem posed in this book. The moral aspect of the God-man/man-god opposition, along with the question of theodicy, is the third problem to be discussed.

In both Soloviev and Dostoevsky, all these problems are organically interconnected and form, together with the other facets of their worldviews, a united whole whose character is defined by the values of Christianity. The thematic division in my analysis of these topics cannot, therefore, have precise watersheds: the themes overflow one into another, and a return to similar aspects from diverse perspectives is inevitable. Nevertheless, these chapter divisions answer, on the whole, the purpose of concentrating attention on each of the above stated problems. In the first chapter I examine Soloviev's works on Dostoevsky and indicate their place among the literary critical writings of Soloviev and in Russian critical tradition regarding Dostoevsky. The second chapter treats biographical questions connected with the period of personal contact between Dostoevsky and Soloviev. The third chapter starts with the conception of God-manhood found in Soloviev's writings and proceeds to an examination of the dynamic antinomy between the God-man and the man-god as artistically developed by Dostoevsky in his four great novels. The discussion leads to the ultimate representation of the man-god in the work of each author: Dostoevsky's "Legend of the Grand Inquisitor" and Soloviev's "Short Tale of the Antichrist" (an intrinsic part of his last major work, *The Three Conversations*). The fourth chapter deals with theocracy: its theoretical foundation by Soloviev and its role in *The Brothers*

Karamazov. The chapter concludes with an analysis of how the theocratic ideal is reflected in Soloviev's and Dostoevsky's views on Russian history and politics. Chapter 5 inquires into the principles of Soloviev's and Dostoevsky's philosophical ethics. It demonstrates the interaction of rationalist and metaphysical ethics in Dostoevsky's novels, including the problem of theodicy, and explicates each thinker's insights into the nature of good and evil.

The degree to which Dostoevsky has been analyzed and explored makes the study of Soloviev pale by comparison. If virtually everything Dostoevsky ever wrote has been completely "inventoried" and furnished with a vast and thorough scholarly apparatus, Soloviev's legacy has not only failed to receive similar treatment, it has not even been published in its entirety.[52] The most complete edition of Soloviev's works is based on the second pre-Revolutionary edition, supplemented by following publications, but still without any scholarly apparatus. Fortunately, the state of Soloviev studies in Russia has been changing, and we are already seeing the fruits of this change. Since the late 1980s, several scholarly editions of selections from Soloviev's writings have appeared, with valuable commentary and notes (see the Bibliography). There has also been considerable activity in the interpretation of Soloviev's work. I should note, however, that this book is intended not to give a compendium of known facts and accumulated scholarly material but to provide textual analysis and a new way of looking at the connections and divergences between Soloviev and Dostoevsky, which to a great extent have defined the subsequent development of both philosophy and literature in Russia.

Russian philosophical thought is primarily anthropocentric. The work of Dostoevsky underscores and to a large extent develops this feature of the Russian consciousness with perfect clarity. In the philosophical system of Soloviev, anthropological ideas are more closely connected with metaphysical, cosmological, and epistemological concepts. Although it would be incorrect in the treatment of Soloviev's work to isolate his anthropology from all these other aspects, for the purposes of this comparative study I have attempted to distill his anthropology so as to facilitate the comparison with Dostoevsky. However, I hope that I have been able to preserve the inherent framework of Soloviev's philosophical vision. The assertion that the central theme of Dostoevsky's work is man has long since become a commonplace. But this cliché is meaningless (one could, after all, say the same thing about any writer) unless one specifies what kind of man it is that Dostoevsky is studying, portraying, and advocating. In 1873 Soloviev called Dostoevsky one of the few writers "who still retains in our time an image and likeness of God."[53] In 1880 Konstantin Leontiev noted that in "our age" people "believe in *mankind,* they no longer believe in *man.* Dostoevsky, apparently, is one of the few thinkers who has not lost his belief in *man himself.*"[54] The man in whom Dostoevsky "believes" exists within the Christian universe, and the underlying foundation for such a "belief" is the biblical tenet that man was created "in the image and likeness of God." Therefore, when comparing Dostoevsky with other thinkers and writers, both Russian and European, it is essential to look at each of them in the light of their individual intellectual conceptions. For example, Lev Shestov, seduced by a similarity regarding certain questions they posed, in their analytical method, and in their enthusiasm for psychological insights, excessively linked Dostoevsky and Nietzsche without taking sufficient note of the fact that each of them, while focusing on identical subjects, viewed these subjects in different dimensions.[55]

We have no need to make a similar stipulation in juxtaposing the names of Dostoevsky and Soloviev. If Nietzsche and Dostoevsky approximated one another while working in different systems, Soloviev and Dostoevsky diverged while working within the same system—the Christological. Exploring the correlations between Soloviev and Dostoevsky—personal, religio-philosophical,[56] literary, and social—one must above all look closely at the foundation they shared, the nature of which may be sketched by a few words from a letter written by Soloviev in 1883: "That love alone is absolute, and that it alone abides—this is said not by me and not by Dostoevsky, but by the Apostles Paul and John."[57]

I

Soloviev on Dostoevsky
A Critic on a Writer

Beauty will save the world.
—*Dostoevsky*

Beauty is the tangible form of good and truth.
—*Soloviev*

Dostoevsky's influence on philosophical thought of the twentieth century is a matter of common knowledge. Problems associated with this theme continue to attract the attention of scholars in the Russian as well as the Western philosophical tradition. At first sight, Dostoevsky's significance for Russian philosophy appears more substantial than Soloviev's significance for Russian literature. However, this imbalance may largely reflect the lack of attention that has been paid to Soloviev's literary contribution. An exception to the general pattern can be made for works on Russian Symbolism, where it is simply impossible to make do without the name of Soloviev. Overall, though, among the many phenomena of Russian literature to which Soloviev is in some fashion related, a fruitful and very interesting topic remains almost unexplored: his literary criticism. It is, therefore, important at least to touch upon the distinctive traits of Soloviev's literary criticism, since a prominent place is occupied in it by his writings on Dostoevsky—our immediate focus of attention.

In discussing Soloviev's writings on Dostoevsky, one needs to bear in mind both authorial intent and the circumstances of the moment. The bulk of what Soloviev said about Dostoevsky was literally spoken, that is, created for oral performance. For this reason Soloviev's literary criticism on Dostoevsky can be divided into two parts. Collectively, the first group of works—"A Lecture Given at the Higher Courses for Women on 30 January 1881 Apropos of the Death of F. M. Dostoevsky," [An Address Given at the Grave of F. M. Dostoevsky], and "Three Speeches in Memory of Dostoevsky"—comprises a kind of eulogy. The second group includes the marginal articles "A Note in Defense of Dostoevsky against the Charge of 'New Christianity'" and "A Few Words Concerning 'Cruelty,'" which represent, respectively, polemics with Konstantin Leontiev and Nikolai Mikhailovskii concerning the latter's influential article about Dostoevsky, "A Cruel Talent."[1]

The main focus of Soloviev the critic was Russian poetry, and his writings on Dostoevsky stand apart, in terms of chronology, form, and intent, from the series of essays he subsequently penned in the 1890s on the work of Pushkin, Lermontov, Mickiewicz, and Aleksei K. Tolstoi. The Dostoevsky essays cannot be divorced from these later works, for they were significant factors in the formation of Soloviev's critical method and tasks. On the other hand, it is necessary to consider what Soloviev says about Dostoevsky within the context of the entire body of critical literature devoted to the writer, both before and after Soloviev.[2] Only by taking both perspectives into account is it possible to evaluate the significance of Soloviev's particular contribution.

THE EARLY CRITICAL RECEPTION

By the time Soloviev's works on Dostoevsky were composed in the early 1880s, a small yet significant body of critical writings on the writer had already formed in Russia. For the most part these were works of critics who later came to be called "radicals" and who, to a great extent, defined both the general direction of Russian criticism during this period and the social and cultural mood of the reading public of their day.

Despite the complexity that obtains in all writer-critic relationships, and despite Dostoevsky's personal resentment and even hostility toward his literary judges, especially in his later years, it was thanks to the critics that his entry into the literary arena followed the dream scenario cherished by every fledgling author. Both from Dostoevsky's own reminiscences and from the numerous testimonies of the other participants in this episode, it is well known how Dmitrii Grigorovich and Nikolai Nekrasov spent a sleepless night in late May 1845 reading *Poor Folk*; how at dawn—which at that time of the year in Petersburg could only be ascertained by checking a clock—they flew to the author's home with their ecstatic congratulations; how Vissarion Belinskii, to whom Nekrasov the very next day handed the manuscript of the "new Gogol," met the work with equal emotion and rapture.[3] Yet this initial recognition of the young Dostoevsky by such prominent literary figures proved to be not only instantaneous but also transitory. When Belinskii, who in his review of the 1846 *Petersburg Almanac* had proclaimed "honor and glory to the young poet whose Muse loves people in garrets and basements,"[4] turned from "opinions apropos of" *Poor Folk* to an appraisal of *The Double,* he substantially moderated his praise and shifted from a eulogizing tone to a didactic one. With the appearance a year later of Dostoevsky's "The Landlady," Belinskii's disappointment grew greater still. In his "Survey of Russian Literature of 1847," the critic limits himself to a caustic retelling of the story's plot, derisively calling it "highly remarkable, only in quite the wrong sense."[5]

We can only surmise how Belinskii, who died in 1848, might have perceived the works Dostoevsky wrote after this date, works which were to determine his place in world literature. Yet the response to *Poor Folk* by the "first Russian critic" set the tone of Dostoevsky criticism for a long time to come (reflecting the predominant approach that was established in the 1840s and later became the basis of Soviet literary criticism). One of Belinskii's statements concerning Dostoevsky's first work is cited with canonical frequency, though not always canonical accuracy: "This first attempt at a Russian social novel has, moreover, been accomplished the way artists usually do things, that is, without themselves suspecting what they have brought forth."[6] Taken together, the commonly quoted beginning of this statement—about the social nature of the novel—and its more rarely mentioned second part characterize perfectly the critical methodology fathered by Belinskii, which at its most extreme led to a not unfamiliar valuational formula of art: artistic in form, social in content. Such an aesthetic view, while implying the presence in the writer of a social consciousness in all its concreteness and all its concern for the material problems of society, relegates the creative process itself entirely to the realm of the unconscious. It is perhaps ironic that such a methodology links content to materialist ideas and categories, whereas form is seen as a product of idealist origin. As a consequence, the aims and purposes of literary critical thought boil down to an investigation of a work's social canvas, while artistic analysis must content itself with emotional and impressionistic deductions and, at best, felicitous stylistic observations.

Nevertheless, Belinskii, who possessed unquestionable artistic intuition, managed despite his aesthetic concepts to see immediately in the early Dostoevsky such essential features of his talent as the combination of humor and the tragic, the absence of a descriptive or satiric bent, and the presence of what Belinskii called "an a priori knowledge of life, and, consequently, a purely poetic, creative" knowledge.[7] Besides this general description of Dostoevsky's talent, Belinskii also noted the distinctiveness of his style and ideas, though in most cases he gave a negative appraisal of the originality of Dostoevsky's artistic methods. (This is not, however, a new phenomenon in the history of artistic criticism: the distinct individual features of an artist are at first viewed as shortcomings, and only with the advent of widespread recognition are they reclassified as the unique and original virtues of his talent.[8])

Belinskii's critical strategy and its tactical application with respect to Dostoevsky were adopted and radicalized by the propagandists of a "revolutionary-democratic approach" to literature, Nikolai Dobroliubov and Dmitrii Pisarev. Both critics died young—Dobroliubov at age twenty-five, Pisarev at twenty-eight. Their youth and the intransigence of their social views call to mind a well-known witticism: "If a man does not become a socialist at twenty, he has no heart; if he is still a socialist at thirty, he has no brains." They did not live long enough to disprove the second half of the aphorism, but they certainly did enough to confirm the first. Dobroliubov's critical method, which he termed "realist criticism," was conditioned not so much by the need to analyze the artistic and formal aspects of literature (a discipline that was essentially nonexistent at this time) as by social needs which he himself formulated as the criteria for evaluating a literary work: "The most important thing for criticism is to determine whether an author is in pace with those natural aspirations which have already been awakened in the people or are to awaken soon in response to the modern order of things."[9] There is little doubt that Dostoevsky, like many others, was sensitive to the "natural aspirations of the people," yet his remark in the essay "Mr. —bov and the Question of Art" might serve as an ironic commentary to Dobroliubov's professional credo: "The main thing is that Mr. —bov is quite content even without artistry, just so long as we speak of the matter at hand. The latter desire is, of course, commendable, but it would be nice if we could speak of the matter well, and not just anyhow."[10] (One cannot help thinking that if Dostoevsky had made one of his characters a literary critic concerned above all with the good of the people, he could not have found a better name than Dobroliubov, formed from the Russian word *dobro,* meaning both "good" and "goods, property," and *liubov',* "love.") An even more graphic demonstration of Dostoevsky's creative position can be seen in his assertion, dating from 1849, that "art has no need of a direction, art is its own goal, an author has only to worry about the artistry, and the idea will come on its own; for it is a necessary condition of artistry. In short, *everyone knows that this direction is diametrically opposed to that of the newspapers and the fire department.*"[11]

Dobroliubov's aesthetic program is so much at odds with the artistic principles of Dostoevsky that the critic, musing on *The Insulted and the Injured* in his famous article "Downtrodden People," doubted the very possibility of applying "rules of strict artistic criticism" to the novel:

> Only someone completely naïve and ignorant could seriously and at length, with proofs, excerpts, and examples, discuss the aesthetic significance of the novel, which even in its narrative betrays the absence of any pretense of artistic significance. Throughout the novel the characters talk like the author; they use his favorite words, his turns of speech; they have the same sentence structure. Exceptions are very rare. . . . This poverty and vagueness of images, this need to repeat oneself, this inability to work out each character even enough to communicate something at least of his proper manner of expression—all this, while revealing, on the one hand, a lack of variety in the author's store of observations, on the other hand directly contradicts the artistic wholeness and integrity of his creations.[12]

Irony often haunts history, including the history of literary criticism. Some seventy years had to pass before the "naïve and ignorant" critic Mikhail Bakhtin put forth the concept of the polyphonic novel of Dostoevsky, a concept founded on the idea of the autonomy and independence of the "voices" of the characters from that of the author. We have come a long way!

Nevertheless, within the framework of his admittedly limited approach, Dobroliubov showed a profound understanding of the characters of the "downtrodden people." In the compassion for man that Dobroliubov correctly noted in Dostoevsky, the critic saw an expression of those humanistic ideals which were already manifested, in his words, "in our literature of the end of the last century in consequence of the dissemination among us at that time of the ideas and writings of Rousseau,"[13] as well as the stimulus for the realization of his own democratic hopes. "We have found," he concluded, "that there are many downtrodden, insulted, and injured individuals among our middle class, that things are hard for them in a moral as well as a physical sense, that despite an outward reconciliation to their position they feel its bitterness, they are ready to chafe and protest, they thirst for a way out. But here we reach the limit of our observations. Where this way out might be, when or how—only life itself can show us this."[14] Dobroliubov's concentration on the social aspects of literature never allowed him to recognize that the humanistic *pity for humankind* is rooted in the religious *compassion for man*. And even though this principle manifested itself with irrefutable clarity in the works Dostoevsky wrote after his camp sentence and exile—that is, after 1859—the idea of religious compassion permeates his work from the very beginning.[15] Still, Dobroliubov, while guided in his literary analysis by social consciousness, was the first critic to give a serious psychological interpretation to the personages in Dostoevsky's early works.

Dmitrii Pisarev wrote two essays about Dostoevsky: "The Dead and the Dying" (1866) and "The Struggle for Life" (1867). The former is based on a comparison of *The House of the Dead* with Nikolai Pomialovskii's *Seminary Sketches*; the latter is an interpretation of the personality and behavior of Raskolnikov in *Crime and Punishment* and is especially interesting both for its content and for its literary and historical significance. Pisarev begins "The Struggle for Life" with a declaration of his position as critic with respect to his subject, which, incidentally, is similar to how Vladimir Soloviev was to open the Foreword to his "Three Speeches in Memory of Dostoevsky" (1881–1883). This formal coincidence is curious in that it reveals with graphic clarity the contrast of "starting points" in the approach to Dostoevsky of two individuals as different as Pisarev and Soloviev. "Before embarking on a critique of Mr. Dostoevsky's new novel," writes Pisarev, "let me announce to my readers that I care nothing about the author's personal convictions . . . or about the overall tenor of his activity. . . . I direct my attention solely to those phenomena of social life which are depicted in his novel."[16] "In the three speeches about Dostoevsky," writes Soloviev in his turn, "I concern myself neither with his personal life nor with a literary critique of his works. I have in mind one question only: what did Dostoevsky serve, what idea inspired the whole of his activity?"[17]

The diametrical nature of the two approaches is perfectly obvious. Yet Soloviev, in limiting the sphere of his investigation, rejects on principle the notion that his "Three Speeches" might even belong to the genre of literary criticism. For Pisarev, on the other hand, his concentration on "phenomena of social life" and his treatment of a work of literature "as a reliable exposition of events that have occurred" apparently do not prevent him from discussing "Mr. Dostoevsky's new novel" in the guise of literary criticism. To be sure, the lack of differentiation between creative and socio-political goals is characteristic not only of Pisarev but of the whole of Russian literary criticism of the second half of the nineteenth century. But it is precisely because Soloviev's analytical approach consciously defines his concrete subject and boundaries of genre that we can regard it as a first step toward a qualitatively different methodology in literary scholarship. I shall touch on this in more detail shortly, but now let us turn back to Pisarev's essay.

Dostoevsky himself could well have named Raskolnikov's journey a "struggle for life." Yet in Dostoevsky's usage, "life" signifies something far greater than the material existence that, according to Pisarev, determines people's fates. By basing his interpretation of the problematics of *Crime and Punishment* exclusively on Raskolnikov's chronic shortage of money, the critic performed an analytical tour de force comparable in its scrupulous investigation and expressive discourse to the analytical studies of Dostoevsky himself. Even in his style Pisarev imitates, whether intentionally or not, the characteristic mannerisms of the author of *Crime and Punishment*, resorting to clarifying repetitions, diminutive nouns, and so on. With the same intensity with which Dostoevsky examines the most minute nuances in the consciousness of his characters, peeling back one after another the psychological layers of human existence, Pisarev examines the nuances of dreary everyday existence and paints with artistic power and precision the wretched and degrading details of the day-to-day process of impoverishment. Thus, if Dostoevsky primarily employs the "close-up" in depicting the grievous psychological condition of his protagonist, Pisarev fills in, as he puts it, the "gaps," setting out the material circumstances of Raskolnikov's life as if under a laboratory microscope. (It is not for nothing that he resorts to a deliberately naturalistic comparison of Raskolnikov's reaction to Marmeladov's story with the reaction of a young medical student to the repellent details of a vivisection.)

At the same time, Pisarev at the start of his essay tries to ignore Dostoevsky's painstakingly elaborated theory (and the psychology linked to it) of the crime and *punishment* of Raskolnikov, then later discredits it as "having nothing to do with those ideas which make up the world-outlook of modern-minded people."[18] Raskolnikov, believes Pisarev, "does not commit his crime in quite the same *way* that some illiterate wretch might commit it; but he commits it for the same *reason* any illiterate wretch would commit it. Poverty is the principal motive in both instances."[19] This is the very attitude of circumstantial justification against which Dostoevsky so steadfastly and at times vehemently fought. Of course, the grounds for Pisarev's interpretation of the central event of the novel lay not only in the onesidedness of the critic's worldview but also in the ambivalence of Raskolnikov's own motivation for his crime. Dostoevsky himself was concerned with this issue, as is clear from his note: "It is essential to bring the course of action to a real stop and do away with indefiniteness, i.e., to explain the whole murder *one way or another* and lay out his character and attitudes clearly."[20] Despite the author's firm intention, the initial ambivalence in the character's reflections on the meaning of his crime does not disappear until the very end.

Pisarev was by no means the only critic and reader of *Crime and Punishment* to disagree with the author's interpretation of the development of Raskolnikov's character. For example, Merezhkovskii, writing later, accepts the ideological justification for his "crime" but completely rejects the religious interpretation of his "punishment." The "future complete resurrection to a new life" on whose threshold Dostoevsky leaves Raskolnikov at the novel's conclusion strikes Merezhkovskii as a less than convincing prospect. Moreover, emphasizing that "for Raskolnikov, the 'crime' is a 'repentance' subordinate to the law of conscience" and identifying this "last living word of the living Raskolnikov" with "Dostoevsky's own last moral deduction from the whole tragedy," Merezhkovskii arrives at a Nietzsche-like conclusion. "Never," he writes, "has a contraband shipment of more dangerous explosives been let pass under the banner of Christian humility, patience, and submissiveness: the misunderstanding that has taken place is roughly the same as if a shell filled with dynamite were taken for a device for putting out a fire. And the more you think about it, the more amazed you are that this misunderstanding continues even to this day: it needed the whole nearsightedness and carelessness of Russian criticism in the realm of religious questions to be so deceived."[21] (More radical still is an assertion by Lev Shestov, who insists, so to speak, on "Raskolnikov being born of the soul of Nietzsche"—synchronically—and "Nietzsche being born of the soul of Dostoevsky"—diachronically.[22]) As we can see, the lack of precision that worried Dostoevsky proved fairly enduring, manifesting itself in various and sometimes contrasting interpretations of Raskolnikov's ideas, character, and fate. However, it would not be a mistake to view this dissent (*raskol*) in opinions as only natural with regard to a character bearing such a name.

SOLOVIEV'S POLEMICS

Considerable influence has been exerted on the critical literature about Dostoevsky—and in particular on the views of orthodox Soviet scholars, with their Marxist hostility toward Dostoevsky's philosophical spirit—by the writings of the populist ideologue Nikolai Mikhailovskii. He wrote several essays about, or rather, against Dostoevsky: "Comments on *The Devils*," in which he sought, among other things, to demonstrate that the novel's young characters were untypical of the modern revolutionary movement (1873);

"On Pisemskii and Dostoevsky," his first reaction to the death of Dostoevsky (1881); and his famous work "A Cruel Talent." The latter article, published in the autumn of 1882, was aimed specifically against Soloviev's lecture on the death of Dostoevsky, delivered at the Higher Courses for Women on 30 January 1881, and in general it targeted all manifestations of panegyrical treatment of the "illustrious deceased."[23] Written in a sharply polemical tone, the article reflects Mikhailovskii's method of subjective sociology, which he developed both in his populist theories and in the realm of literary inquiry. Declaring "Dostoevsky's role as spiritual leader of the Russian people and prophet" to be "rubbish," the critic made his aim the study of Dostoevsky as "simply a great and original writer of enormous literary interest."[24] One would think that such a position would ensure a certain degree of professional objectivity and analytical comprehensiveness. Yet Mikhailovskii directed all his efforts towards the discussion of a single trait in Dostoevsky, which he termed "the cruelty of talent." And it must be said that he carried out his investigation of this particular trait with a fair amount of virtuosity. "Dostoevsky was always preoccupied," writes Mikhailovskii, "with cruelty and torment, and always precisely from the standpoint of their attractiveness, from the standpoint of the voluptuousness seemingly contained within torment." Assigning primary importance in Dostoevsky's creative psychology to "two fundamental properties of human nature: 1) man is a despot by nature and loves to be a tormentor, and 2) man has a passion for suffering," the critic resorted to "an example that is convenient because it is so obvious":

No one in Russian literature ever analyzed the sensations of the wolf devouring the lamb with such thoroughness, depth, one might even say with such love, as Dostoevsky, if one can in fact speak of a loving attitude toward the feelings of a wolf. And he cared very little about the elementary, coarser sorts of wolf feelings—simple hunger, for instance. No, he burrowed down into the very depths of the wolf's soul, hunting for something subtle and intricate in it—not the simple gratification of an appetite, but precisely the voluptuousness of malice and cruelty. . . . Yet despite the fact that Dostoevsky gave us many great and valuable works in this sphere of specialty, he rather contradicts, as it were, another trait commonly associated with his activities. Sticking with our metaphor, someone else might well say that Dostoevsky was, on the contrary, concerned with examining with especial scrutiny the feelings of the lamb being devoured by the wolf. . . . After taking into consideration the whole of Dostoevsky's literary career, we must inevitably come to the conclusion that he quite simply liked setting the wolf on the lamb, and if in the first half of his career it was the lamb that interested him most, by the second half it was the wolf.[25]

Lev Shestov, who called the designation "cruel talent" extremely apt, noted with regret that "the critic wanted with these two words not only to offer a description of the artist, but also to pronounce *sentence* upon him and the whole of his work. To be cruel means to be corrupt, disfigured, and therefore unsuitable. N. K. Mikhailovskii can do nothing but grieve that this is what happened — that Dostoevsky, with his enormous talent, was not at the same time a high priest of humanism. The critic's judgment is based on the idea that humanism is unquestionably higher, better than cruelty."[26] Addressing the theme of "humanism and cruelty," one present-day Russian essayist, in the spirit of Shestov and Leontiev,[27] writes that "Mikhailovskii at least approached one of the enigmas of Dostoevsky's work, even if he did not unravel it. . . . For a critic who traced his ideological line back to the Enlightenment, cruelty was something alien, like dust on the mirror of human nature: this dust is easy to detect, and then to wipe away."[28] More interesting still is an observation by Mikhail Bakhtin, though it implies a certain functionalism of "cruelty" as a device — not, of course, in the social sense intended by Mikhailovskii and roundly criticized, as will be shown below, by Soloviev, but in an artistic and philosophical sense: "The epithet 'a cruel talent,' applied to Dostoevsky by N. K. Mikhailovsky, has some justification, although not as simple a one as it seemed at the time. The special sort of moral torture that Dostoevsky inflicts upon his heroes, in order to force out of them that ultimate word of self-consciousness pushed to its extreme limits, permits him to take all that is merely material, merely an object, all that is fixed and unchanging, all that is external and neutral in the representation of a person, and dissolve it in the realm of the hero's self-consciousness and self-utterances."[29]

Amid this debate, a general inference about the reasons for Mikhailovskii's partial insight is suggested: the subjective sociological method, with its emphasis on individuality and anthropologism, allowed the critic to perceive the psychological details of Dostoevsky's "cruelty," while at the same time its sociological and positivistic nature could not help but be an obstacle to his understanding of the ontological roots of "cruelty." As a result, Mikhailovskii develops in all seriousness the idea that this "cruel talent" could have been utilized for the good of society, if only there was a "social ideal" present in Dostoevsky. It was precisely this speculation in the spirit of Fourier that prompted Soloviev's "mournful reflections." Responding to Mikhailovskii, Soloviev, who fully understood the ontological nature of evil, wrote: "Penetrating more deeply than others into the dark and insane element of the human soul, [Dostoevsky] reflected this in his personages at times with the force of genius, at times with an excessive and truly torturous tension. Yet along with this dark side of the human soul which Dostoevsky perceived and showed to us as psychological *reality,* he had indeed a moral and social ideal, one that allowed no truck with evil forces, that called not for any sort of outward application of evil propensities, but rather for their inner moral rebirth—an ideal not invented by Dostoevsky but bequeathed to all mankind by the Gospels."[30] A utilitarian morality was as absolutely alien to Dostoevsky as it was to Soloviev, who, continuing his argument against Mikhailovskii, predicted the historical consequences of "the new social idea": "At present, revolutionary groups throughout Europe are prepared to direct their unbridled and savage hostility toward the ruling and propertied classes, while the latter, of course, will not hesitate to 'apply' the full force of their cruelty to the revolutionary elements. And there will be no end to this vicious circle of violence, no end to this complicated cannibalism, as long as the social ideal is separated from the moral, and evil passions are justified by the purpose of their application."[31]

If, in his response to Mikhailovskii, Soloviev was defending Dostoevsky from an attack from the left, the polemic with Konstantin Leontiev in his "Note in Defense of Dostoevsky against the Charge of 'New Christianity'" was aimed at defending Dostoevsky from criticism from the right. The departure points of Soloviev's two opponents graphically demonstrate the scope of the perception of Dostoevsky's work by his intellectual contemporaries, the breadth of which was conditioned in large part by the polysemantic (or, in post-Bakhtinian terms, polyphonic) nature of the philosophical and artistic material they were exploring. While Mikhailovskii accuses Dostoevsky of a lack of humanism, Leontiev condemns his "modern aspiration to substitute humanism for Christian dogma."[32] It is obvious that, unlike the observations of Mikhailovskii, Leontiev's formulation reflects a line of argument close to Soloviev's. "The humanism of modern Europe," writes Leontiev, "and Christian humanism are unquestionably antitheses of one another, which indeed are scarcely reconcilable (or reconcilable only aesthetically, in the realm of poetry that is both *realistic* and *artistic,* that is, as a *fascinating and intricate struggle*). We should not wonder at this or be horrified at such a thought. It is quite understandable, though also regrettable. Humanism is a *simple* idea; Christianity is a *complex* notion."[33]

Soloviev is in complete solidarity with Leontiev in his distinctively zealous rejection of "the urge to replace the living fullness of Christianity with the commonplaces of an abstract morality cloaked in the name of Christianity without the Christian essence."[34] Yet he considers Leontiev's accusations misdirected: "Dostoevsky's humanism was not the abstract morality that Mr. Leontiev condemns, for Dostoevsky founded his best hopes for man on a true belief in Christ and the Church, and not on a belief in abstract reason or in that godless and possessed mankind which is reflected in all its abomination more clearly in the novels of Dostoevsky himself than anywhere else. The humanism of Dostoevsky was firmly rooted in the mystical superhuman foundation of true Christianity."[35]

By accepting the objective value of Leontiev's formulation of the question yet rejecting its particular application to Dostoevsky, Soloviev runs up against a position of Leontiev's that left its mark on the whole of the latter's world-view and writings: amoralism. This attribute, Leontiev's "trademark" in nearly every scholarly writing about him, is very often understood in a superficial sense. In fact, the key to understanding Leontiev's amoralism lies in appreciating the metaphysical dimensions of his ethical views. Within his dialectics, "moral philosophy has its worth and its limitations," that is, it is of merely human value. When Leontiev in his essay calls Dostoevsky a "remarkable moralist," he did not intend a compliment. In his opinion, Dostoevsky, with his faith in "the human heart," deviates from the principles of Christianity no less than the advocates of democratic and liberal progress, who hope for the improvement of all mankind through the reconstruction of society. "Christianity, however," writes Leontiev, "believes in neither the one nor the other, that is, neither in the superior autonomous morality of the individual nor in the reason of a collective mankind that must sooner or later create a paradise on earth."[36] This amoral (or, rather, antimoral) point of view reflects in essence "Leontiev's moral philosophy, which is rigorous, colored with a consciousness of the tragic nature of life, and conditioned by his religious perception of the present."[37]

THE THREE SPEECHES

As in his two other addresses on Dostoevsky, in "Three Speeches in Memory of Dostoevsky" Soloviev's concern was neither biographical analysis nor an aesthetic appraisal of the latter's works. Soloviev emphasizes the choice he deliberately made, claiming that he writes thus about Dostoevsky not because he cannot write otherwise but because he does not wish to do so. Moreover, it is significant that the flowering of Soloviev's critical activity came in the 1890s, whereas he was writing about Dostoevsky in the 1880s, when he not only felt little attraction to standard literary criticism but was apparently unsure about his talent for it. In any event, in a letter to Nikolai Strakhov from early 1884, Soloviev says with regard to the publication of his "Three Speeches": "Of course, taken together this will be only 'apropos,' since for a true and complete appraisal of Dostoevsky it is necessary, apart from all else, to be a literary critic, and God has not granted me this, and certainly if you, a first-rate literary critic, have limited yourself to 'recollections' alone, then my rightful portion is but 'an opinion' [*vzgliad i nechto*]."[38] Yet the modesty of Soloviev's self-assessment in no way lessens the objective value of his pronouncements on Dostoevsky during this period. Indeed, it might be conjectured that this confession was in part the product of a desire to please the addressee (Strakhov would, of course, have enjoyed receiving such a compliment from Soloviev, especially as the two men were by no means always generous in their mutual assessments). Later, having achieved mastery in the field of criticism, Soloviev no longer belittled himself; on the contrary, according to Radlov, he was fond of saying that within literary criticism he occupied "a special place, for he had raised it to a new level."[39]

The history of the composition of the "Three Speeches in Memory of Dostoevsky" is bound together with the history of the literary and public attitudes that grew up around the legacy and figure of Dostoevsky, so painstakingly guarded by the writer's widow, who established a tradition of yearly literary evenings in his memory. For three years Soloviev played a chief role in these events. In 1884, however, he declined to participate in the readings, expressing himself in no uncertain terms in a letter to a friend: "I received an urgent invitation from Anna Dostoevskaia to read something at the literary evening, but I refused. Basta!"[40] As has been correctly surmised, "the reason behind Soloviev's abandonment of the gatherings in memory of Dostoevsky was his recognition that the cycle of the progression of thought that had found singular fruition in the apotheosis of Dostoevsky in the 'Three Speeches' was now complete. To go any further with it would for Soloviev have meant entering into a characteristically uncompromising argument with Dostoevsky himself. It is no accident that henceforth all the philosopher's pronouncements on Dostoevsky contained qualifications and were made in passing."[41]

Undoubtedly, Soloviev's progression of thought in the "Three Speeches" increasingly reflects not only Dostoevsky's sphere of ideas but also that of Soloviev himself. The philosopher dedicates his speeches to elucidating "the prevailing idea Dostoevsky carried with him throughout his life, though he only began to master it fully toward the end."[42] Soloviev explains his renunciation of the role of literary critic by referring, first, to the conscious choice of his procedure (as discussed above) and, second, to Dostoevsky's individual stature as a writer. "It seems to me," he says, "that one cannot view Dostoevsky as merely an ordinary novelist, a talented and intelligent man of letters."[43] (Compare this with Mikhailovskii's declaration quoted above:

"Dostoevsky is simply a great and original writer worthy of careful study and offering tremendous literary interest."[44])

The first of Soloviev's "Three Speeches" begins with a brief interpretation of the historically religious role of art and a survey of its present-day condition:

> In the primordial days of humanity, poets were prophets and priests, the religious idea was master of poetry, art served the gods. Then, as life grew more complicated and a civilization founded on the division of labor appeared, art, like the rest of human affairs, stood apart and separated itself from religion. . . . Priests of pure art appeared, for whom the perfection of artistic form became the main thing, apart from any religious content. . . . Artists today are unable and unwilling to serve pure art, to produce perfect forms; they are searching for content. Yet, strangers to the earlier religious content of art, they appeal exclusively to current reality and place themselves in a *doubly* servile relation to it: in the first place, they slavishly try to copy the phenomena of this reality, and, in the second, they strive just as slavishly to serve the topic of the day. . . . In their unsuccessful pursuit of allegedly real details they merely manage to lose the true reality of the whole, while their desire to graft onto art an outward didacticism and usefulness to the detriment of its inner beauty transforms art into the most useless and unnecessary thing in the world.[45]

Of course, everyday realism in literature and, as Soloviev puts it, "partisan encroachments on the idea of beauty" were equally unacceptable to Dostoevsky. It is enough to recall one of his many panegyrics to beauty: "Without the English, life is still possible for humanity, without Germany, life is possible, without the Russians it is only too possible, without science, without bread, life is possible—only without beauty is it impossible, for there would be nothing left in the world."[46] Incidentally, the metamorphosis in *The Devils* of Stepan Trofimovich Verkhovenskii, who utters this panegyric, might serve as an illustration of the idea Soloviev developed of the rebirth of art. Soloviev sets out his vision of a religious and aesthetic synthesis, by which utilitarian and purist approaches find their reconciliation: "The demands for a contemporary reality and a direct benefit from art, meaningless in their present rough and vague application, hint, however, at that heightened and profoundly true idea of artistry which neither the representatives nor the interpreters of pure art have thus far been able to reach. Not content with beauty of form, contemporary artists want, more or less consciously, for art to be a *real force* illuminating and regenerating the entire human world." For the realization of this goal, "art, having separated itself from religion, must enter into a new, free relationship with it."[47] By analogy with Soloviev's construction, the aesthetic position of the elder Verkhovenskii is quite clearly rooted in that humanistic European past when "art became deity and idol." Stepan

Trofimovich's Hamletesque question "Raphael or petroleum?" refers to his own contemporary reality. And in the end, the religious awakening toward which Dostoevsky leads his character must, in Soloviev's triad, transform the art of the future.[48]

Soloviev calls Dostoevsky the forerunner of such art. Unlike many of his contemporaries, who were calling Dostoevsky a prophet while he was still alive, Soloviev bases his conviction not on emotional raptures evoked by Dostoevsky's "religiosity" but on the correspondence (if only in an elementary, developing stage) of the *aesthetics* of the writer to that ideal art of the future whose principles are organically linked with the basic ideas in Soloviev's worldview. (What is more, in the framework of his theocratic idea, which crystallized precisely in the early 1880s, the notion of "prophet" had for Soloviev a real and practical meaning.[49] This fact without question distinguishes Soloviev's use of the word *prophet* from the subsequent clichéd celebrations of Dostoevsky.) Soloviev sees the features of religious art first and foremost in the striving "for the complete embodiment of the idea in its smallest material details to the point of an almost perfect merging with current reality and, at the same time, in the urge to *influence* real life, revising and improving it according to certain ideal requirements."[50] This is the same synthesis of the metaphysical and the physical, idea and matter, conception and practice, that forms the very nerve of Soloviev's philosophy.[51] Therefore, the uniqueness of Dostoevsky the artist consists for Soloviev primarily in the fact that the writer, proceeding from prevailing realism, ultimately reaches a religious truth to which he binds the tasks of his works and from which he derives his own social ideal.

At the same time, wishing to show the difference between Dostoevsky and other "realist" writers, Soloviev makes a highly significant observation about the nature of realism, the essence of which would later find distinct echoes in both Viacheslav Ivanov's theory of realism and Bakhtin's conception of the "author": "Any detail, taken separately, is not real in and of itself, for only *everything together* is real; moreover, the realist artist still views reality *from his own point of view,* he understands it in his own way, and, consequently, it is no longer *objective* reality."[52] Another feature that Soloviev emphasizes in contrasting Dostoevsky's novels with the works of Goncharov, Leo Tolstoi, and Turgenev is the *dynamic* character of his artistic world: "Here, everything is in ferment, nothing is fixed, everything is still only becoming."[53] If in other authors we find a portrayal of the social condition, he writes, the subject of a Dostoevsky novel is social movement. Soloviev does not delve deeply into the artistic aspects that are potentially inferable from this observation; instead, following the task he has set for himself, he traces how social movement in the novels of Dostoevsky reflects a positive social ideal that gradually takes shape in the course of the writer's creative career. "If we want to use one word to designate the social ideal at which Dostoevsky arrived, this word would be . . . the *Church*," says Soloviev, citing an important literary and historical fact: "The Church as positive social ideal was to be the central idea of a new novel or new series of novels, of which only the first was written—*The Brothers Karamazov*."[54]

Soloviev continues to develop the idea of the universal Church in the second of the "Three Speeches." The basic propositions of this second speech center on the characteristic features of Dostoevsky's worldview. In addition, it is important to Soloviev to present not simply Dostoevsky's Orthodoxy but also his creative work as the essence of his personality: "People of fact lead [passive] lives that are not theirs in the full sense, but they do not create life. Those who *create life* are people of faith. It is those called dreamers, utopists, and God's fools who are the prophets, who are the truly better people and the leaders of humanity. It is just such a man we remember today."[55] Soloviev calls the central idea that Dostoevsky serves the idea of universal brotherhood in the name of Christ, noting in this regard Dostoevsky's particular hopes for a universal historical role for Russia in the realization of Christian unity. Yet in his development of this objective assertion, Soloviev, as Aleksei Losev observes, allows "a somewhat looser expression than was characteristic of Dostoevsky."[56] At first he speaks of the universal meaning of Dostoevsky's preaching, then later arrives at the declaration that Dostoevsky "never idealized the people [*narod*] nor worshipped the people as an idol." But as proof of the latter Soloviev cites the thesis Dostoevsky advanced in his Pushkin speech about the capacity of the Russians for assimilating the spirit and ideas of foreign nations, that is, the "worldwide sensitivity" of the Russian people. Unfortunately, the spirit of the Pushkin speech, though unquestionably close to Soloviev and perhaps reflecting his influence, does not eliminate the existence of other contrary and distinctly nationalistic declarations made by Dostoevsky. By the 1890s, Soloviev did not hesitate to draw attention to the incompatibility of many of Dostoevsky's statements with "the universal ideal he proclaimed."[57] But in the speeches in his memory he not only avoided mentioning this incompatibility but even preferred to smooth it over.

In the last of the "Three Speeches," the question of universal Christian unity, representing in general form the highest aim for both Dostoevsky and Soloviev, is tactically defined in purely Solovievian fashion. Moreover, the impression emerges that Soloviev is carrying on a polemic with his late friend, accenting precisely those problems of ecclesiastical union which a nationalistic position is helpless to resolve. For this reason, it seems to me, the generally accepted view that the third speech contains a number of different ideas having little in common with Dostoevsky requires logical (and psychological) correction. In fact, Soloviev's ideas as espoused in that speech have a direct bearing on problems that had troubled and even exasperated Dostoevsky; in it, his dialogue with Dostoevsky attains its culmination, though by no means harmony. It is precisely here that Soloviev begins to develop the theocratic theme which was to become central to him in the coming years. As this theme narrows, so too the polemics touching upon Dostoevsky's relevant views become more pointed. "If Christianity is the religion of salvation, if the Christian idea consists in healing, the inner joining of those elements whose separation is perdition, then the essence of the true Christian cause will be that which in logical terms is called *synthesis,* and in moral terms, *reconciliation.*"[58] Proceeding from this position, Soloviev systematically sets forth his goals: the union of churches, the reconciliation of East and West, and the Christian resolution of the Polish and Jewish questions. At the same time, while saying that the power of God could be seen "not only in the Catholic church but also in the Jewish synagogue," Soloviev does not, of course, maintain that Dostoevsky was as capable as he himself was of recognizing this. However, if Soloviev "dared" to speak out thus in a memorial speech, one must explain it not by a desire to correct a position that had compromised Dostoevsky with a view to his idealization, so much as by the necessity of continuing an unfinished polemic with him, the goal of which was *reconciliation.*

Besides the problems raised in connection with the idea of a universal Church, the third speech contains a description of several aspects of Dostoevsky's worldview which can be realized only within the perspective of Soloviev's own philosophical vision. "To believe in the Kingdom of God," writes Soloviev, "means to combine belief in man and belief in nature with a belief in God."[59] That is, Soloviev sees in the Christian ideal a universal doctrine that unites the Deity, humankind, and nature in a dialectical triad. Dostoevsky, in Soloviev's view,

> more than any of his contemporaries perceived the Christian idea *harmoniously* in its threefold fullness; he was mystic and humanist and naturalist all at once. Possessed of a keen sense of the inner link with the superhuman and in this respect a mystic, he found in this same sense the freedom and strength of man; familiar with the whole of human evil, he had faith in the whole of human good and was, by general recognition, a true humanist. But his faith in man was free of any one-sided idealism or spiritualism: he took man in all his fullness and reality; such a man is intimately bound up with material nature—and Dostoevsky

regarded nature with profound love and tenderness, understood and loved the earth and everything earthly, and believed in the purity, holiness, and beauty of matter. There is nothing false or sinful in such materialism. . . . True humanism is the belief in the *God-man* and true naturalism is the belief in *God-matter*.[60]

In this passage, according to Losev, "Soloviev was expressing his own view of matter, which must be regarded as unique in the history of idealism in general. And he quite rightly noted the same intuition for matter in Dostoevsky as well."[61] Soloviev's speeches in memory of Dostoevsky thus attempt to distill philosophical and religious intuitions and then reconcile them with his own vision. At the same time, Soloviev's aesthetic intuition firmly backed up his deep faith in the comprehensive truth of Dostoevsky's art.

SOLOVIEV AND SUBSEQUENT CRITICS

Of course, external circumstances as well as generic conventions forced the "Three Speeches in Memory of Dostoevsky" to conform to a tone that hampers an appraisal of their author's critical position. Yet even proceeding from the brief analysis of their content offered above, one can draw certain preliminary conclusions about Soloviev's creation of a thoroughly original approach to studying not only the philosophical meaning but also the literary aspects of Dostoevsky's work.[62] The subsequent development of the study of Dostoevsky's writings in Russian criticism has demonstrated the productive and influential nature of the ground laid by Soloviev. Works by Vasilii Rozanov, Akim Volynskii, Dmitrii Merezhkovskii, Lev Shestov, Andrei Belyi, Viacheslav Ivanov, Sergei Bulgakov, Nikolai Berdiaev, Sergei Askol'dov, Lev Karsavin, Nikolai Losskii, Sergei Gessen, Georges Florovsky, and Semen Frank, for all their diversity and originality of thought, are genetically linked to the "Three Speeches" even when their authors disagree with Soloviev or develop their thought in a different direction than did Soloviev himself. On the other hand, certain of Soloviev's observations anticipated the conclusions of Mikhail Bakhtin, the creator of the concept of the polyphonic novel.[63]

For Vasilii Rozanov, Dostoevsky was not merely a major interest and source of inspiration, catalyzing the other fundamental motifs of his writings—religion and sex—but also a fact of his biography. His marriage to Apollinariia Suslova, Dostoevsky's former mistress; their divorce, the complications of which contributed to Rozanov's interest in the "family question"; his first literary success, which came with publication of his study on the "Legend of the Grand Inquisitor"; his choice of *The Diary of a Writer* as his habitual bedside reading—all this speaks of the particular significance of Dostoevsky in Rozanov's life.[64]

Rozanov's monograph *The Legend of the Grand Inquisitor of F. M. Dostoevsky: An Exercise in Critical Commentary,* which appeared in 1891 in
Russkii vestnik, can be considered the first detailed scholarly study of Dostoevsky's art and thought.[65] Developing Soloviev's view of Dostoevsky as an
artist of metaphysical values and a religious prophet, Rozanov subjects the
literary text to a close reading. It has been claimed that the form of Rozanov's
book can be traced to Dostoevsky's *Diary of a Writer,* due to the mix of
genres and themes that characterizes both works.[66] Rozanov's approach is
still employed in analyses of Dostoevsky's work. It is important also to note
the retrospective link of Rozanov's literary critical genealogy to the social
aspect of the work of the *shestidesiatniki,* or "men of the 1860s," and to the
historical (in Strakhov's terminology, "organic") approach to literature offered by Apollon Grigoriev. An example of Rozanov's understanding of the
paths trodden by his predecessors is his 1892 article "Three Moments in the
Development of Russian Criticism," in which he assesses the positive and
negative aspects in the writings of Belinskii, Dobroliubov, and Grigoriev,
dividing the phases of Russian criticism into the aesthetic, the ethical, and
the scientific, respectively. Despite accusing Dobroliubov of a limited understanding of the artistic attitude toward life and of false literary deductions, Rozanov recalls with a faintly elegiac note "the best days of youth,"
when "university lectures and all the wisdom, ancient and great, that could
be gleaned from various old and new books, were forgotten behind a volume
of the works of Dobroliubov."[67]

Rozanov's inquiry into the "Legend of the Grand Inquisitor" is itself
engaging material for analysis. Considering himself a follower of Grigoriev
and Strakhov, that is, of what he defines as the scientific phase of Russian
criticism, Rozanov applied a truly scholarly method to Dostoevsky's work, of
the type traditionally adopted only in classical philology.[68] He replaced the
impressionistic style developed by the criticism of the nineteenth century in
regard to contemporary literature with academic standards based on an exact
method of working with the texts. At the same time, Rozanov's method
evokes associations with the procedures of biblical exegesis, especially if one
considers that the text with which Rozanov was dealing belongs in essence
to the apocryphal genre and has internal ties to the canonical texts of the
New Testament.[69]

It is worth observing the comprehensive accuracy of Rozanov's footnotes
and references (a scholarly aspect almost completely lacking in "impressionistic" criticism). In scholarly terms, even more essential is the ramified
structure of Rozanov's general commentary, which can be classified according to type:

1. Biographical commentary, that is, that in which Rozanov addresses the biography of Dostoevsky, in order to reveal the connection between the writer's personal experience and the ideas and plots found in his work.[70]

2. Historical-cultural commentary, projecting the problems raised by Dostoevsky onto the contemporary state of society and the social and moral problems he foresees.[71]

3. Historical-religious commentary, typically seeking to interpret the role of Orthodoxy in comparison with other confessions.[72]

4. Religious-theological commentary discussing the Christian and metaphysical significance of selected passages.[73]

5. Comparative commentary juxtaposing texts from various works by Dostoevsky.[74]

6. Comparative commentary juxtaposing the works of Dostoevsky with works by other writers.[75]

While not exhausting the characteristics of Rozanov's commentary, the above scheme demonstrates the radical contrast of his method to that of his predecessors. Having taken the "Legend of the Grand Inquisitor" as his central point, Rozanov included in his investigation those of Dostoevsky's other writings which are in one way or another related to it. This allowed him not only to carry out a profound analysis of the "Legend" itself but also to draw general conclusions concerning the whole of Dostoevsky's work within the context of nineteenth-century Russian literature.

Though it is difficult, in any direct sense, to compare Rozanov's study with Soloviev's pronouncements on Dostoevsky, certain intersections can be noted. Besides their shared view of Dostoevsky as a religious artist, both Soloviev and Rozanov offer a very similar description of Dostoevsky's artistic mode in its relation to that of Tolstoi, an issue that is taken up and elaborated by Merezhkovskii, as we shall see below. Soloviev writes: "In [Tolstoi's] motionless world everything is clear and defined, everything is fixed. . . . The artistic world of Dostoevsky is entirely opposite in character. Here, everything is in ferment, nothing is fixed, everything is still only becoming."[76] In the same way, Rozanov says: "Earlier we called Count Leo Tolstoi an artist of life in its finished forms, those which have acquired solidity. . . . On the other hand, Dostoevsky is by contrast an analyst of the *unfixed* in human life and in the human spirit."[77]

Echoes of Soloviev's ideas are also reflected in Rozanov's contrasting of the religious consciousness of the European nations to Orthodox tradition. This theme, however, is so embedded in the currency of Russian thought that it is all but impossible to trace individual distinctions in their respective arguments. In any event, Rozanov did not consciously follow Soloviev; evidence for this is found not only in their later polemics, but also in Rozanov's vulgar interpretation of Soloviev's theocratic idea in a footnote to his study of the "Legend."[78] There can be little doubt that at the time he was writing *The Legend of the Grand Inquisitor* Rozanov's thinking was not merely religious but specifically Orthodox. Consequently, in addition to its worth as literary scholarship, his critical commentary on the work of Dostoevsky possesses no less merit as an Orthodox Christian interpretation of metaphysical concepts and ideas. Rozanov's subsequent evolution led him fairly far from the position from which he "undermined the foundation of the Inquisitor's dialectics." His own "inquisitive" reproaches against Christ in *The Apocalypse of Our Times* for His having refused the temptation to reign over the world, and for having "unbearably aggravated human life," sound bitter and disillusioned. Ironically, in his final book Rozanov was to stumble against his own earlier book.

Soloviev's philosophical treatment of Dostoevsky's legacy was further developed by Dmitrii Merezhkovskii. A prolific man of letters, he devoted a number of works to Dostoevsky, including several large essays[79] and the monumental study *L. Tolstoi and Dostoevsky* (1900–1902). Proclaiming Dostoevsky in 1893 "a prophet unprecedented in history," Merezhkovskii elevated to the ecstatic the solemn tone that had been set by the speeches of Soloviev. (One should not ignore, however, the differences between the conventions of *spoken* rhetoric in which Soloviev was working and those of *written* literary criticism, even as regards the essayistic style chosen by Merezhkovskii.) Later Merezhkovskii went further still and called Dostoevsky "the prophet of the Russian revolution" (which he interpreted in a religious-mystical sense). This was a full departure from both the position of Dostoevsky himself and Soloviev's views on him.

Though Merezhkovskii does not refer to Soloviev in his study of the "life, work, and religion" of Leo Tolstoi and Dostoevsky, the basic idea around which he constructs his analysis is clearly linked to Soloviev's conception of Dostoevsky as the forerunner of a new religious art.[80] The very principle of Merezhkovskii's comparison of the two great writers coincides (as does Rozanov's) with the analogous strategy to which Soloviev resorts in the first of his "Three Speeches," where he reveals the distinctive features of Dostoevsky's artistic world by contrasting it to that of Tolstoi.[81] Despite the difference in what they saw as the main characteristics of each writer, there exists an inner connection: if, for Merezhkovskii, Tolstoi symbolizes the concept of the flesh and Dostoevsky that of the spirit, for Soloviev the former is distinguished by immobility and the latter by motion. However, whereas Soloviev's juxtaposition of Tolstoi and Dostoevsky is auxiliary with respect to his main theme, for Merezhkovskii it serves as a literary platform for his favorite construction of a "new revelation" that is called upon to combine "the truth of the world" with "the truth of heaven."

Soloviev's influence on Merezhkovskii, on the whole rather appreciable, expresses itself here in a transformation of the idea of God-manhood into an idea which would later take the shape of Merezhkovskii's conception of a "Third Testament." The subsequent discussion reveals more localized intersections between Merezhkovskii and Soloviev. Thus, for instance, Soloviev, as if in imitation of scientific terminology, notes that Tolstoi's main strength lies "in a most subtle reproduction of the *mechanism of phenomena related to the human soul [dushevnyi]*."[82] Merezhkovskii, meanwhile, adopting the Apostle Paul's division of a human being into three elements, the corporal, the spiritual, and the soulful (*dushevnyi*), writes that Leo Tolstoi is the supreme portrayer of the "soulful man"—a phenomenon which "in the language of modern science pertains to the realm of psychophysiology."[83] Both Soloviev and Merezhkovskii support their views of Tolstoi's "immobility" and "corporality" by citing *The Cossacks* and *Three Deaths*. No less symptomatic is the correspondence between Soloviev's brief observation concerning the rejection by the author of *War and Peace* of, it would seem, a proper scale in his depiction of Napoleon, a figure of worldwide historical significance, and Merezhkovskii's detailed discourse on the same theme.

Despite the fact that these intersections and coincidences may well be the fruit of each author's individual capacity for observation, the emerging similarity of thought cannot be ignored. Yet it is even more important to point out the divergences in their views. Within the framework of his concept, Merezhkovskii saw "the secret of the whole of future Russian culture" not in the line of Dostoevsky alone but in its confluence with the line of Tolstoi: "They are two great pillars, still solitary and not yet joined, on the threshold of a temple; two opposed parts, each turned toward the other, of a single building already begun but as yet invisible in its entirety—the building of a Russian and at the same time universal religious culture."[84]

Whereas Soloviev contrasted Dostoevsky with Tolstoi in order to demonstrate the uniqueness and the special religious and aesthetic significance of the former, for Merezhkovskii, Tolstoi and Dostoevsky symbolize a coming union of the pagan (or Old Testament!) "sanctity of the flesh" with the New Testament "sanctity of the spirit." And although the historical vision, necessary for Merezhkovskii's model, of paganism as a phenomenon that is "only pre-Christian and, at the same time, inevitably leads to Christianity"[85] formally coincides with an analogous conclusion in Soloviev's historical concept, the general sense of Merezhkovskii's construction diverges fundamentally from the ideas of Soloviev. (It should be noted that Soloviev's view of paganism as a prefiguration of Christianity has little in common with the ideas with which Merezhkovskii was preoccupied at the time—and which were partly consonant with Rozanov's arguments concerning two truths, one "pagan" and one "Christian," which were disjoined in the historical past but were to be made whole in the "new religious consciousness" of the future.) This general conceptual difference is clarified by Soloviev's polemic with Merezhkovskii over the latter's essay on Pushkin.[86] In his notorious article "Pushkin's Fate," Soloviev wrote: "The present-day admirers of Pushkin, without abandoning the bad critical method of *arbitrary* demands and *chance* criteria, reason thus: Pushkin is a great man, and since *our criterion* of true greatness is found in the philosophy of Nietzsche and demands that a great man be a teacher of the buoyant wisdom of paganism and a prophesier of the new or renewed cult of heroes, Pushkin must have been such a teacher of wisdom and such a prophesier of the new cult, for which he suffered at the hands of the stagnant and brutish masses."[87]

Probably stung by Soloviev's words, Merezhkovskii sought to explain himself in his introduction to *Tolstoi and Dostoevsky*: "When, some years ago, in an essay on Pushkin, I expressed the idea that his chief feature by comparison with other European poets consists in the resolution of universal contradictions, in the combination of two elements, pagan and Christian, in a hitherto unprecedented harmony, I was accused of attributing to Pushkin my own, allegedly 'Nietzschean' ideas, though it would seem that no idea could be more contrary or inimical to the definitive conclusions of Nietzscheanism than precisely that of the combination of the *two* elements."[88] Linking his earlier work to the present one, he concludes: "Studying Tolstoi and Dostoevsky means unraveling the riddle of Pushkin in the new Russian poetry."[89]

Tolstoi and Dostoevsky did not see the light of day until after Soloviev's death (only the first part, published in *Mir iskusstva* in early 1900, might have found its way into his hands). And although Soloviev, had he chanced to make the acquaintance of this study, scarcely would have accepted those of Merezhkovskii's Nietzschean tendencies that had made it into the new work from his Pushkin essay, certain of Merezhkovskii's analogies might have been found acceptable by the author of the *Three Conversations*—for instance, Merezhkovskii's statement concerning the common starting point of Tolstoyan and Nietzschean anti-Christianism.[90]

VIACHESLAV IVANOV AND MIKHAIL BAKHTIN

Viacheslav Ivanov was the first writer to elaborate a full conceptual basis for the critical approach which Soloviev initiated. In his "Dostoevsky and the Novel-Tragedy"—a landmark in the history of Russian criticism—he was the first to compare Dostoevsky's "principle of worldview" with his "principle of form." Where others had noted, at best, the specifics of style, Ivanov saw the specifics of genre. Focusing on the figures and events of Dostoevsky's novels, rather than on some abstract doctrines extracted from them, Ivanov in scholarly fashion distinguished three levels of analysis: the fabulistic, the psychological, and the metaphysical.[91] His main theoretical concern lay in an attempt to elucidate in Dostoevsky a synthesis of form and content by analogy with Greek tragedy.

If Soloviev's vision of Dostoevsky as "the forerunner of a new religious art" found a vital response in the works of Rozanov, Merezhkovskii, and others, in Ivanov this vision was creatively adapted and organically tied to the conception of theurgic art and to his general theory of Symbolism. Of course, it is no accident that Soloviev's thesis regarding Dostoevsky was developed with such profundity within Ivanov's religious and aesthetic system; besides the fact that Russian Symbolism (in its "junior" branch) was inseparably linked to the name of Soloviev, it was precisely Viacheslav Ivanov —the chief theoretician of Symbolism—who was instrumental in the full elaboration of this link. He also recognized the correlation of Dostoevsky with Soloviev and drew his own view of Dostoevsky out of Soloviev's. Ivanov called Soloviev an "artist of the inner forms of the Christian consciousness" and claimed that he was the source of "all the slogans and definitions of our most recent religious quest."[92] One should also mention that for Ivanov, who responded to people with at least as much ardor as he did to their ideas, his personal meeting with Soloviev proved pivotal. His remark about Soloviev, "He was the protector of my Muse and the confessor of my heart,"[93] reflects the continuity of *realiora* through a symbolic affirmation of *realia*.[94]

Ivanov devoted three articles to Dostoevsky—"Dostoevsky and the Novel-Tragedy" (1911), "Excursus: The Principal Myth in the Novel *The Devils*" (1914), and "The Image and Masks of Russia: Toward a Study of Dostoevsky's Ideology" (1917)—in addition to a monograph originally entitled *Dostoevsky: Tragedy-Myth-Mysticism*.[95] Mikhail Bakhtin, who used Ivanov's ideas as a starting point in developing his own conception of the "polyphonic novel" of Dostoevsky, wrote:

> The first to grope his way toward this basic structural feature of Dostoevsky's artistic world was Viacheslav Ivanov—and, to be sure, he only groped. He defined

Dostoevsky's realism as a realism based not on cognition (objectified cognition), but on "penetration." To affirm someone else's "I" not as an object but as another subject—this is the principle governing Dostoevsky's worldview. To affirm some-one else's "I"—"thou art"—is a task that, according to Ivanov, Dostoevsky's char-acters must successfully accomplish if they are to overcome their ethical solipsism, their disunited "idealistic" consciousness, and transform the other person from a shadow into an authentic reality. At the heart of the tragic catastrophe in Dosto-evsky's work there always lies the solipsistic separation of a character's conscious-ness from the whole, his incarceration in his own private world.[96]

Having accepted Bakhtin's comments, I consider it important to show how far Ivanov's approach corresponds to the ideas of Soloviev in general, and in particular to his views on Dostoevsky. Ivanov's programmatic essay "Two Elements in Contemporary Symbolism" (1908) leaves no doubts on this score. Proceeding in a straight line from the ideas put forth by Soloviev in the first of his "Three Speeches," Ivanov wrote:

> Art was religious when and insofar as it directly served the aims of religion. The craftsmen of such art were, for instance, the makers of idols in paganism, the medieval icon painters, the nameless builders of the Gothic churches. These artists were ruled by the religious idea. But when Vladimir Soloviev says of the artists of the future that "not only will they be ruled by the religious idea, but they will themselves rule that idea and consciously direct its earthly incarnations," he sets these *theurgists* a task still more important than that which the ancient artists sought to accomplish, and interprets religious art and creativity in an even more elevated sense.[97]

Soloviev's idea that "artists and poets must again become priests and prophets" becomes Ivanov's point of departure. Moreover, in the process of establishing a goal and working out steps for its realization, Soloviev ap-peared to Ivanov not only the source of theoretical inspiration with respect to the new religious art, but also a practical example of its realization (that is, something analogous to how Soloviev regarded Dostoevsky). And, al-though it is commonly held that Ivanov's conception of realistic symbolism was influenced by German Romantic aesthetics, its Solovievian roots are much more obvious. Suffice it to recall the definition given by Soloviev of "art that is true in essence": "*Any tangible depiction of whatever object or phenomenon from the point of view of its definitive state, or in the light of the future world, is an artistic work*."[98] Indeed, Ivanov's very slogan of realistic symbolism, his famous formula *a realibus ad realiora*, exhibits not only a general kinship to Soloviev but also a direct connection to the first of his "Three Speeches in Memory of Dostoevsky." Soloviev's notion of the nature of realism is clearly reflected in his observation, first, of the existence of two realities, "reality *from one's own point of view*" and "*objective* reality," and, second, of the integral character of reality (meaning, of course, objective reality): "only *everything together* is real."[99]

No less significant is the link between Soloviev's ideas and the concept of the "other I" employed by Ivanov to explain the principles of Dostoevsky's realism. Ivan Lapshin, author of the study "The Problem of the 'Other I' in Recent Philosophy," believed that Vladimir Soloviev "was the first writer in Russian philosophical literature to raise the question of the 'other I.'"[100] Lapshin cites the essay "On the Reality of the External World," where Soloviev makes the solution of the problem of knowing the essence of the Other analytically dependent on the law of identity. "I am spontaneously *certain* and know," he writes, "that the man with whom I am speaking is not the manifestation of some *Ding an sich* unknown to me, but an independent being who has the *same* inner reality as I do myself."[101] At the same time it is assumed that "the cognized is not other to the cognizant, but is he himself, and thus this inner cognition is a spontaneous self-distinguishing and self-cognition of a psychic being."[102] The views expressed by Soloviev find a clear echo in Ivanov's ideas regarding Dostoevsky's realistic world-outlook:

> This realism is founded not on theoretical cognition, with its constant opposition of subject and object, but on an act of will and faith which corresponds approximately to Augustine's *transcende te ipsum*; to designate this act Dostoevsky chose the word "penetration." . . . The symbol of such penetration lies in the absolute affirmation, with all one's will and all one's powers of reason, of another's existence—in "Thou art" [*Ty esi*]. . . . "Thou art" no longer means "you are known by me as existing," but rather "your being is experienced by me as my own, through your being I again know myself to exist."[103]

Thus Soloviev directs a problem that was originally epistemological (which, incidentally, is how it remains in Lapshin's thinking) toward an ontological cognition "of the essence of the Other." Ivanov, accepting Soloviev's general understanding, elaborates on the ethical consequences of the problem of the "Other." Dostoevsky's "penetration," on which, in Ivanov's view, his realism is based, lies "outside the cognitive sphere" or within the sphere of that "absolute cognition which we call faith."[104] Ivanov finds confirmation of his interpretation of Dostoevsky's extrarational realism in Dostoevsky's own words: "With perfect realism one finds the man within the man. . . . People call me a psychologist: this is not true, I am merely a realist in the highest sense, that is, I depict the full depths of the human soul."[105]

It is also in line with Soloviev's thought that Ivanov develops the "theme of Mother Earth." The ideas Soloviev expresses in the "Three Speeches" concerning Dostoevsky's link to material nature, about his "faith in nature" and thereby his "faith in the *Mother of God*," are systematically elaborated by Ivanov within the spirit of Solovievian Sophiology. "The mystical realist," he writes, "is he who knows Our Lady, the beloved Bride, the eternal Woman, and in her many aspects recognizes a single principle. . . . The mystical realist sees Her in love and in death, in nature and in the living community [*sobornost'*] that creates of humankind . . . a single universal body. Through his initiation into the mystery of death Dostoevsky was led, apparently, to the knowledge of this universal mystery, as Dante was through his penetration into the *sanctum sanctorum* of love. And just as death was revealed to Dante through love, so to Dostoevsky, through death, was love revealed. Which is to say that to both Nature was also revealed as a living soul."[106]

The artistic form that allowed Dostoevsky to follow the principles of "high realism" is called by Ivanov the "novel-tragedy." He finds substantiation for this generic definition in the fact that Dostoevsky's works outgrew the his-torically established European novel, which was incapable of surpassing the limitations of the individualism of which it was a "mirror." (That is, individ-ualism in which the "other I" is perceived as an object.) On the other hand, Ivanov sees in Dostoevsky the architectonic features of classical tragedy. It is interesting that Bakhtin, who criticizes Ivanov for his definition of the Dostoevsky novel as a "novel-tragedy" and, in particular, for his application to Dostoevsky of the idea of tragic catharsis,[107] overlooks several propositions in Ivanov's work which could be construed within the spirit of Bakhtin's own polyphonic conception. These include a comparison of the method of the novel to thematic and contrapuntal development in music, as well as Ivanov's argument about the combination in the classical epic form, with which he links the novel of Dostoevsky, of features of the lyric and drama, that is, the voices of the author and of the "other characters."

The principal echoes of Soloviev's ideas in Bakhtin's book *Problems of Dostoevsky's Poetics* arise when Bakhtin intersects with Ivanov. One could say that, to the extent that Bakhtin accepted Ivanov's ideas, he was accepting Soloviev's as well. Therefore, the preceding argument on Ivanov's relation-ship to Soloviev need not be repeated with respect to Bakhtin.[108]

Since interpretation of Bakhtin's concept of the polyphonic novel, which is central to his entire theory, is still a matter of some debate, any discussion of it, especially in a comparative context, requires that the views of the discussants—the "author's position," so to speak—be clarified. My position coincides with that of Morson and Emerson: "Polyphony is often criticized as a theory that posits the absence of authorial point of view, but Bakhtin explicitly states that the polyphonic author neither lacks nor fails to express his ideas and values. . . . The issue here is not an absence of, but a *radical change in, the author's position*."[109] In "Toward a Reworking of the Dostoevsky Book," Bakhtin writes about the author's position in the polyphonic novel: "Dostoevsky frequently interrupts, but he never drowns out the other's voice, never finishes it off 'from himself,' that is, out of his own and alien consciousness. This is, so to speak, the activity of God in His relation to man, a relation allowing man to reveal himself utterly (in his immanent development), to judge himself, to refute himself. It is activity of a higher quality."[110]

As it happens, the statement Bakhtin makes here, especially since it is reinforced by his "theurgic" analogy, is comparable to Soloviev's formulation of the difference between Dostoevsky and "realist artists." For convenience of comparison, let us cite his words again: "The realist artist still views reality *from his own point of view*, he understands it in his own way, and, consequently, it is no longer *objective* reality."[111] Bakhtin's definition of activity not "of oneself" as "an activity of a higher quality," comparable to the "activity of God," implies, clearly, that very *"objective* reality" of which Soloviev speaks. The development of this idea by Bakhtin is consonant with a pronouncement Soloviev makes about Dostoevsky in the second of his "Three Speeches." "His ideal," writes Soloviev, "requires not merely the unity of all people and all things human, but above all their unity *as humans*. The point is not unity but the free *consent* to unity."[112] Bakhtin bases his characterization of the polyphonic novels of Dostoevsky on the same categories: freedom and unity. He believes that Dostoevsky creates "*free* people, capable of standing *alongside* their creator, capable of not agreeing with him and even of rebelling against him" (Bakhtin's italics);[113] moreover, "the artistic image of someone else's personality, . . . the image of many unmerged personalities joined together in the unity of some spiritual event, was fully realized for the first time in his [Dostoevsky's] novels."[114]

Bakhtin draws a conclusion which blends ideally into the system of Soloviev's views on Dostoevsky: "Dostoevsky's world is profoundly *pluralistic*. If we were to seek an image toward which this whole world gravitates, an image in the spirit of Dostoevsky's own worldview, then it would be the church as a communion of unmerged souls."[115] It is interesting that, as a contrast to the "unfinalizability" of Dostoevsky's world, Bakhtin, like Soloviev, chooses the artistic world of Tolstoi (an "immobile world," as Soloviev puts it). What is more, Soloviev's observation that in the artistic world of Dostoevsky "everything is in ferment, nothing is fixed, everything is still only becoming,"[116] would seem to find an echo in a concept broadly developed by Bakhtin and fundamental within the framework of his poetics—the concept of unfinalizability (*nezavershennost'*). "Nothing conclusive," Bakhtin writes about the novels of Dostoevsky, "has yet taken place in the world, the ultimate word of the world and about the world has not yet been spoken, the world is open and free, everything is still in the future and will always be in the future."[117]

Bakhtin's conception of the polyphonic nature of Dostoevsky's novel represents a unique model of literary critical analysis. Yet Bakhtin was the first to acknowledge the historical sources of his conception, starting with Ivanov, who, even within the limits of "philosophical monologization," arrived, in Bakhtin's words, "at a profound and correct definition of Dostoevsky's fundamental principle."[118] Therefore, by calling attention to the links between Bakhtin's theory and particular propositions enunciated by Soloviev, we are speaking not only about specific aspects of his influence on Bakhtin, but also about the continuation of a philosophical tradition in Russian thought connected with the name of Soloviev.[119]

THE "THREE SPEECHES" AND SOLOVIEV'S CRITICAL LEGACY

Despite Soloviev's claim to a conscious abstention from any aesthetic appraisal of Dostoevsky's work, the "Three Speeches" already expound the basic elements of an aesthetic method that were to characterize his later essays in literary criticism. These articles from the 1890s demonstrate with perfect clarity the fundamental principle of Soloviev's artistic criticism: philosophical thought is aimed first and foremost at grasping the *artistic* meaning whose aesthetic objectivity transcends methodological schemes. "The chief, properly critical task," says Soloviev, "consists after all not in the reproduction but in the *appraisal* of a given poetic activity *in its essence*, that is, as a *beautiful object* presenting in some concrete form or another the truth of life, or the meaning of the world."[120]

Soloviev did not live to fulfill his plan of writing a major treatise on aesthetics. It is quite obvious that, had death not taken him at the age of forty-seven, we would have had a *Justification of Beauty* to set alongside his *Justification of Good*. But even so, Soloviev's understanding of the nature of art and of the creative element in life is certainly deducible both from his philosophical system as a whole and from individual essays dealing with aesthetic issues. He sketched an outline for an aesthetic treatise as early as the 1870s, in the "Conclusion" to his doctoral dissertation *A Critique of Abstract Principles:*

> If in the moral realm (for the will) unitotality is absolute good, and if in the cognitive realm (for the mind) it is absolute truth, then the accomplishment of unitotality in external reality, its realization or embodiment in the realm of sensate, material existence, is absolute beauty. Since such a realization of unitotality has not yet been granted within our reality, within the human and natural world, but is only in the process of becoming, and furthermore, becoming through our own participation, it is thus a task for humanity, and its fulfillment is art. The general foundations and rules of this great and mysterious art, which puts everything that exists in the form of beauty, comprise our third and final point of inquiry.[121]

Thus, Soloviev placed at the base of his aesthetics a dynamic principle that is central to his worldview: the fulfillment of unitotality, that is, the intrinsic coherence of all things by virtue of truth, good, and beauty.

Soloviev elaborated his aesthetic views in a series of articles in the 1890s: "Beauty in Nature," "The General Meaning of Art," and "A First Step toward a Positive Aesthetics." In these fundamental works, Soloviev examined the phenomenon of beauty as such, and discussed the role of art in the concrete betterment of reality, in the attainment of the "fullness of life." Referring to art as a transforming force, he essentially developed an aesthetic extension of his chief philosophical ideas, one of which emphasizes the need for a mediatory element between the material and the ideal worlds. In the particular realm of the beautiful, the interaction between matter and idea is fulfilled, according to Soloviev, by art, or rather by the creator of works of art, who participates as the "mediator" in the divinely human process of the perfection of the world. This is why any artist's aspiration—to achieve the aesthetic ideal—acquires in Soloviev special significance: "Every sensate representation of any object and phenomenon from the point of view of its ultimate condition or in the light of the future world is the work of art."[122] And the result of an art that meets this absolute criterion must be, as Soloviev had already stated in "The First Speech in Memory of Dostoevsky," "the illumination and regeneration of the entire human world."[123]

The basic metaphysical constructs and philosophical conclusions of Soloviev's doctrine were naturally reflected in the literary criticism of his last decade. He performed, one may say, a "laboratory experiment" by applying the analytical potentials of "integral knowledge" (a synthesis of theology, philosophy, and empirical science) to the analysis of literature. These critical articles, in particular his essays on Pushkin, anticipated in many respects the methods of twentieth-century literary criticism. Among the innovative aspects of Soloviev's critical approach we can list his attention to oppositions and parallels as revealed through a comparative analysis of different texts; his attention to plot structure and to time-space relationships;

and his concern with style, syntax, and grammar. As one scholar has observed, Soloviev's methods of reading and analysis "helped prepare the way for a modern approach to Pushkin's texts" and can be regarded as "his principal contribution to Pushkin studies and to modern Russian criticism in general."[124]

It should be noted that the poetry of Pushkin becomes, within the framework of Soloviev's aesthetics, almost an empirical criterion of beauty in art. Repeatedly calling the poetry of Pushkin a "diamond," Soloviev is, as it were, referring to his own essay "Beauty in Nature," where an image of a diamond helps to illustrate the main idea with exemplary elegance and clarity.[125]

> The beauty of a diamond, being in no way characteristic of its fabric (for this fabric is the same as that found in an ugly lump of coal), obviously depends on the play of beams of light in its crystals. It does not follow from this, however, that the attribute of beauty belongs not to the diamond itself but rather to the beam of light refracted in it. For that same beam of light, when reflected off some ugly object, produces no aesthetic impression whatsoever. . . . Thus beauty, belonging neither to the material body of the diamond nor to the beam of light refracted in it, is a product of the two things in concert. . . . Neither the earthly substance nor the element of light is predominant in the diamond, but rather each penetrates the other in a sort of ideal balance. . . . In this unmerged and indivisible union of substance and light both things preserve their own natures, yet neither one is seen as separate; we see only light-bearing matter and embodied light."[126]

This startling aesthetic idea appears almost as a conceptual prefiguration of the theories of relations, which constitute a prominent trend in twentieth-century thought. But in Soloviev's "prefiguration" of relational theories the ultimate aim is the aesthetic transfiguration of matter and, therefore, the restoration of its metaphysical status. In effect, in speaking about "Pushkin's diamonds," Soloviev points to the ontological beauty of his poetry.[127] In Pushkin's "rainbowlike" poetry, Soloviev discovers a perfect transformation of creative forces similar to the transformation of a ray of white light when it comes into contact with the crystalline body of the diamond. It is precisely in these terms that Soloviev defines beauty as the transfiguration of matter through the embodiment of the supramaterial principle.

For Soloviev, "it was not enough to postulate a 'real' beauty without postulating also man's ability to know it objectively."[128] Predictably, in the field of literary criticism he conducted an objective, comprehensive study of his chosen topics, presenting in his later essays an amalgam of philosophical and formal approaches to the text. The same quality of analysis can also be

discerned in Soloviev's earliest display of critical style, his essays on Dostoevsky. The "Three Speeches in Memory of Dostoevsky" marked a turning
point in the interpretation of Dostoevsky's oeuvre. Moreover, the ideas and
observations presented by Soloviev in this small triptych have given us generous fruit in diverse areas of modern literary criticism and aesthetics.

2
Years of Friendship

Equality creates friendship.
— *Plato*

ACQUAINTANCE

Vladimir Sergeevich Soloviev and Fedor Mikhailovich Dostoevsky first became personally acquainted in 1873. The earliest evidence of direct contact
is Soloviev's letter to Dostoevsky of 24 January concerning the journal
Grazhdanin, of which Dostoevsky had recently become editor. The letter
provides an important expression of Soloviev's position and, significantly,
presumes Dostoevsky's agreement on certain questions.

> Dear Fedor Mikhailovich!
> Owing to the superstitious worship of the anti-Christian principles of civiliza-
> tion that prevails in our senseless literature, there can be no place in it for free
> judgment of these principles. Meanwhile, such a judgment, even if weak in and
> of itself, would be useful, as is any protest against falsehood.
> From the program of *Grazhdanin*, as well as from some of your remarks in

issues 1 and 4, I conclude that the orientation of this journal must be quite different than in the rest of journalism, though it is still not fully formulated with regards to problems of general concern. Therefore, I feel that I may present to you my own brief analysis of the negative principles of Western development: external freedom, exclusive personality, and rational knowledge—liberalism, individualism, and rationalism.

However, I claim for this small experiment only one unquestionable merit, namely, that the prevailing falsehood is openly called falsehood, and emptiness, emptiness.

With genuine respect I have the honor of being your most obedient servant, Vl. Soloviev. Moscow 24 January 1873.[1]

At this time, Soloviev had just turned twenty. He was a student at Moscow University, where a year earlier he had left the Department of Physics and Mathematics and enrolled as a free auditor in the Department of History and Philology. Eighteen seventy-three was Soloviev's final year of study. He was writing to Dostoevsky a few months before taking his examination and receiving a master's degree in historical philology.[2]

Dostoevsky was fifty-one in early 1873, the greater part of his life already past. Behind him were the years of his early youth and his rather tedious studies at the School of Engineering in Petersburg. Behind him were the socialist illusions of the Petrashevskii Circle that had brought him the death sentence, later commuted to four years of penal servitude in Siberia—though only after a horrible mock execution. Behind him was the overwhelming experience of prison and Siberian exile. Behind him, too, were his difficult first marriage, his dramatic and turbulent relations with the quintessential "Dostoevskian" woman, Apollinariia Suslova, his compulsive gambling, and his endless debts. He had already written *Notes from the House of the Dead*, *Notes from Underground*, and his great novels *Crime and Punishment*, *The Idiot*, and *The Devils*. All in all, by this time the most tumultuous portion of Dostoevsky's stormy life was over, and the 1870s were marked for him by a long-awaited stability in his daily life and work: Dostoevsky was an established writer of paramount significance for the Russian reader, and the great fame awaiting him in the not so distant future was already easy to divine; he was happily married to his second wife, and his lack of money had at least ceased to be chronic. Although these years could not be called years of patriarchal tranquility, still they had an air of conclusiveness about them.

However, neither the difference in age nor the difference in life experience prevented Soloviev and Dostoevsky from fast rapprochement. If Dostoevsky could not have had any preconceived attitude toward Soloviev (the young philosopher's first published work, "The Mythological Process in Ancient Paganism," was to appear later in 1873), he was nonetheless prepared for his acquaintance. In the first place, the reputation of Soloviev's father, Sergei Mikhailovich Soloviev, an eminent historian, rector of Moscow University (1871-1877), and a member of the Academy of Science (from 1872), made Dostoevsky by extension favorably disposed to the Soloviev family.[3] Dostoevsky's esteem for Sergei Soloviev is witnessed, for instance, by a meaningful mention of the historian's magnum opus in the novel *The Idiot:* the prince notices on a table at Rogozhin's home a copy of Soloviev's *History* that "was open and had a book-mark in it."[4] It was a reading, recommended to Rogozhin, as it turns out, by Nastasia Filippovna, who had told him: "You should educate yourself. You might at least read Soloviev's Russian history. You don't know anything at all."[5] But in Prince Myshkin's eyes, Soloviev's *History* symbolizes Rogozhin's ability to understand human suffering and feel pity for Nastasia Filippovna: "Rogozhin reading—was not that 'pity'? The beginning of 'pity'? Did not the very presence of that book prove that he was fully conscious of his attitude toward *her*?"[6] Dostoevsky also recommended Soloviev's *History* as reading for young people in letters to several correspondents and includes it in his "List of Books Essential for the Library of an Adolescent."[7]

In the second place, Vladimir's elder brother, Vsevolod Soloviev, had recently introduced himself to Dostoevsky, whom he greatly admired. Judging by the *Recollections of F. M. Dostoevsky* left by Vsevolod Soloviev, their first meeting on 2 January 1873 was an auspicious one.[8] By this time Dostoevsky's circle of friends had grown smaller and his relations with his relatives were somewhat strained, so the appearance of new young acquaintances could only have pleased the writer, who after all believed that "the main thing is to be loved by the young generation." One can assume that the amiable welcome shown by Dostoevsky to the elder brother presupposed a benevolent interest in the younger as well.

Anna Dostoevskaia describes Vladimir Soloviev's appearance in their home thus:

> At the beginning he wrote Fedor Mikhailovich a letter and later came to us at my husband's invitation. He made an enchanting impression on us, and the more often my husband saw and spoke with him the fonder of him he grew and the more impressed he became with his mind and his sound erudition. Once, my husband told Soloviev the reason he was so attached to him.
>
> "You remind me very much of a certain man," said Fedor Mikhailovich, "one Shidlovsky, who had a tremendous influence on me in my youth. You are so like him in both looks and personality that I sometimes feel his soul has transmigrated to you."
>
> "And has he been dead long?" asked Soloviev.

"No, only about four years."

"Then you think I went about without a soul for twenty years before he died?" asked Vladimir Sergeevich, and burst into loud laughter. In general, he could be very cheerful and had an infectious laugh. But sometimes curious things happened to him because of his absentmindedness. For instance, he assumed that because Fedor Mikhailovich was over fifty I, his wife, must be about the same age. And once, when we were discussing Pisemsky's novel *People of the Forties*, Soloviev said, addressing both of us, "Yes, it must seem to you people of the forties that — -."

At these words Fedor Mikhailovich laughed and said to me teasingly, "Do you hear that, Ania, Vladimir Sergeevich includes you too among the people of the forties!"

"And he doesn't err in the least," I answered. "For I really do belong to the forties, having been born in 1846."

Soloviev was very much embarrassed by his mistake. That was perhaps the first time he looked at me and realized the difference in age between my husband and myself.

Fedor Mikhailovich said of Soloviev's face that it reminded him of one of his favorite paintings by Annibale Carracci, *Head of the Young Christ*.[9]

In her diary for 1867, Anna Dostoevskaia made this entry about one of their visits to the Dresden Gallery: "In another hall is Annibale Carracci's picture *The Savior in His Youth*. Fedia greatly esteems and loves this picture."[10]

Ivan Nikolaevich Shidlovskii (1816-72),[11] of whom Soloviev reminded Dostoevsky, was friendly with the writer during the years 1837–39, when Shidlovskii had been nearly the same age as Soloviev at the time he met Dostoevsky. Shidlovskii was also a highly educated man, with a passion for literary and philosophical matters. He wrote poetry in a "mystical-romantic spirit" that made a great impression on Dostoevsky: "Ah, soon, soon I'll read through all of Ivan Nikolaevich's new poems. How much poetry! How many brilliant ideas!"[12] A letter written by Dostoevsky to his elder brother Mikhail on 1 January 1840 gives a gushing description of Shidlovskii, the ecstatic style of which testifies not only to a cult of friendship but also to a cult of Romanticism.[13] But Ivan Shidlovskii's early promise went unfulfilled: in 1839, leaving Petersburg and his job, he moved to his native Kharkov province, where he studied church history (a subject dear, in turn, to Vladimir Soloviev). But, as his daughter-in-law describes in a letter of 1901 to Anna Dostoevskaia,

> scholarly work was not enough to absorb the entirety of his moral activity. Inner discord, a dissatisfaction with all about him, these apparently were the reasons that prompted him during the 50s to enter the Valui Monastery. Apparently not finding satisfaction and peace of mind even there, he undertook a pilgrimage to

Kiev, where he appealed to a certain spiritual director who advised him to return home to the country, where he lived until his death, though even there not taking off the monastic habit of a novice. His strange life, so full of vacillations, bears witness to his strong passions and stormy nature. Ivan Nikolaevich's profound moral sense stood frequently in contradiction to several strange turns of behavior.[14]

Shidlovskii's "strange turns of behavior" were manifested in wanderings, in highway sermons, and at times in drunkenness.[15] It is interesting to note that several of Shidlovskii's behavioral traits and aspirations are indeed reminiscent of Vladimir Soloviev, though when Dostoevsky met the "young philosopher" he could have guessed only intuitively at the latent presence in Soloviev of Shidlovskii's dispositions and habits. Thus Soloviev's habit of wandering from friend to friend and hotel to hotel, the voluntary homelessness he adopted in his mature years, had yet to emerge at the time of his acquaintance with Dostoevsky. Similarly, Dostoevsky could hardly have known that Soloviev at times permitted himself to drink excessively, though, of course, unlike Shidlovskii he never indulged in what may be called "drunkenness." (Later, in *The Justification of the Good*, Soloviev expounded his "theory of wine-drinking," according to which, at higher stages of moral life, wine is able to raise the "energy of the organism," serving spiritual rather than bodily purposes.[16]) Striking, too, is the presence of Ukrainian roots in both Soloviev and Shidlovskii, which Dostoevsky, in comparing them, would again have been unlikely to suspect: Vladimir Soloviev's mother, Poliksena Vladimirovna, came from a very old and singularly gifted Ukrainian family, to one branch of which belonged the famous Russian-Ukrainian philosopher Grigorii Savvich Skovoroda (1722-94), the first religious philosopher in the history of Russian thought. Even a single province—Kharkov—linked Shidlovskii with Soloviev, whose maternal relatives had property there.

Yet in spite of certain similarities between the character and circumstances of the young Soloviev and Shidlovskii, the dimensions of their personalities and activity were clearly incommensurable. According to Dostoevsky himself, in Shidlovskii "a mass of contradictions lived side by side, an enormous intellect and a talent that was never expressed in a single written word, and that died along with him, binges and drunkenness and the taking of monastic vows."[17] The emotional attachment that colored Dostoevsky's attitude toward Soloviev because of the young philosopher's similarity to Shidlovskii finds its parallel in *The Brothers Karamazov*. Alesha resembles the elder Zosima's brother, "who died in his youth": "this brother was, as it were, a pointer and a destination from above in my fate, for if he had not appeared in my life, if he had not been at all, then never, perhaps, as I think, would I have entered monastic orders and set out upon this path. . . . Alexei seemed to me to resemble him so much spiritually that many times I have actually taken him, as it were, for that youth, my brother, come to me mysteriously at the end of my way, for a certain remembrance and perception."[18]

It is worth noting that Dostoevsky met Vladimir Soloviev shortly after completing his novel *The Devils*. Surely, neither the gallery of young men portrayed in the novel who gave in to "devilish" delusion and temptation nor their real-life prototypes had yet receded from the foreground of the author's attention. One can imagine that for Dostoevsky Soloviev's spiritual attitude would have been especially attractive because it contrasted with that of the characters in his recent novel. At the same time, some of Soloviev's biographers have found in *The Devils* an analogy to his own turbulent transitional period of the early 1870s, when his youthful radicalism had passed through various stages, including a brief yet passionate attraction to materialism. "In Moscow," recalls the philosopher's nephew, "Soloviev had already by that time begun to be surrounded by 'strange people,' mystics wavering between Orthodoxy, spiritism, and drunkenness, who saw in the young philosopher a 'superhuman' being. 'Do they really think,' Vladimir Sergeevich would sometimes say to my father, 'that I haven't the guts to found a sect?' . . . In general this circle of strange enthusiasts was reminiscent of the circle surrounding Nikolai Stavrogin in Dostoevsky's novel *The Devils* and more than one Shatov was prepared to exclaim bitterly: 'You meant much in my life, Vladimir Sergeevich!'"[19] As Soloviev's biographer Sergei Lukianov notes: "In some respects he was not even against outrivaling his peers who were less absorbed than he in questions of a philosophical nature."[20] An episode from Soloviev's biographical story "At the Dawn of a Cloudy Youth" may serve as an illustration of his tendency toward the extreme:

> I fell to talking with a young medical student. He was a provincial nihilist of the most fervent stripe. . . . We were in complete agreement that the existing order must soon be destroyed. But he believed that this destruction would be followed by an earthly paradise where no one would be poor, or foolish, or depraved, and that all humanity would begin to enjoy equally all physical and intellectual blessings in innumerable phalansteries that would cover the earth—whereas I heatedly maintained that his view was not radical enough, that in fact not just the world but the entire universe must be utterly annihilated, that if after this there was to be any life at all, it would be a completely different life, nothing like our present life, but purely transcendent. He was a radical-naturalist, I was a radical-metaphysician.[21]

Would Dostoevsky, however, have been troubled by any radical views? His notebook contains this infuriated response to "leftist" critics of *The*

Brothers Karamazov: "The villains mocked me for an *uneducated* and retrograde faith in God. Those fools haven't even begun to dream of a denial of God as powerful as the one I have placed in the Inquisitor and in the preceding chapter, to which the *entire novel* serves as a response. But I believe in God not as some idiot (fanatic) does. And they wanted to teach me and laughed at my backwardness! Their stupid nature cannot even conceive of a denial as powerful as that which I have gone beyond. What would they teach me!"[22]

If the various factors mentioned above paved the way for Dostoevsky's initially favorable impressions of Soloviev, their subsequent relations show a rapidly emerging mutual attachment. Of course, to Soloviev, Dostoevsky's greatness and singular importance were quite obvious. He wrote to his cousin Ekaterina Romanova on 19 June 1873: "It would be beneficial to read all of Dostoevsky: he is one of the few writers who still retains in our time an image and likeness of God."[23] As Sergei Lukianov notes, "Soloviev advised his cousin to read 'the great poets,' but during his entire two-year correspondence with her he specified by name only F. M. Dostoevsky."[24]

The year 1873 was for Soloviev a momentous one in many respects. On 8 June he was confirmed in the rank of candidate in the Department of History and Philology at Moscow University and invited to remain at the university "in order to pursue advanced study in the subject of philosophy and to prepare for professorial status." He spent part of the summer visiting a friend in Smolensk province and in the autumn began attending lectures at the Moscow Theological Academy, where he was admitted upon application "as an outside student." He continued to study there throughout the academic year 1873-74. In this same year, as has been mentioned, his first article, "The Mythological Process in Ancient Paganism," appeared in *Pravoslavnoe obozrenie* (no. 11). In addition, Soloviev was at this time seriously infatuated with Ekaterina Romanova. The relations between them followed an uneven and difficult path. Family contact and correspondence started between them when Soloviev was nineteen and his cousin just fifteen. Before long, however, their friendship took on a romantic quality, and Vladimir began to consider himself engaged. For more than two years he looked forward to one day marrying Ekaterina Romanova. The main obstacle to the marriage was the objection of Soloviev's parents over their close kinship: Ekaterina's father and Vladimir's mother were brother and sister. But there must have also been other reasons which kept Soloviev from settling down decisively and starting a family. "Let me give you a straight answer," Soloviev wrote to Romanova on 6 July 1873. "I love you as much as I am capable of loving anyone; however, I belong not to myself, but to that cause which I shall serve and which has nothing to do with personal feelings, with the interests and goals of personal life. I am unable to give myself to you entirely, and to offer anything less I feel to be unworthy."[25] It should be noted that Soloviev's letters to Ekaterina Romanova not only give us a memorable impression of the story of their relations but also acquaint us with many aspects of the young philosopher's view of the world. According to Ernst Radlov, "Soloviev attached importance to these letters and used to ask whether they remained intact."[26]

For Dostoevsky, 1873 was primarily marked by his assumption of the editorship of the weekly newspaper-journal *Grazhdanin*. This position, which lasted just over a year, allowed him to realize his idea for *The Diary of a Writer*, as well as providing materially for his family. At the same time, nevertheless, it brought him a good many worries. The conservatism of *Grazhdanin* and the less than irreproachable reputation of its publisher, Prince Vladimir Meshcherskii, caused some to regard Dostoevsky with hostility when he accepted the post. According to Anna Dostoevskaia, it was something that "many people could not forgive him."[27] The liberal press nicknamed the publisher of this notorious publication "Prince Period," because in one of his first editorials Prince Meshcherskii demanded "to put an end to all liberal reforms in Russia. Period." Eventually, in the late 1890s, Vladimir Soloviev would express unequivocal disapproval of Meshcherskii and his publication in caustic epigrams and in the play *The Revolt of the Gentry*,[28] but in the 1870s his relations with *Grazhdanin* were quite peaceful. The journal printed a speech given by Soloviev at a philosophical disputation at Petersburg University, entitled "A Few Words on the Present Task of Philosophy."[29] In addition, following Soloviev's defense of his dissertation in 1874, a highly laudatory article by the prominent critic and philosopher Nikolai Strakhov, "The Philosophical Disputation of 24 November," appeared in *Grazhdanin*.[30]

At the end of 1873, Soloviev and Ekaterina Romanova paid a curious visit to the Petersburg fortune-teller Mrs. Field. The visit itself is not surprising, considering Soloviev's general interest in the hidden potentials of the human spirit, evident in his study of the occult and his early preoccupation with spiritism, from which, however, he was soon "cured": Nikolai Strakhov, in his letter to Tolstoy of 12 September 1876, quotes Soloviev as saying: "Spiritists are such rubbish, I can't stand it."[31] The soothsayer must have made an impression on Soloviev, for in November 1877 Dostoevsky, on his advice, went to see Mrs. Field with Vsevolod Soloviev, who writes in his *Recollections* that the fortune-teller's predictions disturbed Dostoevsky. She foretold "great fame" for him, but also "family grief."[32] Indeed, in the spring of the following year Dostoevsky's youngest son suddenly died. The other prediction, as we know, came equally true.

GROWING FRIENDSHIP

In March 1874, at the suggestion of Prof. Pamfil Iurkevich of the Department of History and Philosophy, the university council voted unanimously that "candidate Soloviev be engaged by Moscow University in order to prepare for professorial rank on the Philosophy faculty."[33] Following his first article in *Pravoslavnoe obozrenie*, the journal began to publish Soloviev's master's thesis, which was published serially between January and October. That summer Soloviev wrote several poems, which marked, in his own words, the beginning of his interest in the composition of poetry.[34] In November 1874 he defended his master's thesis in Petersburg, after which his name was on everyone's lips. Soloviev arrived in Petersburg ahead of time and reported on the situation to his relatives in Moscow in a humorously elevated tone: "In the 7382d summer since the creation of the world, and the 1874th summer since the incarnation of the Word of God, on the twenty-fifth day of this September, at half after the tenth hour ante meridiem, we arrived safely and solemnly in the Imperial capital of Saint Petersburg, which was illuminated by the brilliant northern lights of the sun, in which one could not but see an especial act of Divine Providence."[35]

After a brief stay at the Hotel Anglia, he took up residence with his recently married brother Vsevolod, whose relations with his family, including Vladimir, were anything but serene. From their youth on, the brothers had clashed over a variety of issues, not to mention a rivalry, though not a very dramatic one, over Ekaterina Romanova.[36] Yet on this particular visit to Petersburg, Vladimir Soloviev, to all appearances, received a hearty welcome from his brother and was shown every hospitality. After completing all the necessary formalities, on 24 November he defended his dissertation. The disputation went brilliantly. The eminent historian and ardent proponent of women's education in Russia Konstantin Bestuzhev-Riumin solemnly proclaimed: "Russia can be congratulated on a man of genius."[37] Indeed, in his dissertation, which represented an overview and critique of the primary representatives of contemporary Western philosophy, Soloviev demonstrated both an unusually mature grasp of and a creative approach to fundamental philosophical problems.

Soloviev's official opponent was Prof. Mikhail Vladislavlev, who taught courses at the university in logic, psychology, the history of philosophy, metaphysics, and ethics. At the time of Soloviev's dissertation debate, he took a stance favorable to the author and, despite voicing certain objections, expressed confidence in the ability of the candidate to carve out a new, "independently Russian" path in philosophy.[38] As a student, Vladislavlev had contributed to the Dostoevsky brothers' journal *Vremia*, and friendly relations had been established between them. "My brother and I are both waiting impatiently for you," Mikhail Dostoevsky wrote to Vladislavlev on 1 December 1861. "Your article on English universities is very fine, and we are both very pleased with it."[39] Other letters from this period are equally warm. Having grown close to Mikhail Dostoevsky's family, Vladislavlev proposed to his daughter Mariia and in 1865 married her. After this, however, his relations with Fedor Dostoevsky deteriorated, primarily because Vladislavlev cooperated with his in-laws in their financial claims against the writer, who had taken on reponsibility for supporting the family of his deceased brother. Yet by the 1870s ties of family and friendship had been restored.[40] Indeed, it is an interesting detail that the degree candidate's chief opponent was a relative of Fedor Dostoevsky.[41] In the autumn of 1874, Dostoevsky was living in Staraia Russa, and at the time Soloviev defended his dissertation he was not in Petersburg. But he could have learned of the young philosopher's success from acquaintances as well as from the numerous public responses to the disputation.[42] Preserved in Dostoevsky's library is a copy of the master's thesis, presented to him by the author.

Dostoevsky's editorship of *Grazhdanin* was short-lived. As the final episode in this unfortunate and trouble-plagued tenure, he spent two days under arrest in a detention cell for violating censorship regulations. The punishment, imposed by a Petersburg court in June 1873, was viewed as a formality, and Dostoevsky was allowed to choose for himself a "convenient time" to spend in custody. There, in a special detention cell on Sennaia Square, he was visited by Vsevolod Soloviev. Dostoevsky "felt wonderful," drinking tea, smoking his cigarettes, and reading a book. His visitor, in contrast, arrived looking depressed; noticing this, Dostoevsky said: "See here, I wanted to tell you, you can't go on like this forever, you have to do something with yourself. . . . I understand your condition perfectly, I went through it myself. . . . Why, I've told you how fate helped me back then, how forced labor saved me—I became an entirely new person. . . . Oh! what a lucky thing it was for me: Siberia and forced labor! . . . Only there did I live a healthy, happy life, there I came to understand myself, dear friend. I understood Christ, I understood the Russian man. . . . Ah, if only you might spend some time in forced labor!"[43]

This story is curiously echoed by a conversation between Dostoevsky and Vladimir Soloviev, which the critic D. I. Stakheev recorded in his memoirs:

Fedor Mikhailovich was in a calm mood, speaking in a quiet tone. . . . Vladimir Sergeevich was telling him something, and Fedor Mikhailovich listened without responding, until suddenly he moved his chair closer to the chair on which Soloviev was sitting and, slapping him on the shoulder, said: "Ah, Vladimir Sergeevich! I can see that you are a good man."

"Thank you, Fedor Mikhailovich, for such praise."

"Wait a bit before thanking me, just wait," retorted Dostoevsky, "I haven't finished. I want to add to my praise that you would do well to have about three years of forced labor."

"Good Lord! Whatever for?"

"Because you are not yet good enough: but then, after forced labor, you would be a completely beautiful and pure Christian." . . .

Soloviev laughed and said nothing.[44]

In January 1875 Vladimir Soloviev began lecturing at both Moscow University and the Moscow Higher Courses for Women. In an autobiography Soloviev wrote in 1887, he characterized his lectures at Moscow University as being on the history of ancient and modern philosophy and logic. The title of his first lecture course is unknown, although in a later autobiographical statement of 1890 he calls it a course in the history of modern philosophy.[45]

The lectures Soloviev gave at the Higher Courses for Women, founded in 1872 by a Moscow University professor, the historian V. I. Ger'e, focused exclusively on the history of ancient philosophy. In his first lecture, judging from a surviving transcript, he defined the ability to laugh as the fundamental attribute of human nature. Taking exception to the definition of Aristotle, who called man a social animal, Soloviev defined man as a *laughing animal*: "Man has the ability to stand above any physical phenomenon or object; he regards it critically. Man contemplates a fact, and if that fact does not correspond to his ideal perceptions, he laughs."[46]

Soloviev's teaching brought him success and popularity among the students. Equally successful was his appearance in Moscow literary, scholarly, and social circles. At the same time, he was writing philosophical essays, reading extensively, and doing research. In the spring of 1875, Soloviev fell in love with Elizaveta Polivanova, one of his students at the women's courses, and proposed to her. But as with Ekaterina Romanova, this marriage was never to take place. Polivanova subsequently left reminiscences of Soloviev, in which she describes their conversations of that period: "He spoke also of his broad plans for the future. At that time he believed passionately in himself, and in his vocation to make a change in human thought. He sought to reconcile faith and reason, religion and science, to open up new and hitherto inconceivable paths for the human consciousness."

In connection with this excerpt Lukianov adds that "in 1875 F. M. Dostoevsky's novel *The Raw Youth* was published in *Otechestvennye zapiski*. There the senior Versilov declares, in passing, that 'the highest Russian concept is the universal reconciliation of ideas.'"[47] Lukianov also cites an episode from the memoirs of the well-known socialist-oriented economist Ivan Ianzhul about one of his encounters with Dostoevsky, which probably occurred in early 1875, during an intermission at the Aleksandrinskii Theater:

> He [Dostoevsky] asked me whether I had arrived from Moscow long before and how long it had been since I had seen Vladimir Soloviev, toward whom he was evidently well disposed. Upon learning that we were acquainted, he posed further questions about Soloviev, asking how he was, to which I replied that he seemed to be doing well, that according to the rumors he was spending more and more of his time around Katkov, Leontiev, and Liubimov, where he had found a warm reception, and that many in Moscow were displeased by this, beginning with his elderly father! Dostoevsky was convulsed, and, throwing me a fairly ferocious look, he immediately moved away and I did not see him again.[48]

Referring to Soloviev elsewhere in his memoirs, Ianzhul writes: "Vladimir Sergeevich never tried to hide his intimacy with a circle I found extremely offensive—that surrounding *Moskovskie vedomosti*—and once, I don't recall for what reason, he even naively offered to assist me in obtaining Liubimov's patronage!!!"[49] In contrast, it was not from naiveté that Ianzhul caused Dostoevsky to convulse by mentioning the rumors about Soloviev in a negative light, for it was well known that the editor of *Moskovskie vedomosti* and publisher of *Russkii vestnik*, Mikhail Nikiforovich Katkov, along with his coeditors, Pavel Mikhailovich Leontiev and Nikolai Alekseevich Liubimov, was a member of Dostoevsky's own circle. Despite periodic rough patches in their relations, Dostoevsky remained friends with Katkov to the end of his life.[50]

Soloviev's teaching lasted only half a year, for in June 1875 he went abroad. In his request for an official leave, Soloviev defined his research goals as the study of "monuments of Indian, gnostic, and medieval philosophy."[51] For his place of study Soloviev chose London, specifically, the British Museum. To all appearances, he had no regular exchange with Dostoevsky during this time, until his return to Russia in the summer of 1876. Moreover, in a letter of 14 October Soloviev asks his mother: "Is it true that Aleksei Tolstoi and Dostoevsky have died?"[52] From the tone of the question it is difficult to tell just how perturbed Soloviev was by the rumor, which was true in the case of Tolstoi but premature with regard to Dostoevsky. In this same letter he announces his sudden intention to travel to Egypt. The culmination of his stay in Cairo was a journey into the desert, where he was summoned by the voice of the "Eternal Friend." His famous poem "Three Meetings" (written in 1898) describes the author's mystical experience: his meetings with Sophia, the Wisdom of God. In the narrative, for which he chose an ingenious blend of the romantic and the comic, Soloviev relates how he first saw *Her* in childhood during a church service:

> Pronizana lazur'iu zolotistoi,
> V ruke derzha tsvetok nezdeshnikh stran,
> Stoiala ty s ulybkoiu luchistoi,
> Kivnula mne i skrylasia v tuman.
> (Permeated with golden azure,
> Holding a flower of unearthly lands in your hand,
> You stood with a radiant smile,
> Nodded to me and slipped into the fog.)

The second part of the poem depicts the author's studies at the British Museum "some years later." There, among the books "about her," the second encounter occurs:

> Vdrug zolotoi lazur'iu vse polno
> I predo mnoi ona siiaet snova, —
> Odno ee litso, — ono odno.
> (Suddenly everything was filled with golden azure
> And before me she shines anew, —
> Only her face, — her face alone.)

Finally, the third part is dedicated to the meeting in Egypt. The poetic language here is especially eloquent: the mix of "high" and "low" styles in the poem appropriately enough evokes a certain thesis of the esoteric *Tabula Smaragdina*,[53] which was composed in Hellenistic Egypt and is attributed to the legendary sage Hermes Trismegistus: "What is below is like that which is above, and what is above is like that which is below, to accomplish the miracles of one thing."[54] In general, the philosophical, religious, and poetic context of the third part (as of the poem as a whole) is multidimensional. On the one hand, the very idea of the retreat into the Egyptian desert links Soloviev to the early Christian tradition of the "hermit fathers"; on the other hand, his description of the dream and revelation received in the desert recalls Pushkin's "The Prophet" and Lermontov's "The Dream."[55] However, despite the many possible parallels and associations, Soloviev's account of the third meeting is unique both by virtue of the uniqueness of the event described and by virtue of a poetic intonation that is distinctly Soloviev's.

> Chto est', chto bylo, chto griadet voveki —
> Vse obnial tut odin nedvizhnyi vzor.

Sineiut podo mnoi moria i reki,
I dal'nii les, i vysi snezhnykh gor.
Vse videl ia, i vse odno lish' bylo,—
Odin lish' obraz zhenskoi krasoty.
Bezmernoe v ego razmer vkhodilo,—
Peredo mnoi, vo mne—odna lish' ty.
(What is, what was, what will be forever—
Everything was embraced there in one motionless gaze.
Beneath me I see the blue of oceans and rivers,
And the distant forest, and the peaks of snow-capped mountains.
I saw everything, and everything was one,—
A single image of female beauty.
Its measure encompassed the immeasurable,—
Before me, within me—only you alone.)

Bringing his account of the three meetings to a close, the philosopher-poet writes:

Eshche nevol'nik suetnomu miru,
Pod gruboiu koroiu veshchestva
Tak ia prozrel netlennuiu porfiru
I oshchutil siian'e bozhestva.
(Still a slave to the vain world,
Beneath the coarse crust of matter
I thus first perceived the imperishable crimson
And felt the radiance of divinity.)

Needless to say, if at the very end of his life Soloviev refers to this mystical experience as "the most significant thing that has so far happened to me," it would be difficult to overestimate its influence on the formation of Soloviev's philosophy and on his life as a whole.

We can only guess at the nature of Soloviev's conversations with Dostoevsky upon his return to Russia. However, Soloviev's sojourn abroad, and specifically in the libraries of Europe, was reflected, if only episodically, in Dostoevsky's work. In the May–June 1877 issue of *The Diary of a Writer* Dostoevsky published an excerpt "from the Book of Predictions by Johann Lichtenberger, in the year 1528."[56] The writer reports that this "ancient folio-volume" was "discovered in London, in the Royal Library," by "one of our young scholars." In a draft Dostoevsky makes a further reference not included in the final text: "The same [scholar] traveler who imparted to me the excerpt from the book of Johann Lichtenberger tracked down in Paris, in another library, another book of predictions, also from the sixteenth century and also in Latin."[57] There need be no doubt that the "young scholar and traveler" in question was Vladimir Soloviev.[58] Dostoevsky advertised this excerpt "merely as a fact not devoid of a certain interest." Yet the interpretation of its mystical allegories allowed him to speak once again about the special role of Russia and the Christian spirit of the Russian people: "The great eagle shall arise in the East . . . and make tremble those who dwell by the waters in the West."[59]

After his return Soloviev remained only a short time at Moscow University: in the spring of 1877 he was appointed to the Academic Committee of the Ministry of Public Education and moved to Petersburg, which was well in line with his own desires. Henceforth, the sympathy and friendship between Dostoevsky and Soloviev acquired the depth and significance of a spiritual phenomenon. Soloviev's move to Petersburg coincided with the renewed flourishing of Dostoevsky's journalistic career. In January 1876, publication of *The Diary of a Writer* had resumed, this time as an independent periodical published by the author himself. Such a form seems to have accorded naturally with Dostoevsky's creative aspirations: in his own publication he could freely express his opinions on the most diverse topics, using a variety of genres. His artistic, political, religious, and philosophical views found concrete expression in every chapter. Moreover, thanks to the *Diary* Dostoevsky crossed, as it were, the natural boundary that divides the two participants in the literary process, the writer and the reader. The periodical provoked an extensive correspondence, establishing direct contact between Dostoevsky and his readers and becoming a pulpit of sorts for the writer.

LECTURES ON GOD-MANHOOD

In 1878 (from the end of January through March) Soloviev gave twelve public talks at the Society of Friends of Spiritual Enlightenment entitled *Lectures on God-manhood*. As the program announced: "The aim of Mr. Soloviev's talks will be to show the rationality of positive religion, to show that the truth of faith, in all the fullness of its concrete substance, is at the same time the truth of reason. The central concept of the talks is the idea of God-manhood, or the living God."[60] Soloviev's lectures were a tremendous success. As one contemporary recalls: "Crowds of young people came to hear him. For the first time a defense of the Crucified Word sounded from the rostrum, in defiance of the general tendency of unbelief. These talks stirred up heated argument and debate."[61] Dostoevsky invariably attended the lectures. Anna Dostoevskaia recalls that "these lectures drew a full hall of listeners, among whom were many of our mutual friends. Since things were going well at home, I too went with Fedor Mikhailovich to hear the lectures."[62]

It was at one of these lectures that the famous "nonmeeting" of Dostoevsky and Leo Tolstoi took place. The fate of their personal acquaintance,
according to Anna, appears to have rested with Nikolai Strakhov, who accompanied Tolstoi to Soloviev's lecture. Returning home, Dostoevsky and
Anna noted that Strakhov had not approached them and during the intermission had "barely greeted" them. A few days later the reason became clear:
Tolstoi had "asked not to be introduced to anyone," and Strakhov, very likely
guided by a desire to preserve his role as exclusive intermediary between
the two greatest living Russian writers, had resolved to carry out Tolstoi's
request to the letter and make no exception for Dostoevsky. It is worth
quoting in connection with this episode Vladimir Soloviev's view of Strakhov:
"He has a most incomprehensible and complex nature: at once honest and
false [*i dobrosovesten, i fal'shiv*]."[63] Later both Dostoevsky and Tolstoi very
much regretted not having met that evening.[64]

In 1878, probably in early spring, Dostoevsky received a letter from a
certain Nikolai Peterson expounding the ideas of his teacher, Nikolai
Fedorov. This remarkable and decidedly most original thinker had developed a unique doctrine of the "common task," which, according to him,
would lead mankind to the ultimate goal—the resurrection of all the dead.
Fedorov worked at the Rumiantsev Library in Moscow and was well known
to patrons there as a phenomenally erudite expert in the most diverse fields
of knowledge. His philosophical ideas, however, were familiar to almost no
one. In Dostoevsky's reply to Peterson, written on 24 March 1878, we find,
alongside the main topic—a discussion of the ideas of Fedorov, who had
"extremely interested" Dostoevsky—a report of the lectures and, above all,
of the intense and fruitful contact between Soloviev and Dostoevsky and
their unanimity in the most important questions of faith and existence.

> First of all, a question: who is this thinker whose ideas you conveyed? . . . Then
> I'll tell you that in essence I am in complete agreement with these ideas. I read
> them as though they were my own. I read them (anonymously) today to Vladimir
> Sergeevich Soloviev, a young philosopher of ours who is now giving lectures on
> religion—lectures that are attended by a crowd of nearly a thousand. I waited for
> him specially so as to read to him your summary of the thinker's ideas, since I
> found much similarity in his views. That gave us a marvelous *two hours*. He is in
> profound sympathy with the thinker and meant to say almost the same thing for
> his next lecture (he has four lectures left out of twelve). . . . I will alert you that
> we here, that is, Soloviev and I, at least, believe in an actual, literal, personal
> resurrection, and in the fact that it will take place on earth.[65]

In his eighth lecture, Soloviev does indeed examine human immortality.
However, he "does not mean natural man or man as phenomenon."[66] For

all the enthusiasm with which Dostoevsky and Soloviev received the exposition of Fedorov's ideas (unfortunately, Peterson's letter to Dostoevsky—the source of the writer's initial acquaintance with Fedorov's doctrine—is unknown), the statement that Soloviev "meant to read almost the same thing for his next lecture" seems hasty. The boundaries of Soloviev's agreement with and divergence from Fedorov were subsequently defined quite clearly. In Fedorov's doctrine, "resurrection as an action is positivism in the realm of ultimate causes; whereas positivism in the usual sense, that is, the positivism of knowledge, has to do with the realm of initial causes."[67] Soloviev, meanwhile, remained forever faithful to his position "against the positivists" even in Fedorov's idealist version. "Our work must be religious, not scientific, in nature," he wrote to Fedorov in the mid-1880s.[68]

"VLADIMIR KARAMAZOV"

In May 1878 the Dostoevskys' beloved three-year-old son Alesha died. For Fedor and Anna this was a "terrible tragedy." The child perished from an attack of the epilepsy he inherited from his father. Dostoevsky's wife writes in her *Reminiscences*:

> My husband was crushed by this death. . . . In an effort to comfort him a little and divert him from his black thoughts I begged Vladimir Soloviev, who used to visit us in those days of our mourning, to persuade Fedor Mikhailovich to accompany him to Optina Pustyn, the hermitage where Soloviev was planning to go that summer. A pilgrimage to Optina had been a long-time dream of Fedor Mikhailovich's, but very difficult to realize. Soloviev agreed to help me and began talking my husband into making the trip to Optina with him. I added my own entreaties to his, and it was decided then and there that Fedor Mikhailovich would go to Moscow in mid-July (he had been planning to go there anyway to offer his future novel to Katkov), and use the occasion to make the trip to Optina with Soloviev. I would not have dared to let Fedor Mikhailovich make such a distant and wearisome (in those times) journey by himself. But I felt that Soloviev, even though he was a man "not of this world," would be able to look after Fedor Mikhailovich if he should have an epileptic seizure.[69]

In his letters from Moscow, Dostoevsky describes for his wife his preparations and then the journey itself to the hermitage at Optina Pustyn with Soloviev. But these letters reflect, on the whole, the day-to-day, external side of the trip. We know, however, that on the journey Dostoevsky discussed with Soloviev "the main idea and in part the plan of his new work."[70] In the first of his "Three Speeches in Memory of Dostoevsky" Soloviev wrote: "The Church as a positive social ideal was to be the central idea of a new novel or a new series of novels, of which only the first was written—*The Brothers Karamazov*."[71]

Nearly every commentator on Dostoevsky's last novel has pointed to real-life prototypes of the characters in *The Brothers Karamazov*. There can be no doubt that Vladimir Soloviev was among those whose features were imprinted on the pages of the novel. In the view of many scholars, Dostoevsky embodied him "in Alesha Karamazov—in the image that he held most dear and closest to his heart and that he most cherished."[72] However, according to Anna Dostoevskaia in 1881, "Fedor Mikhailovich saw in the person of Vladimir Soloviev not Alesha, but Ivan Karamazov."[73] This "double attribution" should not strike us as contradictory: the "young philosopher" represented a rare combination of the brilliant acuity of an analytical mind armed with every possible intellectual method of cognition and a profound religiosity springing from a kind and cheerful nature. It is likely that Dostoevsky simply "divided fraternally" Soloviev's intellectual and spiritual features between Ivan and Alesha. The philosopher's nephew Sergei Soloviev proposes an even broader analogy, by pointing to a correspondence between the relations of Dmitrii and Ivan Karamazov and those of Vsevolod and Vladimir Soloviev, noting that "although Vsevolod bears even less of a resemblance to Dmitrii than Vladimir to Ivan, it is quite possible that Dostoevsky wrote *The Brothers Karamazov* under the influence of his acquaintance with the Soloviev brothers. Especially as the third brother, Mikhail, about whom Dostoevsky might have heard from both brothers, undoubtedly bore certain traits of Alesha Karamazov, playing the role of general peacemaker and consoler within the family."[74] Incidentally, might it not have been the young Soloviev whom Dostoevsky had in mind, if only by superficial association, when Ivan remarks that "Russian professors today are quite often the same Russian boys"?[75]

It is interesting that the celebrated jurist Anatolii Koni left recollections of Soloviev that evoke comparison with Ivan Karamazov's conversation with the devil. Koni recounts how one evening in the winter of 1899 he was returning home with Soloviev after dinner. Along the way Soloviev expressed a desire to stop in at Koni's for a glass of red wine. "Leaving him for a minute to see to the wine," writes Koni,

> I hardly recognized, upon my return to the study, the pale man with alarmed and wandering eyes as the same Soloviev who had been cheerful and joking with me just moments before. "What's the matter, Vladimir Sergeevich? Are you ill?" He shook his head negatively, and covered his eyes with his hand. They brought in the wine, but he pushed the filled glass away with an abrupt motion and, after sitting silent for a while, suddenly asked me whether I believed in the actual

existence of the devil, and when I replied in the negative, he said: "Well, for me his existence is indisputable: I have seen him just as I am seeing you now." "When and where?" "Why, right here, just now, and several times before. He spoke to me." "Your nerves are shot, Vladimir Sergeevich—it's just a hallucination." "Believe me, I am capable of distinguishing a trick of my senses from reality. This time it was fleeting, but some time ago I saw him quite close and spoke with him. I was returning by ship from the Finnish shore and, having woken up early one morning, I was sitting on the bed in my cabin, slowly getting dressed and now and then becoming lost in thought, when suddenly I felt the presence of someone beside me and turned around. Sitting cross-legged on the crumpled pillows was a grey shaggy creature watching me with piercing yellow eyes. I knew at once who it was, and stared back at him unflinchingly. 'Do you know,' I said to him, 'that Christ has risen?!' 'Christ may have risen,' he replied, 'but you I shall harness!' And leaping onto my back, he grabbed me by the neck and pressed me to the floor. Choking in his grip and under his weight, I started uttering the invocation of Peter Moghila,[76] and he began to weaken, growing lighter, until finally his grip failed and he fell from me. In a state of terror I ran out onto the deck and fainted."[77]

Concluding this intriguing story about Soloviev, the pragmatic Koni adds: "Ordinary superstition was alien to him." Naturally, these particular episodes cannot have been reflected in any way in *The Brothers Karamazov*, which was written long before. Yet this curious coincidence underscores the significant refraction received in the figure of Ivan by, first of all, Soloviev's capacity for mystical experiences—a capacity of which Dostoevsky was well aware—and, second, by Soloviev's unconcealed certainty in the actual existence of the devil.[78] Of course, one should not expect a literal reproduction of Soloviev's personality in the characters of the novel: Dostoevsky did not copy his characters. Nevertheless, it is easy to see in the young philosopher that synthesis of "head and heart" without which Alesha is naive while Ivan is cruel.

TWO SOPHIAS

In discussing the personal relations between Soloviev and Dostoevsky in the late 1870s, one cannot ignore their mutual friend—Countess Sofiia Andreevna Tolstaia, the widow of the poet Aleksei Konstantinovich Tolstoi. Her obvious intelligence and charm were remarked upon in numerous testimonials by her contemporaries. According to the writer Nikolai Leskov, "Countess Tolstaia's home was one of the most pleasant and was frequented by the most interesting people. Among the men of letters who would visit the countess formally or informally were Vicomte Vogüé, Dostoevsky, Boleslav

Markevich, Vladimir Soloviev, and myself. Once Turgenev stopped by. Sometimes in that home we would read, but more often we conversed and sometimes argued—not without passion and interest."[79]

The importance of Countess Tolstaia's home for Soloviev at this time is evident from Nikolai Strakhov's letter to Leo Tolstoi of 4/5 April 1877, in which he writes: "Yesterday, that is, the 4th, Vladimir Soloviev came to see me, and it seems he and I shall strike up a friendship. The trouble was that until recently Countess Tolstaia, the widow of Aleksei Tolstoi, lived here. She, along with another lady, a friend of hers [apparently, Strakhov has in mind Tolstaia's niece, Sofiia Khitrovo], are enormously fond of philosophy and read a great deal, even visiting the Public Library for this purpose. And so Soloviev was continually at the home of this Tolstaia."[80]

In her turn, Anna Dostoevskaia recalls her husband's attachment to this home and its hostesses, Sofiia Tolstaia and Sofiia Khitrovo: "But more and more often during the years 1879 and 1880, Fedor Mikhailovich used to visit Countess Sofiia Andreyevna Tolstaia, widow of the poet A. K. Tolstoi. She was a woman of great intellect, highly educated and well read. . . . Fedor Mikhailovich was fond of visiting with Countess Tolstaia also because of the very lovely family around her: her niece, Sofiia Petrovna Khitrovo, an extremely warmhearted young woman, and her three children—two boys and a darling little girl. . . . Countess Tolstaia possessed a tender and responsive heart; and the joy she was able to give my husband on one occasion was something I remembered in gratitude all through my life." Dostoevsky's wife further relates a fascinating episode in which Vladimir Soloviev once brought her a large reproduction of the Sistine Madonna. Countess Tolstaia had obtained it for Dostoevsky after he called this painting the greatest work of art. Anna Grigorievna remarks that "Fedor Mikhailovich was touched to the depths by her heartfelt kindness."[81]

For Vladimir Soloviev, Countess Tolstaia became nearly as close as a relative. He was a frequent guest at her estates of Pustynka and Krasnyi Rog. Soloviev probably met Sofiia Tolstaia and Sofiia Khitrovo in Moscow in 1876.[82] His acquaintance with them had a particular influence on the whole later life of the "confessor of Saint Sophia." Soloviev once called his attitude toward Sofiia Khitrovo "icon-worship." Their twenty-year-long relationship remains a mystery, especially as they both saw to the concealment of their correspondence from outside eyes—no trace of it has yet been found.[83] The recollections of contemporaries are scrappy and colored with perplexity. "What could we think of her, this married woman, whom he loved?" writes, for instance, the philosopher Lev Lopatin's sister Ekaterina, who knew the entire Soloviev family from childhood.[84] "As usual, everyone spoke of this love, criticizing and pitying. People said that she was 'tormenting' him, that she wasn't good-looking, that she had the appearance of a large cat or tigress and strikingly beautiful hands. . . . There was no question, however, that she was a remarkable woman, with a sharp mind, great culture and great taste, interested in everything and able to attract the most prominent people, and exceptionally charming. She lived with her aunt, the Countess Tolstaia, the widow of the poet Aleksei Tolstoi. The very air which Soloviev breathed in the company of these two women, the atmosphere of art, of subtlety of relations and spiritual refinement, was essential to him."[85] For many years Soloviev waited and hoped that "the woman he called his intended would bring herself to take the final step and become his wife,"[86] yet, as he himself foretold in lines dedicated to Ekaterina Romanova before her marriage to another man, destiny had prepared for him the role of fiancé but not husband:

> Chto rokom suzhdeno, togo ne otrazhu ia
> Bessil'noi detskoi voleiu svoei,
> Proiti ia dolzhen put' zemnoi, toskuia
> Po vechnom nebe rodiny moei.
> (What fate has decreed, I shall not fight
> With my powerless childish will,
> I must travel this earthly path, yearning
> For the eternal heavens of my homeland.)

Whatever the outward aspect of the relations between Vladimir Soloviev and Sofiia Khitrovo, it is clear that in his love for her, personal emotion intertwined with a philosophical and mystical vision of the world. One can recall the names of Laura and Petrarch, Beatrice and Dante, but behind the mystery of such amazing relations lies the mystery of an amazing personality. Meditating on this theme, Sergei Bulgakov wrote: "In the history of poetry, mysticism, and philosophical speculation, Vladimir Soloviev is the only figure who not only had poetic and philosophical contemplations regarding Sophia but also ascribed to himself personal relationship with her, which took on an erotic character, in, of course, the most sublime sense. For this reason, he viewed earthly love for himself as, in general, a sort of fall or betrayal."[87]

THE DEFENSE

On 6 April 1880 Soloviev defended his doctoral dissertation, *A Critique of Abstract Principles,* at St. Petersburg University. In his preface the author defined the subject and tasks of the proposed work: "By abstract principles,

I mean those individual ideas (the particular aspects and elements of a universal idea) which, when abstracted from the whole and confirmed in their exclusivity, lose their true character and, entering into opposition and conflict with one another, plunge the world of man into that state of intellectual disorder in which it has hitherto found itself."

Soloviev states his intention to focus on the epistemological and ethical aspects of a critique of such abstract principles. He claims that moral activity must have a concrete object as well as abstract sources. The group and individual have each other as moral objects: "The moral significance of society . . . is determined by the religious or mystical principle in man, by virtue of which all members of a society do not form limits to one another but inwardly complete one another in a free unity of spiritual love, which must have immediate realization in a spiritual society or church. Thus the foundation of a normal society must be a spiritual union or church that itself defines the indisputable aims of society."[88]

The idea of a positive unity is the fulcrum, the philosophical principle of Soloviev's critique. Clearly, the problems examined in the dissertation were also among the most important in Dostoevsky's work and worldview. And indeed, according to Anna Dostoevskaia, her husband "was very much interested in Vladimir Soloviev's forthcoming defense of his doctoral dissertation, and wanted to be present without fail for that solemn occasion. . . . The debate was a brilliant one and Soloviev successfully parried the attacks of his formidable opponents. Fedor Mikhailovich stayed until the audience had dispersed, so as to have the opportunity to shake the hand of the hero of the hour. Soloviev was obviously pleased to see that Fedor Mikhailovich, despite his frail health, had wanted to be there at the university among his friends on such a memorable day in his life."[89] The "formidable" opponents, among whom was again M. I. Vladislavlev, did not, however, present any "formidable" objections and Soloviev easily parried individual criticisms. Thus at the end of the disputation a member of the Mathematics Department, Vladimir Vulfson, "reproached the doctoral candidate for not mentioning, in declaring the principle of love to be the foundation of a normal society, that this foundation had been pointed out before him by Auguste Comte. The doctoral candidate remarked that considerably earlier than Auguste Comte the principle of love had been proclaimed by Jesus Christ."[90]

Dostoevsky's presence at the disputation was noted in the papers *Novoe vremia* and *Sovremennye izvestiia*.[91] A few days after the defense, Dostoevsky wrote in a letter to his acquaintance Ekaterina Junge: "At the recent disputation here by the young philosopher Vladimir Soloviev (son of the historian) for the Doctor of Philosophy I heard from him one profound phrase: 'Mankind, I am deeply convinced,' he said, 'knows far more than it has hitherto managed to express in its science or its art.' Well, it's the same with me: I feel that there is far more hidden in me than I have hitherto been able to express as a writer."[92] The phrase to which Dostoevsky refers probably corresponds to Soloviev's arguments in the first chapter of *A Critique of Abstract Principles:*

> As long as the general principles defining the value and significance of our thoughts, deeds, and works remain questionable or obscure, mankind with all its acquisitions resembles a rich man who possesses fully genuine treasures, but only through disputed or even quite illegal documents, in consequence of which he cannot well and truly manage his property as he pleases, and it is of but trifling value to him. Furthermore, to continue this comparison, our rich man's ancestors have left him similar secret hoards about which he knows nothing and wants to know nothing, thinking them a tale from childhood and regarding those who tell him about them as superstitious people or charlatans.[93]

Soloviev's sister recalls that when Soloviev, after defending his dissertation, began distributing copies of it to his friends and acquaintances, he came up with three inscriptions: 1) "As a token of respect, but also for you to read"; 2) "Perhaps for you to read, but more as a token of respect"; 3) "Not at all for you to read, but only as a token of respect." It is reasonable to assume that Dostoevsky fell into the first group.

THE UNIVERSAL MAN

In May 1880 a monument to Pushkin was scheduled to be unveiled in Moscow. The celebration connected with this turned into a tremendous event in Russian cultural life. Of particular historical importance was Dostoevsky's Pushkin speech, which aroused extraordinary public enthusiasm. Dostoevsky did not immediately agree to take part in the festivities. In a letter to the president of the Society of Friends of Russian Letters, Sergei Iuriev, in response to the latter's news of the forthcoming Pushkin celebrations, he wrote: "I really have said here loudly that for the day of the dedication of the Pushkin Monument a serious article about him is needed in print. And I have even *dreamed,* in the event it were possible for me to go to Moscow for the day of the dedication, *of saying* a few words about him, but orally in the form of a speech. . . . Writing, after all, is not the same as speaking. One needs to write something weighty and substantial about Pushkin."[94] In his next letter to Iuriev, Dostoevsky accepted, though with some reservations, the invitation to the ceremony: "I think I will venture to go to Moscow. . . . Regarding an 'Address" or a speech by me, I don't yet know what to say. I can see from your letter that there will be plenty of speeches and all by such outstanding people. If I say something in memory of our great poet and great Russian, I'm afraid of saying too little, but I wonder whether the time will be found for me to say more (of course with reasonable limits) after speeches by Aksakov, Turgenev, Ostrovsky, and Pisemsky."[95]

Both his caution and his craftiness ("whether the time will be found for me") were no doubt dictated by considerations of literary politics: having placed the two Ivan Sergeeviches—Aksakov and Turgenev—in the same line, Dostoevsky certainly could not have expected any ideological unanimity at the ceremony. He expressed himself more frankly in a letter to the famous publisher of the newspaper *Novoe Vremia*, Aleksei Suvorin: "The news that you *may* not be going is very unpleasant for me: we Petersburg guests would have a better time if we were there in a *large group*."[96] As the celebration drew closer, Dostoevsky's misgivings began to prove justified, and there were growing signs of a "scandal" (the method of plot development so dear to the writer's heart). Dostoevsky's reaction to what was happening and his mood were quite unequivocal. "And it turns out, just as I already had a premonition of, that I'll be going not for pleasure, but perhaps even for downright unpleasantness," he wrote to the renowned statesman Konstantin Pobedonostsev, newly appointed chief procurator of the Holy Synod. "Because the matter concerns the dearest and most basic convictions. I had already heard in passing even in Petersburg that there is a clique raging there in Moscow. . . . Even the newspapers have already published things about the rumors of certain intrigues. I have prepared my speech about Pushkin, and precisely in the most *extreme* spirit of my (that is, *our*, I make bold to thus express myself) convictions, and therefore I expect, perhaps, a certain amount of abuse."[97]

On the way to Moscow Dostoevsky learned of the death of Empress Mariia and assumed that "the Pushkin festivities cannot take place." But the unveiling of the monument, scheduled for 26 May, was merely postponed until 5 June, and Dostoevsky, finding himself longer than he had reckoned among literary figures of every stripe, gives in his letters to his wife a detailed and characteristic description of the clashes behind the scenes of the celebration. He is obviously annoyed at "certain intrigues." For example, when telling of the organizing committee's obstruction of Katkov, Dostoevsky is filled with indignation: "It's vileness, and if I weren't so involved in these festivities, I would perhaps break off relations with them.[98] Without doubt, the mutual intolerance of many writers and groups of the Russian intelligentsia contrasted both with the generally desired unity of Russian cultural forces and with the widespread, genuine enthusiasm surrounding Pushkin's name. Some of the speakers at the ceremonies did not hesitate to voice their opinions on this subject. For instance, Katkov, who in the end was present at the dinner on 6 June, though only in his capacity as a member of the Moscow town council, called for the reconciliation of hostile parties. However, the idea of harmonious relations was given universal perspective in the brilliant speech of Dostoevsky, which provoked unprecedented enthusiasm from the audience. The surviving drafts and versions of the speech attest to Dostoevsky's painstaking preparation for his appearance, to say nothing of the fact that Pushkin's personality and significance for Russia had for many years been on his mind.

In his Pushkin speech, as Dostoevsky summarized it for its publication in the 1880 *Diary of a Writer,* he "meant to emphasize four points in my discussion of Pushkin's significance":

> 1. That Pushkin . . . was the first to uncover and indicate the essential, pathological activity of our educated society, historically detached from its native soil and elevating itself above the People. He captured and graphically set before us our negative type: a restless and alienated man, lacking faith in his native soil and its native strength, rejecting Russia and, ultimately, himself . . . , wanting no dealings with others and genuinely suffering. . . .
> 2. He was the first . . . who gave us artistic types of Russian beauty. . . . All these types of positive Russian beauty, the beauty of the Russian soul, were derived entirely from the spirit of the People. . . . And so, . . . having diagnosed the ailment, he also gave us great hope: 'Trust in the spirit of the People and expect salvation from it alone, and you shall be saved.'
> 3. The *third* point . . . concerns that special and most characteristic trait of his artistic genius, found nowhere else and in no one else—the capacity to respond to the entire world and to assume completely the form of the genius of other nations in a reincarnation that is almost total. . . .
> 4. This capacity is an altogether Russian one, a national one, and Pushkin merely shares it with our entire People; and, like a perfect artist, he is also the most perfect expression of this capacity.[99]

The final part of the speech reveals Dostoevsky's basic idea with particular clarity. "For what is the strength of the spirit of Russianness if not its ultimate aspirations toward universality and the universal brotherhood of peoples?" he asks. "Indeed, the mission of the Russian is unquestionably pan-European and universal. To become a real Russian, to become completely Russian, perhaps, means just . . . to become brother to all people, *a universal man* [*vsechelovek*], if you like. Oh, all our Slavophilism and Westernizing is no more than one great misunderstanding between us, although it was histori- cally necessary. . . . To become a genuine Russian will mean specifically: to strive to bring an ultimate reconciliation to Europe's contradictions, to indi- cate that the solution to Europe's anguish is to be found in the universal and all-unifying Russian soul, to enfold all our brethren within it with brotherly love, and at last, perhaps, to utter the ultimate word of great, general har- mony, ultimate brotherly accord of all tribes through the law of Christ's Gospel!"[100]

Reactions to Dostoevsky's address, both in the press and in the letters and memoirs of contemporaries, comprise an entire stratum of critical material connected with the writer.[101] Let us confine ourselves to his own description of his triumph, which he sent to his wife a few hours after giving the speech:

> What are my Petersburg successes! Nothing, *zero*, compared to this! . . . I read loudly, with fire. . . . When I spoke at the end, however, of the *universal unity* of people, the hall was as though in hysteria. When I concluded—I won't tell you about the roar, the outcry of rapture: strangers among the audience wept, sobbed, embraced each other and *swore to one another to be better, not to hate one another from now on, but instead to love one another.* . . . "Prophet, prophet!" people in the crowd shouted. Turgenev, for whom I put in a good word in my speech, rushed to embrace me with tears in his eyes. Annenkov [the critic, literary historian, friend and literary adviser to Ivan Turgenev] ran up to shake my hand and kiss my shoulder. "You're a genius, you're more than a genius!" they both told me. Aksakov (Ivan) ran up onto the platform and declared to the audience that my speech *was not just a speech, but a historic event!*[102]

That the name of Aksakov is placed alongside those of Turgenev and Annenkov now testifies to the moment of genuine unanimity among both friends and foes of Dostoevsky under the influence of his speech. (The truce, to be sure, did not last long; already on August 17 Ivan Aksakov was writing to his fellow Slavophile, the historian of Russian literature Orest Miller: "Of course, there's no need to name me when mentioning the impression Dosto- evsky's speech produced on Turgenev and Annenkov. It's awkward."[103])

On June 10, Sofiia Tolstaia, Iuliia Abaza, and Vladimir Soloviev sent Dostoevsky a telegram from Sablino:[104] "Forward to Fedor Mikhailovich. We rejoice at everything. Do understand. Accept from us more than words. Sofiia, Iuliia, Vladimir Soloviev."[105] This text reflects a degree of intimate mutual understanding that does not require verbose or even friendly effu- sions. Dostoevsky's swift letter of thanks in reply to the telegram confirms just such a level of relations: "How good it is on your part that you (all) remembered me. When you become aware that you have such kind friends,

your heart grows bright." Dostoevsky goes on to give a fairly detailed description of the enthusiastic reception given him by the most diverse people,
then exclaims: "My heart is full—how can I help telling my friends! I'm still
stunned" At the close of the letter he writes about Soloviev: "And I kiss
Vladimir Sergeevich ardently. I got three photographs of him in Moscow: in
his early years, in youth, and the last one in old age. What a handsome fellow
he was in his early years."[106] Dostoevsky has evidently forgotten that Soloviev
the "old man" is not yet thirty. In portraits taken in the 1880s Soloviev does,
in fact, look older than his years, but he certainly could not be called old.
One recalls the absentmindedness of Soloviev himself, who at one time
included Dostoevsky's wife among "people of the forties." However, it is
possible that it is not a question of either being absentminded. Anna Dostoevskaia, for her part, went to some effort to look older and to make the age
difference between her and her husband less noticeable. And, by all accounts, she succeeded. As for Soloviev, it is plausible to assume that Dostoevsky, not sensing a gap of an entire generation between them, included him
not only in his own circle but in his own age group. But something else is
curious: why did Dostoevsky need to obtain three separate photographs of
Soloviev, and at different ages? Was this a sign of friendly emotions ("I kiss
Vladimir Sergeevich ardently")? Or did Dostoevsky, at work on the continuation of *The Brothers Karamazov,* want to scrutinize the visual changes
over the years in the face that was reflected in the main characters of his
novel? If the latter, the sequence of boyhood, youth, and old age is more
explicable—it corresponds not with the actual age of Vladimir Soloviev but
with the chronology of *The Brothers Karamazov.*

For Soloviev, the fundamental ideas of Dostoevsky's Pushkin speech were
not merely close, they were "his own." The themes of "universality and the
universal brotherhood of peoples," of an "ultimate brotherly accord of all
tribes through the law of Christ's Gospel," were developed by Soloviev
throughout his writings. Like Dostoevsky, he believed (at least at this period)
that a special role awaited Russia in the path toward "great, general harmony." Obviously, the same ideas had been expressed in one form or another
by other Russian thinkers, particularly in connection with the hopes for
Russia's historico-Christian mission. Ivan Aksakov, speaking about Dostoevsky's address, did not fail to note: "The thoughts contained in [the speech]
are not new to anyone among the Slavophiles. This question has been posed
more profoundly and more broadly by Khomiakov and by my brother Konstantin Sergeevich."[107] However, Dostoevsky's enunciation of a panhuman
national ideal is in fact closest in spirit to Soloviev. As Konstantin Mochul'skii
observes in his study of Dostoevsky: "The concept of the universality of the

Russian spirit, which lies at the base of Dostoevsky's Pushkin speech, was formulated by Soloviev before him."[108] Years later, in the essay "The Russian National Ideal," Soloviev wrote:

> Not only did [Dostoevsky] approach this ideal in the basic character of his views to a greater extent than the old Slavophiles (to say nothing of the more recent nationalism), he even gave it—in his Pushkin speech . . .—a completely true, though a most general form. . . . His formula of an all-embracing, all-uniting, and all-reconciling Russian and Christian ideal was . . . announced amid unusually solemn circumstances. One should have considered a way to realize and justify this ideal, one should have applied it as the highest standard by which to regulate all the practical questions of social life. . . . But for such a task, if only in the literary field, Dostoevsky would have had to relinquish the host of deep-rooted prejudices, preconceived ideas, and elemental national instincts that were within him.[109]

Soloviev expresses himself still more sharply in the essay "Of Questions of Culture": "Dostoevsky, who in his Pushkin speech pointed more emphatically than all the Slavophiles to the universal all-human character of the Russian idea, at the same time became in any concrete statement of the national question an exponent of the most elementary chauvinism."[110] True, all this was written by Soloviev in the 1890s, while in the "Three Speeches in Memory of Dostoevsky" (1880-83) he not only failed to point to Dostoevsky's inconsistency but insisted that his work was dominated by the universal Christian idea, the Christian act, the essence of which "in logical terms is called synthesis, and in moral terms, reconciliation."[111] With Soloviev himself, the idea of universal humanity is reflected in one form or another in all of his work. In *The Justification of the Good*, for example, he offers the following formulation: "In Christianity the consciousness passes from the abstract *uniform man* [*obshchechelovek*] of philosophers and jurists to the actual *universal man* [*vsechelovek*] and thereby utterly abolishes the old enmity and alienation among various classes of people. . . . *Universal humanity . . . is not an abstract concept, but the harmonious plenitude of all positive features* of the new or reborn creation—which is to say, *not only personal but also national features*" (Soloviev's italics).[112]

After defending his doctoral dissertation, Soloviev did not obtain a chair in philosophy as he had hoped. In the capacity of Privatdozent he began teaching at Petersburg University and at the Bestuzhev Higher Courses for Women. On 20 November 1880 he gave his inaugural lecture at the university, "The Historical Situation of Philosophy." In it Soloviev emphasized the constructive character of philosophy as such: "Philosophy has existed in mankind for more than two and half thousand years. One asks: what has it done for man during this long time? . . . It makes man fully man."[113] He does not repudiate Western "abstract principles" and includes in the general creative process both rationalistic and mystical philosophy. The whole of European philosophy "has served Christian truth." Naturally, given such a synthetic view of philosophy, "all our Slavophilism and Westernizing is no more than one great misunderstanding." However, unlike Dostoevsky, who had said this, Soloviev was consistent in his reasoning.

Soloviev's lectures were a tremendous success, the audience increased at each session, and soon the course had to be transferred to the assembly hall. Soloviev established personal friendships with many of his students. One of them, N. Nikiforov, recalls visiting Soloviev at his home to defend his own "realist worldview" and bringing a list of authors of that school. Soloviev found the list incomplete and at once proposed to the "realist" a more detailed list, with references to the sources.[114]

Dostoevsky at this time, the autumn of 1880, also found himself surrounded by young people. "Honorary tickets for concerts and balls organized by higher educational institutions were sent to him constantly. . . . Young people followed him in throngs, kept putting questions to him to which he had to respond almost in speeches."[115] New success awaited Dostoevsky at the literary soirées to which he began to be frequently invited. On 30 November, for example, he spoke in the hall of the Credit Society for the students of St. Petersburg University—that is, before the same audience and within the same walls as Soloviev (his much talked about appearance in this hall—a speech on capital punishment—would take place two months after Dostoevsky's death). In December 1880 Dostoevsky was busy preparing the January issue of *The Diary of a Writer*. He planned to publish the *Diary* for two years, then begin work on the second part of *The Brothers Karamazov*. According to Anna Dostoevskaia: "During the first half of January Fedor Mikhailovich felt extremely well. He visited friends and even agreed to participate in the home theatricals that were to take place at Countess Tolstaia's at the beginning of the next month."[116] On 29 January Soloviev was scheduled to visit: he planned to introduce to Dostoevsky a student from his university course, Prince Esper Ukhtomskii.[117]

IN MEMORIAM

Soloviev was not to see Dostoevsky alive again: on the night of 26 January 1881 Dostoevsky's pulmonary artery burst, and on 28 January he died. Dostoevsky's funeral was a historic occasion. The tens of thousands of people following the casket, the numerous choirs, the "long procession of wreaths carried on poles," the burial service in the church of the Aleksandr Nevskii Monastery—all gave witness to Dostoevsky's enormous fame and the national grief caused by his death. "After the funeral service the coffin of Fedor Mikhailovich was lifted and borne out of the church by his admirers, among whom the young philosopher Vladimir Soloviev was conspicuous for his anguished face. . . . After the coffin was lowered, speeches were made over the grave. First to speak was A. I. Palm, a former member of the Petrashevskii Circle. He was followed by Orest Miller, Professor K. N. Bestuzhev-Riumin, Vladimir Soloviev, P. A. Gaideburov, and many others."[118] Soloviev's speech, judging by the recollections of eyewitnesses, was marked by a particular expressiveness and significance: "The apostolic figure of Vladimir Soloviev, his curls falling across his brow, was impressive. He spoke with great emotion and expression."[119] In the eulogy he spoke over the tomb, Soloviev, calling Dostoevsky "the spiritual leader of the Russian people," appealed to love and universal forgiveness: "Dostoevsky believed in God and the God-man, . . . he preached the all-reconciling and all-forgiving power of love as the basis for the uniting of all people into one universal brotherhood, for the realization on earth of the kingdom of truth, for which he longed and toward which he strove all his life."[120] It is significant that Soloviev's brief speech is reminiscent of Dostoevsky's own Pushkin address. Here we encounter a phenomenon, essential to an understanding of Soloviev's general interpretation of Dostoevsky: the idea of a universal man, of an all-uniting brotherhood of nations, which Dostoevsky formulated in his Pushkin address and which Soloviev pursued in his whole life and work, appears in the graveside speech as Dostoevsky's definitive and immutable credo.

On 1 March 1881 Emperor Alexander II was assassinated. This event precipitated a political and moral ordeal for Russian society. Anna Dostoevskaia, recalling her husband's final days, wrote: "It is possible that my husband might even have recovered for a time, but his recovery would been of short duration. He would undoubtedly have been deeply shocked by the news of the villainous deed of 1 March, for he idolized the Tsar as liberator of the serfs. His barely healed artery would have burst again, and he would have died."[121] On 13 March Vladimir Soloviev gave a lecture at the Bestuzhev Higher Courses for Women in which he unequivocally condemned the revolutionary movement: "If modern revolution begins with violence, if it uses violence as a means for bringing about some new truth, it thereby reveals the obvious lie hidden within it. . . . The violences of modern revolution betray its impotence. For man, from a human perspective, any violence, any external exercise of a power alien to him, is impotence. Such external force is strength to a beast, but to a spiritual being it is impotence, and if man is not fated to return to a bestial state, then a revolution based on violence has no future."[122]

The reception of Soloviev's speech is not known, but the next lecture he gave, on 28 March, entitled "A Criticism of Modern Education and the Crisis of the World Process," caused a public sensation. The substance of the lecture, which is better known as his speech on capital punishment, has come down to us in the notes of those who were in the audience. In addition, Soloviev wrote two explanatory letters with a brief account of what he said: one to the governor of St. Petersburg, N. M. Baranov, and the other to Emperor Alexander III. Summarizing the main point of his speech, Soloviev wrote that "capital punishment . . . is an unforgivable act and in a Christian State must be abolished,"[123] and that

> the Russian people live and move in their totality by the spirit of Christ. . . . The tsar of Russia is the representative and exponent of the national spirit, the bearer of all the finest strengths of the people. . . . The present painful time offers the Russian tsar a hitherto unprecedented opportunity to proclaim the power of the Christian principle of universal forgiveness and so accomplish the supreme moral deed, which will raise his power to an inaccessible height and establish his rule on an unshakable foundation. By pardoning the enemies of his power in spite of all the natural feelings of the human heart, . . . the tsar will stand upon a super-human height and by that very deed will show the divine meaning of imperial power.[124]

A few months before the assassination, Dostoevsky, who himself had only a short time left to live, made a note for the 1881 *Diary* in connection with the execution on 4 November 1880 of Kviatkovskii and Presniakov, terrorists from the group People's Will: "What is capital punishment? In the state, it is sacrifice for an idea. But if there is the Church, there is no capital punishment."[125] Clearly revealed in these words is the idea which Dostoevsky discussed with Soloviev during their journey to Optina Pustyn in 1878, "the central idea of a new novel—the Church as a positive social ideal." In calling on Alexander III to carry out the Christian commandment of universal forgiveness, in linking Christ's truth, the Russian people, and the Russian tsar, Soloviev appealed to the main ideas of Dostoevsky (though these ideas, of course, were not his alone).

It is interesting that Anna Dostoevskaia, according to her friend M. N. Stoiunina, was very displeased by Soloviev's address and even joined others by "banging her umbrella" as a sign of indignation. When Stoiunina "ventured to rebuke her for booing the very thinker whom Fedor Mikhailovich so loved, whom indeed he embodied in Alesha Karamazov—in the image that he held most dear and closest to his heart and that he most cherished—Anna Grigorievna exclaimed: 'No, no, Fedor Mikhailovich saw in Vladimir Soloviev not Alesha, but Ivan Karamazov!'"[126]

The speech against capital punishment proved a turning point in Soloviev's life, though the address itself should not be viewed as an event with irreversible consequences. The measures imposed on Soloviev were not severe: Alexander III ordered "that Mr. Soloviev, through the agency of the Ministry of Public Education, be reprimanded for the inappropriate opinions expressed by him in a public lecture concerning the crime of 1 March, and, apart from this, be ordered to refrain for a certain time, according to the discretion of the same Ministry, from public talks."[127] It appears that the tsar was disturbed not so much by what Soloviev said as by the public's reaction to it. This explains the official advice to Soloviev to abstain from public speaking for a time—a measure aimed not against the philosopher himself but toward the prevention of further political trouble. Consequently, when in November 1881 Soloviev handed in his resignation, the minister of education remarked to him: "I did not demand this."[128] But Soloviev appraised the significance of the situation in his own way: his renunciation of his position as professor of philosophy was in a sense the conscious act of a philosopher.

The "Three Speeches in Memory of Dostoevsky" can be considered the postscript to a period of friendship, in which the likemindedness of Soloviev and Dostoevsky prevailed over their differences. In this sense they are more panegyric than criticism. Soloviev himself stressed the specific nature of his work: "In the three speeches on Dostoevsky I do not concern myself with either his personal life or a literary criticism of his writings. I have in mind only one question: What did Dostoevsky serve, what idea inspired the whole of his work?"[129] Like a triple echo, they reflect the profundity and complexity, sincerity and partiality, reality and ideality of a human relationship which, although it lasted for less than ten years, determined the relationship between Russian literature and Russian philosophy for decades to come.

3

God-man or Man-god?

Man is the measure of all things, of those that are, that they are, and of those that are not, that they are not.
—*Protagoras*

Behold, the Man!
—*John 19:5*

THE CONNECTING LINK

"Dostoevsky believed in man and mankind only because he believed in the *God*-man and *God*-manhood—in Christ and the Church."[1] What did Soloviev understand by the terms *God-man* and *God-manhood,* and to what extent did his conception coincide with Dostoevsky's?

   Soloviev's *Lectures on God-manhood* provide a concise introduction to his entire metaphysical system. In these lectures, which Dostoevsky attended conscientiously, Soloviev touches upon nearly all the themes that would receive further development and interpretation in his later works. In particular, this is true for Soloviev's idea of God-manhood, which "constitutes the center of his entire doctrine, philosophical and religious, the basic substance of his entire teaching, of everything he preached about the life-path of man and mankind."[2] Though the *Lectures on God-manhood* were not the first work of importance written by the young philosopher—besides his dissertation and several articles, he had already published in 1877 *The Philosophical Principles of Integral Knowledge*—they undoubtedly marked the beginning of Soloviev's recognition and fame. The *Lectures* defined not only Soloviev's personal philosophical positions but also one of the chief models of Russian religious philosophy.

Soloviev views the world process as a religious process within mankind, the goal of which is the transfiguration of the world into the Body of Christ. "This Body of Christ, first appearing as a tiny embryo in the form of the small community of the first Christians, is gradually growing and developing, until in the end it will embrace all mankind and all nature in one universal divine-human organism."[3] With the aid of an etymological reminder (in Latin, *religare* means "to unite"), the philosopher formulates the idea that religion reunites man, the world, and the Absolute. "Reunion or religion consists in bringing all the elements of human existence . . . into a proper relation to the absolute central principle and, through it and in it, to a proper harmonious relation among themselves."[4] Naturally, this "reunion" cannot be realized through onesided efforts, and the Orthodox doctrine of the presence of the Living God in the world finds logical reflection in Soloviev's conclusion: "Religious development is a positive and objective process, it is the real interaction of God and man—a divine-human process."[5] At the same time, man's metaphysical responsibility in the formation of the world appears here in all its uniqueness. But what are the grounds for assigning man such an exclusive role? Soloviev provides an answer to this question by proceeding from the very nature of man. "Man is at once divinity and nonentity," he says,[6] without dwelling at length on a theme that is best summarized by Derzhavin's famous line: "I am king—I am slave, I am worm—I am God." Soloviev sees in man the connecting link between the divine and the natural worlds, and his task is not to describe man, but to show his significance in the common link of true being.

Soloviev ontologically deduces the existence of mankind from the need of the Absolute for "other," nonabsolute existence. It is only by virtue of the "other," only in relation to it, that the Absolute can affirm itself. According to Soloviev, the connection of the world (the "other") to the Absolute would be impossible were it not for man, who belongs to both the divine and natural realms. Thus man becomes the natural mediator between God and material existence, and the only means for realizing unitotality.[7] It is in man, more specifically in human consciousness, that the process of unitotality begins. The potential urge of the natural world toward unitotality attains actuality, albeit still ideal, in human consciousness. "In man nature grows beyond itself and passes (in consciousness) into the realm of absolute being."[8] However, man's unique ability to achieve "positive absoluteness," the divine nature possessed by God in eternity, is a source not only of inspiration but also of suffering. Indeed, on the one hand it presents the potential absoluteness of the human *I*, a belief in the self, in human personality, and at the same time a belief in God. But on the other hand it entails an awareness of the actual insignificance of that very same *I*. Soloviev sees in this opposition the root of man's evil, nonfreedom, and inner slavery. It is not difficult to perceive that on the whole this conception of the exclusivity of human consciousness links the psychological problematics of existence to man's metaphysically exclusive role in the world process, thus bearing an internal similarity to the philosophical position of Dostoevsky.

This interplay between actual insignificance and ideal potentiality is the source of practically all the conflicts that tear apart the consciousness of Dostoevsky's characters. This is by no means to say that they all consciously relate their own limited possibilities as individuals to the a priori infinite potentiality of mankind and attribute the insignificance of their personal existence to their participation in the material world. Yet the deeper meaning of the quest and suffering of "Dostoevskian characters" always lies in their unrestrained aspiration toward the absolute in themselves and through themselves by means of a mobilization of all their powers of consciousness. Before elucidating this statement, it is necessary to note the multiple meanings of the concepts "absolute" and "consciousness" as used here. Endowing his characters with the power to aspire to the absolute, Dostoevsky sends them in different, sometimes diametrically opposed directions. Each of them, in perceiving his absolute (superhuman) potential, envisions his realization in a different way, which inevitably results in an ironic paradox— the individual absolute. And only in the overcoming (real or potential) of the individual absolute does there arise the image of the divine-human absolute—Christ. The term *consciousness* is here used to mean a single form of apperception that is associated with transcendental, rational, and empirical knowledge (in Russian, the word *so-znanie* conveys semantically the notion of a compound, comprehensive knowledge).

THE SELF-MADE MAN-GOD: RECIPE ONE

What happens in *Crime and Punishment*? The obvious answer would seem to lie in the very title. However, while the act committed by Raskolnikov is undoubtedly a crime, what can be considered his punishment? Juridically, it is forced labor. Yet it is precisely at the hard labor camp that Raskolnikov's name appears alongside the word *happiness* for the first time in the whole novel. It is there, on the last page of the story, that Dostoevsky frees his character from the yoke of his past deeds, even from his name, so far as the very name Raskolnikov is associated with dissidence (*raskol*), splitting (*raskolot'*), and with the blow of an ax (*kolot' toporom*). In "a new story, the story of the gradual renewal of a man," which, according to the author, might "be the subject of a new tale," there can no longer be the name Raskolnikov, and Dostoevsky on the threshold of this "gradual regeneration" calls his character "he," as if he were a newborn, as yet unnamed infant.[9]

Should the punishment be considered the agonies of fear, spite, and despair in which Raskolnikov finds himself after committing his crime? Psychologically, this is possible, but if we allow ourselves to depart from customary logic and shift the cause-and-effect pair of "crime-punishment" over one notch, we can claim that Raskolnikov's murderous act is in fact already the punishment for a crime he has committed against himself, against what stands in opposition to the lower creature within him. "I murdered myself, not the old woman!" he tells Sonia.[10] Raskolnikov fully discerns the presence of two elements in man, one omnipotent and the other insignificant: "I want to find out . . . whether I am a trembling creature or whether I have the *right*."[11] But his consciousness, having grasped the formal element of man's nature, monstrously distorts its substance. Throughout the novel Raskolnikov returns repeatedly to the motivation of his crime (*prestuplenie*), though almost to the very end he continues to see it as a mere overstepping of bounds (*perestuplenie*).[12]

Dostoevsky at first provides only snatches of his protagonist's reasoning, which without familiarity with Raskolnikov's "main idea" seem more or less acceptable and even slightly banal: "All is in a man's hands and he lets it all slip from cowardice, that's an axiom. It would be interesting to know what it is men are most afraid of. Taking a new step, uttering a new word."[13] The following conclusion is more diffuse, both in its essence and in its exposition: "What if man is not really a *scoundrel*, man in general, I mean, the whole race of mankind—then all the rest is prejudice, simply artificial terrors and there are no barriers and it's all as it should be."[14] But even here another, non-"Raskolnikovian" interpretation is possible: the human race, man as a whole, is not a scoundrel, not a creature (only), consequently there are no barriers to his attaining—what? The good, to be sure, "if he is not a scoundrel"! Yet gradually it becomes ever clearer that while he proceeds from objective grounds, Raskolnikov arrives at completely arbitrary conclusions.

It is as if a single wrong sign has been substituted in a correctly formulated problem, and the entire solution, directed along a false path, leads to fundamentally mistaken results. Such a comparison is fairly fitting, as Raskolnikov himself thinks of his "idea" in arithmetic terms: "Granted, granted that there is no flaw in all that reasoning, that all that I have concluded this last month is as clear as day, as just as arithmetic."[15] This "arithmetical justice" is indeed the sign, the confusion and displacement of ideas that leads the whole solution of the problem along a false path. The very word *spravedlivost'*, "justice" (stemming from *pravda*, "truth," but also "correctness"), incorporates an ambivalence. One of its senses is abstractly rationalistic, the other moral. By assuming the moral truth of arithmetic, Raskolnikov falls into an obvious contradiction. Yet this very contradiction indicates, as it were, the precariousness of his worldview and thereby the potential of changing it.

One could say that ideological confusion in the consciousness of the former student is a mark of his intellect, but at the same time it is clear that behind Raskolnikov's precarious views lie entire systems of utilitarian ethics: the "moral arithmetic" of Bentham, according to which morality amounts to the utility of an action and can be calculated as the balance of pleasure and pain; the ethics of Mill, with its preference of intellectual delights in a qualitative evaluation of pleasures; the theory of Comte, who held that mental and moral phenomena relate exclusively to "the mental and moral functions of the brain"; and other positivistic ethical doctrines. In principle, rationalism, if implemented consistently, should reject all objective elements of morality. "The sole vital element becomes the unconditional, exclusive self-assertion of the individual, of the *I*. To myself I am a god; to me everything is of importance only as my means; I recognize no limit to my egoism in anyone else: the only limit for me is the limit of my might. I derive all right and all justification from *myself*: I have a right to everything that is in my power"—thus Soloviev, in *The Crisis of Western Philosophy,* projects the ultimate rationalistic outlook.[16]

Raskolnikov's vacillations in explaining the reasons behind the murder he has committed to a certain degree reflect those of Dostoevsky himself. While working on the novel, he made this note: "It is essential to bring the course of action to a real stop and do away with the indefiniteness, that is, *one way or another* to explain the whole murder and lay out his character and attitudes clearly."[17] In his confession to Sonia, Raskolnikov finally pushes aside the secondary, concomitant motives and defines his central idea "without casuistry": "It wasn't to help my mother I did the murder—that's nonsense—I didn't do the murder to gain wealth and power and to become a benefactor of mankind. Nonsense! I simply did it; I did the murder for myself, for myself alone. . . . I wanted to find out then and quickly whether I was a louse like everybody else or a man. Whether I can step over barriers [*perestupit'*] or not!"[18] Thus it becomes clear that Raskolnikov murders for the sake of principle, that is, he commits *ritual* murder. He sacrifices the old woman, together with Lizaveta (whom he consistently forgets, as she has no place in his scheme, rigid like any ritual), to a new god—himself. Yet his sacrificial offering is not part of an established religious ceremony but represents a requisite condition for the creation of a new cult. That is, sacrifice is assigned not the role it usually fulfilled in ancient religions but that which it plays in Christianity: without the sacrifice of Christ, the New Testament is impossible. Raskolnikov, brought up in the Christian tradition, intuitively follows precisely this logic of sacrifice. But only the logic! (Dostoevsky would develop this logical construction still further in Kirillov, who elucidates the dependence of the Incarnation on sacrifice even more clearly: in his case, the sacrificial rite as such becomes a rite of self-sacrifice.) The ritual component of Raskolnikov's action is also reflected quite distinctly in the way that Raskolnikov in his self-analysis reveals the symbolic function of the object he has sacrificed: "I didn't kill a human being, but a principle!"[19]

A number of details both in Raskolnikov's theory itself and in the narrative of the novel bear a superficial likeness to religious typology. His very surname evokes, among other associations, the idea of an ecclesiastical phenomenon—the Orthodox schismatics, or *raskol'niki*.[20] Typical is Raskolnikov's attitude toward the "new word," the "new step" as an unprecedented phenomenon capable of changing the world order. This notion is played up in one form or another several times in the novel and at the end is given a definitive expression: "Then for the first time in my life an idea took shape in my mind which no one had ever thought of before me, no one! I saw clear as daylight how strange it is that not a single person living in this mad world has had the daring to go straight for it all and send it flying to the devil!"[21] In other words, Raskolnikov has suddenly realized "clear as daylight" the metaphysical weight of this extraordinary step that "no one ever before" had made. The metaphysical dimension lends a special connotation to the very concept of the "new word" through which Raskolnikov fancies to transform himself into a new being. This "word" is supposed to play the role of his New Testament.

The first tangible appearance of "Raskolnikov's idea" occurs in the conversation he overhears in a tavern between an officer and a student. The student advocates the idea's utilitarian side: "Kill her, take her money and with the help of it devote oneself to the service of humanity and the good of all. What do you think, would not one tiny crime be wiped out by thousands of good deeds? . . . One death, and a hundred lives in exchange—it's simple arithmetic!"[22] This coincidence of ideas, in which Raskolnikov suspects "predestination" and "a sign," is far from the only one in the novel. Raskolnikov's theory has also other prophets, with the difference that they see only the practical benefit of its realization, whereas Raskolnikov sets his hopes on a metaphysical result. Dostoevsky, as is typical with him, apportions similar ideas to quite different characters, thus revealing the invariant conclusion of any proposition. In Luzhin the mercantile aspect of the idea predominates: "Science now tells us, love yourself before all men, for everything in the world rests on self-interest. You love yourself and manage your own affairs properly. . . . Economic truth adds that the better private affairs are organised in society, . . . the firmer are its foundations and the better is the common welfare organised too."[23] In Svidrigailov the moral benefit of the same theory is first and foremost: "Here's . . . a theory of a sort, the same one by which I for instance consider that a single misdeed is permissible if the principal aim is right."[24] Thus we are dealing, as it were, not with a personal idea, born within a single maniacal consciousness, but with an emergent doctrine, the true meaning of which is revealed only to the bearer of the "new word."[25] Vladimir Soloviev accurately defined the fundamental reason leading Raskolnikov to commit murder: "the inner sin of self-deification."[26]

The basis, then, of Raskolnikov's crime is sin, but this sin develops as the consequence of an absolute, divine human personality. "Absoluteness" (*bezuslovnost'*), says Soloviev,

> just like other similar concepts, such as infinity—has two meanings: negative and positive. Negative absoluteness, which undoubtedly appertains to the human personality, consists in the ability to transcend any finite, limited content. . . . By not being satisfied with any finite conditional content, man in fact declares himself free from any internal limitation. . . . But this dissatisfaction with any finite content or partial, limited reality is thereby a demand for all of reality, a demand for a fullness of content. And the *possession* of all of reality, of the fullness of life, constitutes *positive* absoluteness. Without it, or at least without the possibility of it, negative absoluteness signifies nothing, or rather—it signifies an unending internal contradiction. It is in such a contradiction that the present-day consciousness finds itself.[27]

From this point of view, Raskolnikov's tragedy stems not from the fact that he "has no right" but from the fact that he does "have the right." However, while asserting the "divine rights" bestowed on him as a human individual, he does not possess the "divine content." By declaring his "negative absoluteness," Raskolnikov casts aside man's potential for attaining "positive absoluteness."

THE SELF-MADE MAN-GOD: RECIPE TWO

Another of Dostoevsky's characters to "get stuck" on the idea of God-man-hood is Kirillov in *The Devils*. "There will be full freedom," he says, "when it will be just the same to live or not to live. That's the goal for all. . . . For whom it will be the same to live or not to live, he will be the new man. He who will conquer pain and terror will himself be a god. . . . Then there will be a new life, a new man: everything will be new. Then they will divide history into two parts: from the gorilla to the annihilation of God, and from annihilation of God to . . . the transformation of the earth and of man physically. Man will be God, and will be transformed physically, and the world will be transformed and things will be transformed and thoughts and all feelings."[28] This awkward theoretical formulation and its fanatical im-plementation do not so much distort as oversimplify a number of fundamen-tal philosophical problems. The correlation of being with nonbeing, the conditions of freedom and the role of human consciousness in the world process had become basic topics of philosophical study long before they occurred to the mad engineer. Given, however, the "time and place" in which Dostoevsky situated his character, it is logical to assume that Kirillov is basing himself not, for example, on Aristotelian metaphysics (according to which being equals nonbeing *in potentia*) but on his own misapprehension of Hegel's thesis that the *concept* of nonbeing passes to the *concept* of being and vice versa. Although it is impossible to state with certainty that Dosto-evsky consciously "armed" Kirillov with straightforward Hegelianism, there is no doubt that in contemporary Russia philosophical minds were seeking to resolve the question of the correlation of being and nonbeing within the framework of the German philosophical tradition. At the same time, the lack of any systematic education in this field often led to a blind acceptance of many influential trends, with no attempt at critical interpretation. Thus, for example, behind Kirillov's statement that "there will be full freedom when it will be just the same to live or not to live," one can glimpse the ideas of Schopenhauer and Hartmann.

This is not to say that Kirillov arrived at his conception after studying the pillars of European thought or through encounters with Russian philosoph-ical amateurs. Rather the reverse—everything we know about him testifies to his lack of learning and even illiteracy: for example, he speaks Russian "not quite correctly."[29] But, as Dostoevsky writes in the *Diary* for 1876: "Ideas live and are spread in accordance with laws too difficult for us to grasp; ideas are infectious, and do you know that within the general mood of life a certain idea, a certain concern or longing accessible only to a highly educated and developed mind, may suddenly be passed on to a creature who is semiliterate, coarse, and who has never been concerned about anything; and that such an idea may suddenly infect that person's soul with its influence?"[30] Therefore, whether Kirillov hit upon his theory himself or picked up scraps of other people's thoughts is immaterial; what is important is that through his unbalanced consciousness Dostoevsky introduced a number of timely ideas into the philosophical problematics of the novel. In a draft of the preface to *The Devils* Dostoevsky noted: "In Kirillov there is the national idea of immediately sacrificing oneself for truth. . . . To sacrifice oneself and everything for truth—that is the national trait of the generation. May God bless it and send it an understanding of truth. For the whole point is what one considers to be truth. That is why the novel was written."[31]

Kirillov's "truth," like the "truth" of Raskolnikov, exhibits a semblance of coherent metaphysical construction. In both the manuscript drafts of the novel and the final text, Kirillov's "truth" is elaborated in detail: "If there is no God, then I am God. . . . If I am God, then the highest thing is self-will. I must, I cannot help but manifest my self-will, if I acknowledge myself a god. I am obliged before people, before the world. When there was God, I did not dare to be the master of my life. When he is not, I am obliged by conscience to manifest my will to myself and to everyone (even if by myself) in its highest manifestation."[32] According to Kirillov, the "highest manifestation of will" is to kill oneself, while the lowest is to kill someone else. Thus Kirillov's sacrifice can be viewed as the perfection of Raskolnikov's. In both cases the right to exert control over human life becomes the maximum manifestation of self-will. Each hopes for a transformation of the world order as a result of his personal act of volition. Yet unlike Raskolnikov, who endeavors with the help of various justifications to define his aim within sound —that is, rational—limits, Kirillov carries the thought through, never troubled that in going beyond its logical development he is overstepping the boundary between mentally sound and unsound. Dostoevsky calls Kirillov a "Russian idealist,"[33] and though by this he is defining his character's nature rather than his worldview, Kirillov exists wholly in the world of idealistic conceptions. To him the essence of the cognizable depends entirely on the consciousness of the cognizer: "Man is unhappy because he doesn't know he's happy. It's only that. That's all, that's all! If anyone finds out he'll become happy at once, that minute. That mother-in-law will die: but the baby will remain. It's all good. I discovered it all of a sudden."

Stavrogin, with whom he is speaking, asks a question that immediately shifts Kirillov's "discovery" from the epistemological sphere to the ethical: "And if anyone dies of hunger, and if anyone insults and outrages the little girl, is that good?" "Yes!" answers Kirillov. "And if anyone blows his brains out for the baby, that's good too. And if anyone doesn't, that's good too. It's all good, all. It's good for all those who know that it's all good. If they knew that it was good for them, it would be good for them, but as long as they don't know it's good for them, it will be bad for them." It is interesting to note how Dostoevsky develops and transforms the theme with the aid of the word *good*. In Kirillov's response, the sense in which *good* is used still correlates with the concept of happiness set forth above: "If they knew that it was good for them, it would be good"; "Man is unhappy because he doesn't know he's happy." But the subsequent discussion imperceptibly changes the connotation of the word: "They're bad because they don't know they're good. . . . They'll find out that they're good and they'll all become good, every one of them." That is, the emphasis has been shifted from the becoming happy to becoming good.

Relatively speaking, the scheme sketched by Kirillov presents the paradisical ideal of a happy mankind incapable of doubting that "all is good." ("And God saw every thing that he had made, and behold, it was very good"—Gen. 1:31.) But to attain this ideal mankind must return to its pre-fall nature, "they must find out that they're good." He who frees man from sin, "who teaches that all are good, will end the world." This train of thought would seem to be set within the framework of the Christological teaching of universal salvation. Stavrogin responds to Kirillov's construction accordingly: "He who taught it was crucified." But he is told in reply: "He will come, and his name will be the man-god." "The god-man?" Stavrogin repeats. "The man-god. That's the difference."[34] In *The Crisis of Western Philosophy*, Soloviev demonstrates the link between the ultimately materialistic idea of the man-god and the idealistic conception of the human-divine *I, as cognizer.*

> From a subjective standpoint, the assertion of Hegelian philosophy that the essence of everything is a logical concept was tantamount to the assertion that the essence of the human *I* is logical *cognition,* that the subject, or the individual, has meaning only in cognition as a cognizant being. But . . . if cognition has no relation to any being, has no content separate from itself as form, then . . . it becomes a purely *subjective* activity by the cognizer, to whom, in this way, passes absolute meaning. In place of the objective essence of old metaphysics, the only true being is declared to be the cognizant *subject.* . . . And the *proper* essence of the subject is his *self-assertion* or will. . . . Thus, supreme meaning passes to *man* as such, in his subjective, personal existence. This transition ad hominem was accomplished in German philosophy, as is well known, by Feuerbach, a former pupil of Hegel. "The essence of man," says Feuerbach, "is his *higher essence*; although religion calls the higher essence God and views it as an object essence, in truth this is only

man's own essence, and therefore the turning point of world history is that for man God must henceforth be not *God* but *man*."[35]

Kirillov believes that he has reached the "turning point"; all that remains is for him to exercise his right of free choice between being and nonbeing, that is, to exercise the divine function and thereby achieve the divine nature.[36] Dostoevsky carries the process of self-consciousness to its logical limit: consciousness cognizant of itself and locked within itself. But if, to paraphrase Pascal, the god speculatively deduced by Feuerbach can be called the man-god of the philosophers, Kirillov's man-god is painfully arrived at by him as an antithesis to the God of Abraham, Isaac, and Jacob, incarnated in Christ. Kirillov's very conviction that his *individual* incarnation into the man-god depends upon his *individual* consciousness is rooted (whether he realizes it or not) in the Christian doctrine of the incarnate Logos: the Word made flesh. Several times Kirillov is mentioned as reading the Apocalypse, the Revelation of St. John the Divine. We may assume that in reading St. John's Gospel, he would agree with one of the variants of the first line proposed by a still more celebrated character—Faust: "In the beginning was Thought."[37]

PRINCE ANTICHRIST AND PRINCE CHRIST

If Raskolnikov's theory is constructed on a rationalistic justification of the idea of the man-god, and Kirillov finds a more mystical explanation for it, with Stavrogin this theme is developed in both directions, though not by him but rather through him. "The metaphysical significance of Stavrogin is such that he must dramatically dominate everything about him, while he himself remains inactive."[38] The mission to which Raskolnikov and Kirillov lay claim and condemn themselves alone is imposed upon Stavrogin by others. In his case it is not a question of reincarnation or transfiguration at any cost, but merely the fulfillment of a man-god's role. Stavrogin's lack of his own face, his own soul, is noted by the author from the very beginning: "It was said that his face suggested a mask."[39] Somewhat later we find a description of Stavrogin asleep, "sitting strangely motionless": "His face was pale and forbidding, but it looked, as it were, numb and rigid. His brows were somewhat contracted and frowning. He positively had the look of a lifeless wax figure."[40] The frightening "motionless lethargy" of the sleeping Nikolai Vsevolodovich (and we observe behind Stavrogin the eyes of his mother, Varvara Petrovna, who is "seized with terror" at the sight of her son) becomes a visible expression of his nature: "neither cold nor hot." To Stavrogin life and death (in the broad sense), good and evil are indeterminate categories: "I am still capable . . . of desiring to do something good, and of feeling pleasure from it; at the same time I desire evil and feel pleasure from that too."[41]

The unpredictability of his behavior reflects less the mysteriousness of a soul than the irreality of an automaton, dispassionately carrying out evil and good deeds.[42] However, the evil in Stavrogin's actions clearly prevails. Nikolai Vsevolodovich's anger "was a calm, cold, if one may say so, *reasonable* anger, and therefore the most revolting and most terrible possible."[43] Even his bravery is devoid of expression: "Stavrogin would have shot his opponent in a duel, and would have faced a bear, . . . but it would be without the slightest thrill of enjoyment, languidly, listlessly, even with *ennui*."[44] Toward the end of the novel Stavrogin himself admits in a letter to Dasha: "From me nothing has come but negation, with no greatness of soul, no strength." And he immediately corrects himself: "Even negation has not come from me. Everything has always been petty and spiritless."[45] Now and then some emotion does break through the automatism of Stavrogin's amorality, but such bursts of "warm" reaction are associated with feelings of hatred, anger, and, once, fear. This is most clearly revealed in the chapter "At Tikhon's."[46] Stavrogin wakes up the morning after raping a girl in his own lodgings: "My first thought upon awakening was whether she had told or not; for a moment I was really frightened, though not intensely. I was in very good spirits that morning, and awfully kind toward everyone, and the whole crew was very well pleased with me. . . . Toward evening I felt afraid again, but this time the fear was incomparably more intense. Of course, I could deny everything, but I might still be found guilty. I had visions of prison camp. I was afraid and indeed experienced terror, I don't know why, for the first time in my life—a most agonizing sensation. Besides, in the evening, when I was in my lodgings, I began to hate her so that I decided to kill her."[47]

But the chief emotion ruling Stavrogin is boredom, having degenerated over time from the "vague sensation of that eternal, sacred yearning" with which the author endowed this young "Prince Harry." It is precisely this trait that Dostoevsky singled out in his note on "Stavrogin as a character": "all passions (*always together with boredom*)."[48] "The main thing was that life bored me to the point of stupefaction," says Nikolai Vsevolodovich himself after his shocking description of Matresha's suicide.[49] If Dostoevsky chose an excerpt from Pushkin's "The Demons" (along with a Gospel parable) as an epigraph to the entire novel, he could have used another line from Pushkin as a motto on Prince Harry's coat of arms: "Mne skuchno, bes" (I'm bored, demon).[50]

The emotional void accompanying his incredible fortune of possessing every conceivable external gift allows all the other characters in the novel to fill this brilliant shell of an outstanding personality with whatever content they like. To be sure, Stavrogin himself also plays with his many-sidedness, provoking the most diverse ideas and emotions in people. But Dostoevsky, while repeatedly declaring Stavrogin's truly magnetic charm, under which practically all those around him fall, never once offers a satisfactory explanation for it. As a result, his mysterious attractiveness in conjunction with the unmotivated nature of most of his actions makes this ambiguous image even more strange (an epithet to which the author very often resorts when describing Stavrogin).

But what role does Nikolai Vsevolodovich Stavrogin play in people's fates? "Remember what you have meant in my life, Stavrogin," Kirillov, who is possessed by the idea of the man-god, says to him.[51] "You meant so much to me in my life," repeats Shatov, the advocate of the idea of a "Chosen People."[52] Shatov's "main theme," his notion of Orthodoxy, his belief in Russia's exclusive vocation, were all adopted from Stavrogin's words. "It was a teacher uttering weighty words, and a pupil who was raised from the dead. I was that pupil and you were the teacher," declares Shatov.[53] The entire scene of the late-night conversation at his home is extremely important for a portrait of Stavrogin. At the same time, it does not facilitate an understanding of his character but rather complicates it: his behavioral paradoxes, his view of the world, his relations with people stand out as if illuminated by the flame of a candle; yet the whole figure remains in shadow, à la Rembrandt.[54] Dostoevsky makes Stavrogin's character still more mysterious by handing him some of his own words: "Didn't you tell me," asks Shatov, "that if it were mathematically proven to you that the truth excludes Christ, you'd prefer to stick to Christ rather than to the truth?"[55] Dostoevsky had expressed this very thought, in a somewhat different form, as early as 1854 in a letter to N. D. Fonvizina.[56] Equally close to the author's own ideas are other "quotations" from Stavrogin: "An atheist can't be a Russian, an atheist at once ceases to be a Russian"; "A man who is not Orthodox cannot be Russian."[57] At the same time, when Shatov asks, "Are you an atheist? An atheist now?" Stavrogin replies: "Yes." "And then?" (that is, when Stavrogin was "sowing" the idea of "God and the Fatherland" in Shatov's heart and "infecting [Kirillov's] heart . . . with poison"). "Just as I was then."[58] Despite the enormous substantive and spiritual contradiction, which Shatov clearly sees, and despite his accusation that Stavrogin has lost the "distinction between evil and good," he "cannot tear Nikolai Stavrogin out of his heart."[59] "Shan't I kiss your footprints when you've gone?" exclaims Shatov. ". . . Why am I condemned to believe in you through all eternity?"[60] The tone of religious ecstasy stands out distinctly in this frenzied declaration.

With equal fanaticism, though with quite different goals, Petr Verkhovenskii pins his hopes on Stavrogin: "Do you know, I have thought of giving up
the world to the Pope. . . . The Pope at the head, with us around him, and
below us—Shigalevism. . . . It's an ideal: it's in the future. . . . Listen. The
Pope shall be for the west, and you shall be for us, you shall be for us! . . .
You are my idol! . . . You are an awful aristocrat. An aristocrat is irresistible
when he goes in for democracy! To sacrifice life, your own or another's, is
nothing to you.[61] You are just the man that's needed. It's just such a man as
you that I need. I know no one but you. You are the leader, you are the sun
and I am your worm."[62] Intoxicated by his scheme, Verkhovenskii reveals his
plan for its execution.

> We will proclaim destruction. . . . We'll set fires going. . . . Russia will be over-
> whelmed with darkness, the earth will weep for its old gods. Well, then we shall
> bring forward—whom? . . . Ivan the Tsarevich. . . . We shall say that he is "in
> hiding." . . . But he will appear, he will appear. . . . He exists, but no one has seen
> him. Oh, what a legend we can set going! . . . Listen. I'll let no one see you, no
> one. So it must be. He exists, but no one has seen him; he is in hiding. And do
> you know, one might show you, to one out of a hundred thousand, for instance.
> And the rumor will spread over the land: "We've seen him, we've seen him." . . .
> You are beautiful and proud as a god; you are seeking nothing for yourself, with
> the halo of a victim round you, "in hiding." The great thing is the legend. You'll
> conquer them, you'll only have to look, and you will conquer them. He is "in
> hiding," and will come forth bringing a new truth. . . . And the whole land will
> resound with the cry: "A new just law has to come," and the sea will be troubled
> and the whole gimcrack show will fall to the ground, and then we shall consider
> how to build up an edifice of stone. For the first time! We are going to build it,
> we, and only we![63]

Petr Verkhovenskii, who, in Fedka's phrase, is an "evil seducer and so-
called atheist," wants, essentially, to embody his quasireligious ideal in Stavrogin. Sometime in his childhood he had known the feeling of religious fear:
"When he said his prayers going to bed he used to bow down to the ground,
and make the sign of the cross on his pillow that he might not die in the
night."[64] Over time Verkhovenskii has grasped the psychological nuances of
the correlation of fear, love, and faith. "I want you to help from goodwill and
not from fear," he says, tempting and being tempted by Stavrogin.[65] In
himself "good will" is absent altogether. His childhood fear without love has
degenerated into a hatred of Christ. Now, attempting to create an "Ivan the
Tsarevich," he experiences the same combination of worship, fear, and hatred toward his new "idol." "Surely you don't want to offer yourself just as
you are as a substitute for Christ?," his father cries to him. But Petr Ver-

khovenskii's plans are even more "autocratic" (*samovlastnee*): what he wants is "one magnificent, despotic will, like an idol, resting on something funda-mental and eternal."[66] As a "substitute for Christ" he wants to "offer" Nikolai Vsevolodovich Stavrogin.

Lebiadkin too joins to the chorus of idolaters, honest and crafty: "You meant so much in my life!"[67] His servility basically stems from straightfor-ward cupidity: Stavrogin is for him a "milch cow," though in the captain's clowning and knavish heart mercantile self-abasement exists side by side with the most high-flown romanticism, inspiring Lebiadkin to poetic pearls worthy of the pen of Koz'ma Prutkov.[68] This literary romanticism unques-tionably brings a note of sincere admiration to his attitude toward Stavrogin: "You've been scattering clever sayings your whole life. . . . Imagine Liputin, imagine Petr Stepanovich saying anything like that!"[69] Lebiadkin is a comic character, whom the author flatly calls a fool, but in Dostoevsky's works "the spirit moves where it will," and conceptually weighty opinions and comments are often placed in the mouths of insignificant and even base characters. Lebiadkin is a jester, and jesters are traditionally able to utter truths. He gives us a significant description of Stavrogin: "With such a wonder-worker anything may come to pass; he lives to do harm."[70]

Even Fedka, the murderer and thief, while accusing Petr Verkhovenskii of blasphemy, expresses his admiration for Nikolai Stavrogin: "Master Stav-rogin stands at the top of the ladder above you, and you yelp at him from below like a silly puppy dog, while he thinks it would be doing you an honor to spit at you."[71] Fedka never calls Stavrogin anything but Master (*Gospodin*, Master, Sir, Lord), and in his conversation with Stavrogin himself twice repeats: "I stand before you, sir, as before God [*Istinnyi,* the True One]."[72]

"Wonder-worker," "Master," "Lord," "True One," "God"—all these seem-ingly chance titles have a distinctly cultic flavor and strengthen the religious atmosphere around Stavrogin. The idolatry Stavrogin inspires in those around him acquires the added force of erotic emotion in his relations with women: "All our ladies were wild over the new visitor. They were sharply divided into two parties, one of which adored him while the other half regarded him with a hatred that was almost bloodthirsty: but both were crazy about him."[73] Female emotions toward Stavrogin are concentrated in three characters: Dasha, for all her "common sense" and grasp of life, adores him with sacrificial devotion, while Liza is gripped by a passion in which hatred boils beneath love. Only the emotion of Mariia Timofeevna is simple and sublime, but then she loves not the real Nikolai Vsevolodovich but her own myth of him—not Stavrogin but what he should be, his *eidos* (if one may use Platonic terminology). But present in the attitudes of all three toward

Stavrogin is a mystical element. "God save you from your demon," he is told by Dasha,[74] whom in his last letter he asks to come to "live forever" in a narrow valley in the mountains.[75] (An association with Lermontov's "Demon" springs inevitably to mind.) "I'll believe your word as though it were God's," swears Liza, who, like Dasha, is prepared to follow Stavrogin "to the end of the earth."[76]

When one sums up all the aspects of the novel connected, on various levels, with Stavrogin, there emerges a significant, Gospel-like scheme of disciples awaiting revelations and sacrifices, selflessly devoted women, and a mother who is invariably accompanied by her faithful companion: in this case Stepan Trofimovich Verkhovenskii. Even the choice of some of the names reveals certain parallels. Ivan (Shatov) is the name of Christ's beloved disciple, John. The name Petr (Verkhovenskii) is the symbol of the Catholic Church, which Dostoevsky believed had given in to "the Devil's third temptation"—power, and whose head, the Pope, is an integral part of Verkhovenskii's plan for world supremacy. Among female characters one can note Mariia and Elizaveta. Finally, there is Stavrogin—whose surname comes from the Greek for "cross," and whose patronymic, Vsevolodovich, symbolizes absolute power. The problematics of Stavrogin's image are profoundly linked with the idea of the man-god. Here, in contrast to the general terms used to create the problematics of Raskolnikov and Kirillov, Dostoevsky depicts the idea in detail, showing how the Gospel model is adopted to create the image of the man-god. Such a logical thematic development leads in Dostoevsky to an obvious conclusion: the idea of the man-god is ultimately identical to the idea of the Antichrist. Of course, Stavrogin himself is too insignificant for such a role, but he is still "of the same nature," as the General notes about yet another prince in Soloviev's *Three Conversations*.: "in the writings of St. John the Divine: you have heard, little children, that the antichrist will come, even now are there many antichrists. So is he one of these many, these very many."[77] Stavrogin's incapacity for total evil is conditioned less by a capacity for good (or, more precisely and more prosaically, "the habits of a gentleman,"[78] as he himself puts it) than by his inability to "believe in an idea."[79] "I know I'm a worthless character, and I don't pretend to be a strong one," he admits to Kirillov. "You'd better not," Kirillov replies, "you're not a strong person."[80] Having provoked, whether intentionally or not, a stream of people to worship him, Stavrogin has neither the desire nor the opportunity to fulfill the various hopes they have placed in him. "Impostor," shouts the holy fool Mariia Timofeevna, who, like her jester brother, is permitted to utter truths.

While in Stavrogin the idea of the man-god acquires the features of the

Antichrist, the image of the God-man, Christ, is most visible in the protagonist of Dostoevsky's novel *The Idiot,* Prince Myshkin. A number of significant parallels point to an intentional correlation between these two
characters. The author introduces the reader to both Myshkin and Stavrogin
shortly after they return from Switzerland, while at the close of the stories
both characters are due to return there (although Stavrogin at the last
moment chooses suicide over departure). The "Swiss connection" has even
more geographic precision: in both novels the canton of Uri is mentioned:
Stavrogin intends to settle there,[81] while Myshkin recognizes a view of the
canton in a landscape in General Epanchin's study.[82] Myshkin bears the title
of prince; Stavrogin is called a prince by his deranged wife. (In both cases
the title of prince suggests certain symbolic associations: Prince of Peace,
Prince of Darkness, of the World, and so on.) Prince Myshkin suffers from
epileptic fits that "made him almost an idiot";[83] Stavrogin earns a reputation
as a madman in society by his inexplicable actions.[84] Myshkin's anti-Catholic
statements are repeated almost verbatim by Stavrogin (in Shatov's paraphrase): "Catholicism . . . preaches the Antichrist. . . . Roman Catholicism
believes that the Church cannot hold its position without universal political
supremacy";[85] "Announcing to all the world that Christ without an earthly
kingdom cannot hold his ground upon earth, Catholicism thus proclaimed
the Antichrist and ruined the whole Western world."[86] Both Stavrogin and
Myshkin are drawn into complicated relations with competing women.
Moreover, Myshkin at the beginning of the novel recalls his purely Christian
love for the unfortunate Marie (the analogy to the Gospel story in John 8
about the adulteress sentenced to be stoned is quite transparent),[87] while
Stavrogin is bound to the mad Mariia Timofeevna by a strange marriage.
Her brother Lebiadkin in both his disposition and his function in the novel
has something in common with Lebedev from *The Idiot*, a kinship underlined by the similarity of their names. During the course of the novels both
Stavrogin and Myshkin receive slaps in the face: the former from Shatov, the
latter from Gania.

   Clearly, such an accumulation of similar elements serves as a sign either
of the characters' closeness or of their maximal divergence, their antinomy.
It is essential to note that in the original plan of the novel the Idiot has more
in common with the future Stavrogin than with the future Myshkin: owing
to a superabundance of inner strength, he is capable of extreme manifestations of both good and evil.[88] Thus from the outset *The Idiot* was to display
a protagonist of two symmetric characters with "opposite signs."

   In Prince Myshkin (of the final version) Dostoevsky embodied with
unique cogency his vision of an "imitation of Christ." Numerous analyses of

the novel have vividly clarified the image of a character whom the author in
his later drafts had begun to call "Prince Christ."[89] The idea of portraying "a
truly beautiful person"[90] naturally came close to the idea of the God-man
Christ, who for Dostoevsky was the only "truly beautiful individual."[91] At the
same time, by placing his "Prince Christ" within modern society, the writer,
as it were, simulated the situation described by Belinskii in their old quarrels:
"But believe me, you naïve man, . . . were your Christ born in our time he
would be the most insignificant and ordinary man; thus he would fade into
the background in the face of contemporary science and of what presently
makes up the moving forces of mankind."[92] Belinskii sought on the basis of
this supposition to demonstrate the deficiency of Christ, whereas Dostoevsky
is showing the deficiency of those who are unable to accept not only the
God-man but also His reflected light in the "insignificant and ordinary"
Prince Myshkin. It is possible that the biographical situation connected with
Belinskii also underlies the symbolism, so essential in the novel, of Pushkin's
"Poor Knight." Dostoevsky was never able to forget the mocking lines with
which Panaev, Nekrasov, and Turgenev greeted him in the name of the
famous critic:

> Rytsar' gorestnoi figury,
> Dostoevskii, milyi pyshch!
> Na nosu literatury
> Rdeesh' ty, kak novyi pryshch.
> (Knight of sombre figure,
> Dostoevsky, darling pomp!
> On the nose of literature
> You glow like a new pimple.)

Besides retrospective personal associations with the image of the "poor
knight," one cannot avoid considering the association that emerges in view
of Dostoevsky's relationship with Soloviev. As we know, Vladimir Soloviev
himself had a vision "transcending understanding" (*nepostizhnoe umu*): during his visit to London in 1875 a "voice" called the young philosopher to
Egypt, where he saw "a single image of womanly beauty"—the "Eternal
Friend."[93] Certainly Dostoevsky, who put in Aglaia's mouth his own admiration for "the grand conception of the platonic love of medieval chivalry,"[94]
would recognize the profound mystical meaning of this unique experience
in Soloviev's life.[95]

Religious intuition allowed Dostoevsky to reflect on the very essence of
Christianity by creating not a theological treatise but a literary character—
Prince Myshkin. And most certainly in the fulfillment of this task his religious
intuition was matched by an artistic one. Dostoevsky's intention to depict "a

truly beautiful person" is clear enough, but nevertheless it is illuminated even more with the appropriate argument from Soloviev's *Lectures on God-manhood*:

> Nowadays in the Christian world . . . one very often finds people who call themselves Christians but declare that the essence of Christianity is not in the person of Christ, but in His teaching. . . . But in what does Christ's teaching consist? . . . Long before Christianity the Indian religious teachings—Brahmanism and Buddhism—were already preaching love and charity, and not only toward men, but toward everything that lives. In the same way, the characteristic content of Christianity cannot be considered Christ's doctrine of God as the Father, God as a preeminently loving and good being, since this teaching too is not specifically Christian. . . . If we examine the entire theoretical and moral content of Christ's teaching that is found in the Gospel, the only thing we shall find that is new and specifically different from all other religions will be Christ's teaching about Himself, His indication of Himself as the living incarnation of truth. . . . Thus, if the characteristic substance of Christianity is sought in the teaching of Christ, we must here acknowledge that this substance amounts to Christ Himself.[96]

Thus also for Dostoevsky the essence of Christianity lay precisely "in the person of Christ," whose vivid features he saw in the fictitious Prince Myshkin.

THE FINAL ENCOUNTER: "THE LEGEND OF THE GRAND INQUISITOR" AND "A SHORT TALE OF THE ANTICHRIST"

In *The Brothers Karamazov* Dostoevsky "reached the culmination in the development of his major ideas and the artistic images in which he embodied them. Of course, this is not meant to imply a final solution to the philosophical problematics of Dostoevsky's novels, the presence of philosophical closure, "not because the author has failed in his attempts to achieve it, but because it did not enter into his design."[97] But *The Brothers Karamazov* commands the finality that Dostoevsky had intended for it (though in the conjectural context of a "great novel" or cycle of novels under the general title of "Atheism"): "Let me write this last novel, then may I die—I shall have said all that I have to say."[98] The allegorical devils give way to an actual character—the Devil—while the development of the man-god/God-man antinomy reaches its logical conclusion with the appearance in the pages of the last novel of the real Christ and His antipode, the Grand Inquisitor.

As mentioned above, Dostoevsky discussed "the main idea and in part the plan of his new work" with Soloviev during their journey to Optina Pustyn in the summer of 1878. The reflection of Soloviev's philosophical and religious ideas and even his personal character in *The Brothers Karamazov* has been repeatedly addressed by scholars.[99] Soloviev's influence revealed itself most directly in Ivan Karamazov's article on theocracy. The intersection of other themes, while less incontrovertibly presupposing the presence of "influence," provides ample objective grounds for reflecting on the shared aspects of the two thinkers' world-outlooks.

"The Legend of the Grand Inquisitor" and "A Short Tale of the Antichrist" (a section of Soloviev's last work, *Three Conversations*) can be considered the culmination of Dostoevsky's and Soloviev's immersion into the metaphysical confrontation between the God-man, Christ, and the man-god, the Antichrist. A comparison of these two works is invariably found wherever the names of their authors are juxtaposed. There is little to be gained from attempts to determine the priority of the formal developments of the main ideas reflected in the "Legend" and the "Tale." Although Soloviev wrote the *Three Conversations* more than twenty years after the appearance of *The Brothers Karamazov*, retrospective analysis of both texts moves the question of priority into "time immemorial." As one scholar observed: "It may be that Soloviev wrote his *Lectures on God-manhood* not without the unconscious influence of the cult of Christ in Dostoevsky, which does not rule out that the *Lectures* themselves were later reflected in the 'Legend,' with which, in turn, the *Three Conversations* are unquestionably linked."[100] Let us examine again the texts of the two works which are crucial for our topic.

Early in the chapter of *The Brothers Karamozov* that is called "Grand Inquisitor" we find three verse quotations. They play, as it were, the role of epigraphs to Ivan's poem, which he has "made up and memorized":

Ver' tomu, chto serdtse skazhet,
Net zalogov ot nebes
(Believe what your heart tells you,
For heaven offers no pledge)
—from the last stanza of Schiller's poem "Yearning," in Vasilii Zhukovskii's translation.

Udruchennyi noshei krestnoi
Vsiu tebia, zemlia rodnaia,
V rabskom vide tsar' nebesnyi
Iskhodil blagoslavliaia
(Bent under the burden of the Cross,
The King of Heaven in the form of a slave
Walked the length and breadth of you,
Blessing you, my native land)
—the last stanza of Fedor Tiutchev's poem "These poor villages."

V velikolepnykh avtodafe
Szhigali zlykh eretikov
(In the splendid auto-da-fe
Evil heretics were burnt)
—somewhat altered lines from Aleksandr Polezhaev's poem "Coriolanus."[101]

An account of the symbolic meaning of the "epigraphs" helps us to see more distinctly at least three aspects of this polysemous chapter. The lines from Polezhaev's poem serve as "historical commentary" to the Legend: they indicate location—Western Europe, most likely Spain; historical time—the Middle Ages; and relative time—the past. The quotation from Tiutchev's famous poem serves as a commentary to the "Grand Inquisitor" chapter within the context of the whole novel of *The Brothers Karamazov*: place of action—Russia; time—the unspecified past. Moreover, if one recalls the second stanza of Tiutchev's poem:

Ne poimet i ne zametit
Gordyi vzor inoplemennyi,
Chto skvozit i taino svetit
V nagote tvoei smirennoi
(The stranger's proud gaze
will neither comprehend nor notice
what shows through and secretly shines
in your humble nakedness)

the past tense of the stanza quoted by Dostoevsky becomes linked semantically to the present. Thus "ideal" Russia, the "native land," is in the present, having been blessed by the "King of Heaven" in the past, a blessing that presumably applies to the future as well. (It is worth noting the semantically antonymous pairs that emphasize an implied opposition between the West and Russia, which is revealed in a comparison of the two poetic quotations: blessing/evil [*blago-slovliaia/zlykh*], in slavish/in splendid [*v rabskom/v velikolepnykh*].) Finally, the lines from Schiller have a universal connotation—they can serve as an epigraph to the Legend, to the "Grand Inquisitor" chapter, and to the entire novel. The gist of the ingenuous and naive, at first glance, peroration, which is spoken in the present tense and thereby retains a perpetual urgency, is the superiority of faith over reason. It is interesting that Dostoevsky cuts off Schiller's stanza just before its end: "Only a miracle will show us the way / Into that magical land of miracles." The text that immediately follows the quotation in the novel, though, displays an internal connection with the final words of "Yearning": "True, there were also miracles then. There were saints who performed miraculous healings; to some righteous men, according to their biographies, the Queen of Heaven herself came down. But the devil never rests, and there had already arisen in mankind some doubt as to the authenticity of these miracles."[102]

This peculiar dismissal of the miracle theme that traditionally accompanies religious stories and legends is not accidental. True faith does not rest on miracles. Indeed, Dostoevsky places *miracle* at the disposal of the Grand Inquisitor, who uses it along with *mystery* and *authority* to "correct" Christ's deed.[103] Vasilii Rozanov, reflecting on the "Legend of the Grand Inquisitor," writes: "Christ left to men His image, which they might emulate with a free heart, like an ideal corresponding to their own (secretly divine) nature and answering their vague inclinations. This emulation must be free, for therein lies its moral virtue. Meanwhile, any new revelation from Heaven would appear as a *miracle* and would introduce *compulsion* into history, depriving people of the freedom to choose and, with it, moral merit."[104] The Grand Inquisitor in his program bases the realization of a "universal kingdom" and "universal peace" not on mankind's divine element but on its human nature, with all its attendant weaknesses. His theory of a "happy mankind" is diametrically opposed to the conception of the God-man. He consistently distorts the fundamental propositions of Christianity on the nature of sin, the essence of redemption, and salvation and resurrection.[105]

The concept of human freedom is tied to the notion of sin. Nikolai Berdiaev, whose philosophical worldview is imbued with the spirit of freedom, observes:

> There exist two freedoms: the first is primordial freedom and the second is ultimate freedom. . . . Saint Augustine in his struggle against Pelagianism taught of two freedoms: *libertas minor* and *libertas major*. The lower freedom was for him the primordial, first freedom, which is freedom to choose good, and is linked with the possibility of sin; the higher freedom was the final, ultimate freedom— freedom in God, in goodness. . . . The human image endures by means of a nature higher than itself. Human freedom achieves its ultimate expression in higher freedom, freedom in Truth. Such is the inevitable dialectics of freedom. It leads to the path of God-manhood. In God-manhood human freedom is united with divine freedom, the human image with the divine image.[106]

Scholars examining the question of freedom posed in the "Legend" often fail to consider that while infringing, in the final analysis, on the second freedom—freedom in Christ—the Grand Inquisitor starts by doing away with the condition of the first, primordial freedom: "there is no crime, and therefore no sin, but only hungry men."[107] As a rule, these words are seen to provide the grounds for destroying man's sense of responsibility. Yet they also infringe upon man's freedom. As Berdiaev noted: "Free goodness, which is the only goodness, presupposes the freedom of evil."[108] By proclaiming the absence of sin, the Grand Inquisitor is depriving people of the freedom to choose. The irony of this proposition lies in the fact that the appearance of Christ is "also" aimed at delivering mankind from sin. But the idea of redemption is founded not on the illusion of the absence of sin but on the fact of its presence in the world. Therefore, the process of redemption is impossible without the "first freedom," the freedom to choose, just as salvation is bound up with the "second," ultimate freedom, to which refer the words: "And ye shall know the truth, and the truth shall make you free" (John 8:32).

The Grand Inquisitor is too skilled in theology not to understand the internal dialectics of Christianity: mankind's deliverance from sin requires redemption and sacrifice. Yet since the program he expounds sets as its object not the redemption of sin but the illusion of its absence, cause has been skillfully replaced by effect: the concept of sin has been replaced by the concept of punishment for sin. "We will tell them that every sin will be redeemed if it is committed with our permission; and that we will allow them to sin because we love them, and as for the punishment for these sins, very well, we take it upon ourselves."[109] This plan for "redemption," like any parody, is constructed upon the basic elements of the chosen model. Just as the illusory absence of sin parodies the idea of redemption, so the sufferings of "the hundred thousand of those who govern" parody the idea of sacrifice. "Only we, we who keep the mystery, only we shall be unhappy. There will be thousands of millions of happy babes, and a hundred thousand sufferers who have taken upon themselves the curse of the knowledge of good and evil."[110]

Transformed with similar consistency is the idea of Christian love for mankind, in whose name the sacrifice is ostensibly made. Vladimir Soloviev, meditating on the good in human nature, notes: "Love in a purely psychological sense . . . is deep-rooted and abiding pity or compassion. . . . Long before Schopenhauer the Russian people identified these two concepts in their language: for them 'to pity' [*zhalet'*] and 'to love' [*liubit'*] signify one and the same thing."[111] One may note that Dostoevsky, by placing a profession of love for mankind into the "bloodless, ninety-year-old lips" of the Grand Inquisitor, is playing with two connotations of a single word. Semantically present in "pity," besides "love," is the notion of contempt (compare the adjective "pitiful," *zhalkii*). It is precisely this "meaning of love" that is advocated by Christ's antagonist: "I swear, man is created weaker and baser than you thought him! . . . Respecting him so much, you behaved as if you had ceased to be compassionate, because you demanded too much of him—and who did this? He who loved him more than himself! Respecting him less, you would have demanded less of him, and that would be closer to love, for his burden would be lighter. He is weak and mean."[112] (It is worth noting that it is precisely love as compassion for man and mankind that Schopenhauer, whom Soloviev mentions, contrasts with the "primordial criminality" of the World Will. Pity-love leads the philosopher to the idea of the destruction of the World Will. Nietzsche, on the other hand, who was reared on Schopenhauer's philosophy and perceived the tragedy of human existence as his own, arrived at the idea of the destruction of Christ. As in much else, Dostoevsky prophetically pointed out the latent anti-Christian and Antichrist-ian potential of a love-pity originating in a recognition of man's pitifulness.)

The Grand Inquisitor's tempting speculations concerning the basic concepts of Christianity culminate in his alternative idea of salvation: "Peacefully they will die, peacefully they will expire in your name, and beyond the grave they will find only death."[113] These words might be simply the ordinary expression of an atheistic worldview, were they based only on "godlessness."[114] And the following promise—"But we will keep the secret, and for their own happiness we will entice them with a heavenly and eternal reward"—sounds indeed like a *lozh' vo spasenie*, a lie in the name of salvation. "It is said and prophesied that you will come and once more be victorious, you will come with your chosen ones, with your proud and mighty ones, but we will say that they saved only themselves, while we have saved everyone," concludes the self-proclaimed "savior." But what kind of salvation is it for those who "beyond the grave find only death"? The Grand Inquisitor replaces the idea of the salvation of God-manhood with the salvation of mankind; instead of salvation in Christ, who "is the Resurrection and the Life," he proposes a quasisalvation outside of Christ—the "universal happiness of men" and death. Indeed, how could it be otherwise, if he says to Christ, "We are not with you, but with *him*" ("the dread and wise spirit," that is, the devil)? Alesha, after listening to Ivan's "little poem," exclaims: "Your Inquisitor doesn't believe in God, that's his whole secret!" "What of it! At last you've understood," agrees Ivan.[115]

But the world of philosophical problematics in which Dostoevsky's characters exist does not allow for religious neutrality. Unbelief signifies not atheism but antitheism, and turning away from Christ signifies a turning toward the Antichrist. Therefore, even the Grand Inquisitor, though dooming mankind to death, hopes for salvation for himself "in the next world": "For even if there were anything in the next world, it would not, of course, be for such as they."[116] The Christian doctrine of mankind's salvation and resurrection is transformed into a theory of salvation for those who have sided with the Antichrist. It is appropriate, in connection with this theme, to recall a characteristic episode from the final section of Soloviev's "Short Tale of the Antichrist": "Meanwhile, a terrible subterranean rumbling was heard in the northwestern corner of the central palace beneath the *kubbet-el-aruah,* that is, the *dome of souls,* where according to Muslim legend the entrance to the underworld is located. When the assembly, at the invitation of the emperor [the Antichrist], moved in that direction, everyone clearly heard countless voices, thin and shrill-half childish, half devilish-crying: 'The time has come, release us, *our saviors, our saviors!*'"[117]

To return to the Grand Inquisitor, one cannot ignore the logical error in his reasoning: if salvation is understood to mean eternal life, inseparable from the image of Christ, then in the Antichrist's antistructure "life" must have its antipode, that is, "antilife," which it is thus difficult to call salvation. One conceivable explanation for this outwardly illogical proposition is given by the elder Zosima, who can be viewed as an antipode to the Grand Inquisitor, in his "mystical reasoning": those who "have cursed themselves by cursing God and life . . . cannot look upon the living God without hatred, and demand that there be no God of life, that God destroy himself and all his creation. And they will burn eternally in the fire of their wrath, thirsting for death and nonexistence. But they will not find death."[118] In such a context, "antilife"—that is, nonexistence—truly looks like salvation. It is interesting that within the framework of the artistic reality created by Dostoevsky the idea of antipodality, expressed most fully in the ideological antinomy of Christ-Antichrist, is consistently implemented in the novel's structure as well. The Grand Inquisitor essentially abides within nonexistence—his existence has been "made up" by Ivan—whereas the elder Zosima is a real character in the novel. Moreover, "The Legend of the Grand Inquisitor" has not been written down by its author, Ivan, while "The Life of the Hieromonk and Elder Zosima, Departed in God" exists in manuscript form and was "composed from [the elder's] own words" by Aleksei Karamazov, who in turn is here set in opposition to Ivan.[119]

Before turning to a comparison of the theme of God-manhood in Dostoevsky's "Legend of the Grand Inquisitor" and Soloviev's "Short Tale of the Antichrist," let us compare the formal aspects of the two works. They are both written in the spirit of the apocryphal genre. The "Legend" has three quasi-epigraphs, while Soloviev prefaced the "Tale" with the first stanza from his own poem "Panmongolism." Both works represent a text within a text. However, if with Soloviev the "text" of the "Tale" is presented palpably, its actual existence emphasized by a stage direction—"(*Mr. Z began reading the manuscript that had been brought to him)*"—Dostoevsky has just as clearly noted the absence of an actual "text": as I have shown, Ivan "didn't write" his poem but "made it up and memorized it." The action of the "Legend" occurs in the past; the action of the "Tale" relates to the future. In both cases the narrative breaks off and a scheme is given for its conclusion. In Soloviev's "Tale," "the manuscript does not continue," and Mr. Z summarizes the end of the tale "in its main features." Ivan also announces a brief summary: "I was going to end it like this: . . ." In *The Brothers Karamazov* the "Legend" occupies (almost entirely) the fifth chapter of the fifth book, and thereby does not stand out in form from the overall structure. The "Tale of the Antichrist" lies in a more complicated structural correlation with the main text of the *Three Conversations*. The dialogue form chosen by Soloviev was conditioned, in all likelihood, by the classical tradition, and particularly the dialogues of Plato, which commonly featured an inserted myth. Assembling five Russians by the Mediterranean, that is, by Plato's native Aegean Sea, Soloviev draws them into a dialogue constructed around the classical questions of philosophy, politics, and religion.

In his article "Soloviev and Dostoevsky," Ernst Radlov maintains: "If the 'Tale of the Antichrist' can be likened superficially to the 'Grand Inquisitor,' the views expounded in them are very different."[120] While the two works are indeed quite different, their treatment of the God-man/man-god antinomy, central to the thought of both writers, is actually compatible. For both Dostoevsky and Soloviev, the threat of the Antichrist was not only real but pressing. An acquaintance of Dostoevsky, V. Timofeeva, recalls him saying: "*They* do not even suspect that soon the end of everything will be here, the end of all their 'progress' and chatter!" . . ."They don't even dream that indeed the Antichrist is already born—and *is coming!* . . . And the end of the world is near—nearer than they think!"[121] Soloviev speaks of the same thing, even using some of the same words, when he foresees the imminent "dénouement of our historical process, consisting in the emergence, glorification, and ruin of the Antichrist": "Well, there will still be a great deal of chatter and bustle on the stage, but this drama has already long since been written full to the end, and neither the spectators nor the actors are permitted to change anything in it."[122]

The general eschatological idea of the *Three Conversations* is revealed with apocalyptic force in the "Tale of the Antichrist." "This tale (which I have already read in public)," writes Soloviev in his foreword, "prompted both in society and in print a great deal of confusion and misinterpretation, the main reason for which is very simple: a lack of familiarity among us with the testimony of the Word of God and the Church tradition concerning the Antichrist. The inner significance of the Antichrist as a religious impostor,

. . . his connection with the false prophet and thaumaturge, . . . the dark and especially sinful origin of the Antichrist himself, . . . the general course and the end of his activity, along with certain individual traits characteristic of him and of his false prophet . . .—all this can be found in the Word of God and in ancient tradition."[123]

The "Tale" not only illustrates Soloviev's links to Church tradition but also his consistent espousal of an apocalyptic historical conception. Not for nothing was he the son of Sergei Soloviev, an exponent of metaphysical views in Russian historiography, who believed that world history was nearing an end. The positive meaning of history is embodied for Vladimir Soloviev in the image of the God-man, Christ. Just as the cosmic process in material nature led to the emergence of the "natural man," so the historical process has made ready the appearance of the "spiritual man": "The whole of nature has aspired and gravitated toward man, the whole history of humanity has been directed toward the God-man."[124] Therefore, the appearance of the Antichrist in a work whose central idea is contained in the words "The end of the world is the final battle and ultimate victory over evil" is a logical necessity. "Where absolute Good appears as a Personality, there also must the extreme manifestation of evil be a personality: absolute evil is the complete and thorough falsification of good."[125]

Such a comparison of Christ and the Antichrist includes not only the antinomy of good and evil, but also what is for Soloviev the important philosophical postulate of the secondary nature of evil. The "remarkable man" Soloviev depicts, whom "many called a superman," *volens nolens* sees himself not as an independent personality but as an antipode to Christ: "Christ, preaching moral goodness and exhibiting it in his own life, was *the reformer* of mankind, but I am called to be *the benefactor* of this partly reformed, partly unreformed mankind. I shall give men everything they need. Christ, as a moralist, divided men by means of good and evil; I shall unite them by means of earthly blessings, which are every bit as necessary as good and evil."[126] Soloviev ironically plays up the question of "secondness" in the Antichrist's argument: "Christ came before me; I am second; but then, that which appears later in order of time is in essence the first. I have arrived last, at the end of history, precisely because I am the perfect, ultimate savior."[127]

Like the Grand Inquisitor, the Antichrist initially assumes the role of mankind's savior, but if in Dostoevsky the essence of such a "salvation" is revealed only at the end of the Inquisitor's monologue, after he has summed up his entire program, with Soloviev's "proud righteous man" the hope "to begin his salvation of mankind" disappears the moment "a furious and gripping spirit of hatred" replaces his "reasonable, cold respect for God and Christ": "'I, I, not He! He is not among the living, is not and never will be. He never rose, never rose, never rose! He rotted, rotted in the tomb, rotted like the least of—.'And with foaming mouth and convulsive jumps he sprang out of the house, out of the garden, and raced down the rocky path into the heart of the black night. . . . Suddenly something stirred within him. 'Should I summon Him, ask what I am to do?' And amid the darkness a meek and sorrowful figure appears before him. 'He pities me. No, never! He did not rise, he did not!' And he threw himself from the precipice."[128]

This entire scene is clearly associated with the Gospel parable that Dosto-evsky placed as an epigraph to *The Devils*: "Now a large herd of swine was feeding there on the hillside; and they begged him to let them enter these. So he gave them leave. Then the demons came out of the man and entered the swine, and the herd rushed down the steep bank into the lake and were drowned" (Luke 8:32–33). But in Soloviev's "Tale," superman is "saved" by his father, whose voice, "constrained and at the same time distinct, metallic and utterly soulless, as if from a phonograph," proclaims to him: "Do your work in *your* name and not in mine. . . . He whom you consider God demanded of his son obedience, and obedience without limit —even unto death on the cross, and he did not help him on the cross. I demand nothing from you, and I shall help you."[129] Thus occurs the "transformation" of the "great man" into the Antichrist. His proud but still moral desire to be the savior of mankind is changed into a Satanic thirst for the realization of "boundless self-love."

In one of the few detailed works offering a comparative analysis of "The Legend of the Grand Inquisitor" and "A Short Tale of the Antichrist," it is suggested that "Soloviev's protagonist is a figure of genius, but that he con-tains nothing of the tragic. The secret he keeps (his desire to set himself in place of Christ) does not evoke in him the sufferings that are inherent to the Inquisitor, a tragic figure."[130] The word *tragic* is used in a conventional sense, which implies that the tragedy is based on suffering. Indeed, in such param-eters, the agonizing doubts the Inquisitor has experienced in his quest to control mankind's fate raise him, as it were, onto a "tragic" pedestal. But even here his sufferings can be called tragic only with reservation, since the Inquisitor, carried away by the idea of humanism, dooms "universally happy mankind" to "only death," while at the same time counting on justice for himself: "Judge us if you can and dare."[131] However, if we accept V. Ivanov's elaborate interpretation of tragedy as based on antinomy and a notion of guilt rooted in the absolute, mystical reality, Soloviev's Antichrist could not be denied his tragic status so easily.

The chief measure of the entire complex of ideas and events realized both by the Grand Inquisitor and by the Antichrist is Christ. Whatever the philanthropic motives, whichever methods they choose to manipulate mankind, they both encroach upon the metaphysical significance of the God-man's incarnation into history. The one "corrects the deed" of Christ, while the other wants to replace Him outright. The tactical difference in their aims should not overshadow the unity in their positions: they are both not with Christ but "with *him*," as the Inquisitor puts it.

It is essential to note that the problematics of the two figures reveals the individual approaches of Dostoevsky and Soloviev to the theme of God-manhood. The Inquisitor is guided in the program he has proclaimed by human nature, as he understands it. The Antichrist is basing the realization of his plan on *super*human (that is, metaphysical) nature.[132] The choice of time and place in the "Legend" and in the "Tale" foreshadows the vantage point from which the two authors view the interconnection of elements contained in the idea of God-manhood. Dostoevsky's action unfolds in Spain, more specifically, in Seville, fifteen centuries after the events of the Gospel. What Soloviev relates occurs at the end of time, on a global scale. The "Legend" ends with Christ departing into the "dark squares of the city," leaving humanity with the prospect of the continuing historical process. The "Tale" concludes with the Second Coming, "the accession of Christ for a thousand years" and, consequently, the end of historical humanity. According to one apt observation, Soloviev moved from God to man, and Dostoevsky from man to God.[133] This orientation with respect to the divine-human process, evident in an examination of the writings of Dostoevsky and Soloviev as a whole, was reflected in their final works as well.

If up to now I have been speaking about aspects of the conception of God-manhood that are comparable for both thinkers, it is necessary at least to mention an element of Soloviev's doctrine of God-manhood that is only indirectly relevant to Dostoevsky. As I have mentioned, all the fundamental propositions of Soloviev's philosophy were reflected in this doctrine. "The idea of God-manhood is not simply the center of the crystallization of his thoughts, or the focal point at which they meet and commingle, but a living and creative path, one could say—a heuristic principle."[134] The whole system of "positive unitotality," the synthesis of "integral knowledge," rests upon the conception of God-manhood. God-manhood, according to Soloviev, is first and foremost the incarnation of the Absolute. In the natural world the absolute divine element—the unitotality—exists only potentially; in man it first attains self-consciousness, its ideal actuality. This realization of the divine element, its image and likeness, is ideal humanity (Sophia) or the soul of the world.

Mankind, united with God in the Blessed Virgin, in Christ, in the Church, is the realization of the essential Wisdom or the absolute substance of God, its created form, its incarnation. Indeed, we have here one and the same substantial form (designated by the Bible as the *seed of the Woman,* that is, of *Sophia*), which is revealed in three progressive and abiding manifestations, distinct in reality but in essence inseparable, and which takes the name of Mary in its female incarnation, that of Jesus in its male incarnation—even while preserving its own name for its full and universal appearance in the perfect Church of the future, the Bride and the Wife of the Word of God. This triple realization of the essential Wisdom in mankind is the religious truth that Orthodox Christians confess in their doctrine and manifest in their divine worship.[135]

Thus, according to Soloviev, perfect mankind is the supreme manifestation of Sophia—of the wisdom of God, with which it is hypostatically united. A. F. Losev, who considers precisely Sophia to be the central idea of "Soloviev's whole philosophizing," discloses the meaning of the image "as the indivisible identity of the ideal and the material, as the materially realized idea or as ideally transformed matter."[136]

The principle of Sophia, by virtue of its universality, has different interpretations depending on the philosophical context.[137] For Soloviev, the poet and mystic, Sophia symbolizes first and foremost the Eternal Feminine, which as a relatively passive element, devoted to God, receives its form from Him. Although in his doctrine Soloviev continues the ancient tradition of the Christian mystics, including the biblical conception of "Wisdom" (Hokhmah), Augustine's development of the idea of the "Wisdom of God," and the religious experience of Boehme, Swedenborg, and Baader, from the standpoint of canonical theology many tenets of his Sophiology remain questionable. Some Russian thinkers, in their development of Soloviev's doctrine of Sophia, interpret many of Dostoevsky's female characters and his use of such conventionally female images as Mother Earth symbolically as expressions of the idea of the Eternal Feminine.[138] But their arguments are directly bound up with the idea of "mystical realism" applied to Dostoevsky and the symbolist theory of realism as a whole (based on the principle formulated by Viacheslav Ivanov as *a realibus ad realiora*) and cannot be analyzed outside their specific context. Essentially, Dostoevsky shared little of Soloviev's Sophiology, even from an anthropological point of view. Among the various aspects of Sophia there is, it would seem, only one that in its pure form falls within the sphere of Dostoevsky's interests: the issue of the Russian national spirit. "Alongside the *individual,* human image of the Divinity," writes Soloviev in *Russia and the Universal Church,* "alongside the Virgin and the Son of God, the Russian people knew and loved, under the name of Saint Sophia, the *social* incarnation of the Divinity in the Universal Church. . . . By dedicating their ancient churches to Saint Sophia, the incarnate Wisdom of God, the Russian people gave this idea a new expression unknown to the Greeks (who identified Sophia with the Logos)."[139] Dostoevsky would have felt a profound attraction to such a combination of metaphysics and patriotism.

The philosophical and artistic work of both Soloviev and Dostoevsky is defined, first and foremost, by that which in general defines religious consciousness—faith in God and faith in man. And if one of them moved from God to man and the other from man to God, this movement from opposite directions along a single path has one unique point of contact—Christ. For Dostoevsky as for Soloviev, it is the God-man Who is the measure of all things.

4

Theocracy
Vision and Reality

Two laws suffice to rule the whole Christian Republic better than all the laws of statecraft (Love your Lord with all your heart, with all your soul, with all your mind . . . Love your neighbor as yourself).
—Blaise Pascal

THE PERFECT WORLD ACCORDING TO SOLOVIEV

In his unfinished yet seminal work *The Philosophical Principles of Integral Knowledge* (1877), the first full statement of the basic ideas of his philosophical system, Soloviev wrote:

> The aim of philosophy can only be the knowledge of truth, but the fact is that this very truth, genuine complete truth, is at the same time necessarily good and beauty and might, and for this reason true philosophy is inseparably linked with genuine creativity and with moral action, which give man victory over lesser nature and dominion over it. Taken by itself, philosophy can give man neither bliss nor superior might, but true philosophy, that is, integral knowledge, that which is free theosophy, *cannot* be separated from other spiritual spheres. . . . Thus, although

free theosophy can find the beginning of its development within the bounds of its own theoretical sphere, it can accomplish this development only in conjunction and simultaneously with the development of free theurgy and theocracy.[1]

If the idea of ideal mankind was crystallized for Soloviev in the concept of God-manhood, the social form of ideal mankind was theocracy. Within Soloviev's philosophical system, theocracy occupies a natural place as the expression of the principle of unitotality in human society. In developing his conception of theocracy, Soloviev proceeds from "man's theocratic position in the world."[2] Only man, who "by his dual constituency balances inner might and outward need in genuine freedom," is capable of "genuine union with God." A being who is free, rational, and aspiring to perfection, as is man, must pass through three successive stages on the way to true theocracy: "First, the being voluntarily submits to the action of God as the supreme *power,* then it consciously accepts this action of God as the true *authority,* and finally it participates independently in the action of God, or enters into a living *council* with God."[3] Society, for Soloviev, is "the supplemented or expanded individual, while the individual is the condensed or concentrated society."[4] Therefore, the path to perfection of individual man is inseparable from the process of the perfection of the whole of society. The perfect theocratic synthesis is the free and universal union of God and humanity. It is fulfilled through the functions of the three theocratic powers represented by Priest, King, and Prophet. Jesus Christ, the Priest of the Lord, the King of the world, and the Prophet of the future life revealed the triune way of God-manly union that was inherent in the first Adam. Christ restored to fullness the three forms of theocratic service that are not performed by natural man, who as priest has desecrated the sanctuary, as king has lost his power, and as prophet has betrayed his calling. By embodying the theocratic unity, Christ realized the fullness of time, since the priestly anointment is defined by the tradition of the past, the kingly anointment by service to the present, and the prophetic anointment by knowledge of the future. Christ is the One "who reconciles with God the reality of our past and our present state. He alone can fulfill the ideal of our future."[5] Naturally, in Soloviev's theocratic vision the individual appearance of the Kingdom of God in the one God-man stands as a promise of the universal appearance of the Kingdom of God in mankind collectively.

Many students of Soloviev's thought have agreed with E. Trubetskoi that the philosopher based his vision of social transformation upon a belief in the possibility of achieving the Kingdom of God within the historical limits of mankind's life.[6] In accordance with this view, the entire middle period of Soloviev's work, devoted largely to the elaboration of the theocratic idea, is often called utopian. Soloviev himself, however, vigorously objected to such an interpretation of his theocratic conception: "Any attentive reader can see that I have not given the slightest grounds for serious critics to ascribe to me the absurd identification of the Kingdom of God with historical Christianity, or the visible Church (which one exactly?). This identification, like recognizing any baptized scoundrel to be a 'spiritual' man, or a 'son of God,' is excluded from my thought not only *implicite* but also *explicite*."[7] Though this statement dates from the 1890s, it cannot be regarded as a deviation from the earlier theocratic project. For Soloviev, this project was always bound up primarily with the very process of a practical Christian transformation of society, the preparation of humanity for the Kingdom of God. In this sense, the goal of a theocratic society is no more utopian than that of the perfection of mankind in God-manhood. "The kingdom of the world must be subordinate to the Kingdom of God, the worldly forces of society and of man must be subordinate to the spiritual force: but what is meant here by subordination, and how—by what means and methods—is it to be accomplished?" With this thought Soloviev indicates quite clearly both the goal he has proclaimed and his awareness of the problems associated with its attainment.[8] At the same time, he indeed speaks repeatedly of the attainment of the Kingdom of God on earth as "the aim of Christian activity," with the reservation that "we must not take this aim as reality, for in reality the Kingdom of God on earth has not yet been fulfilled and God reigns over men more than in them."[9]

It appears that the confusion concerning means and end, present in interpretations of Soloviev's theocratic idea from the very beginning, was in no small part caused by the philosopher himself. As noted in the commentary to a recent edition of Soloviev' s works, "Soloviev's use of the concept of *theocracy* has a peculiar character and frequently disorients not only ordinary readers but also scholars. By theocracy Soloviev meant not the broad authoritative prerogatives of ecclesiastical institutions, which, according to his conception, denoted merely 'abstract clericalism,' but the essential, though not compulsory, guiding role of Christian values in the life of human society."[10] In *The Great Dispute and Christian Politics,* Soloviev emphasizes: "In order to understand and formulate the task of Christian politics correctly, it is necessary to consider positive Christianity or the visible, earthly Church in its two aspects: that of its abiding [*prebyvaiushchaia*] foundation and that of its practical action in the world."[11] The same approach is obviously necessary when considering theocracy, which, properly speaking, *is* the Church as a positive social ideal. For Soloviev, the aim (the abiding foundation) was theocracy in the sense of the Kingdom of God, while the means (the practical action) was theocracy in the sense of a form of society that is capable, due to its attained perfection, of entering into the Kingdom of God. Soloviev returns time and again to the aspect of theocracy that is marked by becoming rather than by eternal being: "the fulfillment of the Church is free *theocracy*";[12] "the essence of theocracy is the free interaction between the Divinity and mankind";[13] "theocracy creates a just social environment in which human freedom, achieved through sacrifice, is limited for the sake of love";[14] "the fulfillment of the Kingdom of God proceeds through a process of organic growth, by virtue of which the barely perceptible embryo of faith develops into the enormous and all-embracing formation of new life."[15] It is clear from the contexts of these passages that Soloviev is speaking not of the eschatological Kingdom of God whose approach was heralded by Christ, but about the Kingdom of God which, in the words of Christ, is within us. "To enter into the Kingdom of God that is outside us, though it has already drawn near to us, to possess it and make it our own, requires labor and effort"[16]— that is, "practical action." That does not, however, imply the existence of two kingdoms of God, but refers to individual concepts that complement one another in a single comprehensive idea.

To sum up, one can say that Soloviev employs the word *theocracy*, depending on the context, to mean both the substance and the form of the Christian transformation of mankind into the Kingdom of God. Failing to take this conceptual distinction into account leaves many of his statements open to ambiguity. At the same time, the logic with which Soloviev views the history of mankind seems to stipulate an uninterrupted passage from the physical world into the metaphysical. This feature of the philosopher's position as regards the philosophy of history naturally accords with the character of his epistemology. As Konstantin Mochul'skii observes: "All knowledge— even the knowledge of the natural sciences, the empirical study of the external world—is regarded by him as a revelation of divine essences, that is, as [a matter of] religious contemplation [*umozrenie*]. . . . This lack of distinction between types of knowledge and their mingling in the single category of theosophy can be explained by Soloviev's personal experience. For him the otherworldly was an everyday fact of consciousness."[17]

Soloviev has frequently been reproached for mingling the rational and the mystical, including in the most vulnerable area of his conception of the "unitotal"—theocracy. But in accusing Soloviev of "losing sight of the boundaries" separating this world from the Divine world, his opponents direct their criticism at his infringement of "spatial" principles, that is, at his attempt to establish a heavenly kingdom *on earth*. Yet if one correlates Soloviev's theocratic plan with the factor of time, it turns out that the philosopher regards the entire historical process as preparation for the Kingdom of God. In other words, he sees the realization of theocracy (the rule of God) only at the end of time, which fully agrees with the tradition of millenarianism based on the Book of Revelation, and, consequently, at the end of *earthly* humanity.[18] Soloviev himself foresaw possible objections to his theocratic idea and as early as the *Critique of Abstract Principles* (1877–80) wrote:

> Laying aside any metaphysical considerations and limiting oneself solely to the realm of phenomena, and specifically of historical phenomena, it is easy to see that any event in the life of human society, before becoming a fact of reality, was an ideal of the thinking intellect. . . . Idea and fact, utopia and reality are relative terms which constantly shift from one to the other, and if certain utopias can and must be ignored, it is not because they are utopias, that is, because they have no place in the given external reality or appear in it merely as ideas, but because they are bad ideas; and in this respect not only are they inapplicable within the existing reality, but they also have no legitimate place in the world of ideas.[19]

Of course, the position stated here does not exclude the presence of a utopian element in Soloviev's theocratic project; rather, it shifts the question from the transcendental substance of the idea itself onto the practical steps Soloviev posits for its realization. A literal interpretation of Soloviev's hope for the realization of the Kingdom of God on earth is comparable to a reductionist (and thereby distorted) understanding of Saint Augustine's conception of the City of God. Augustine's contrast of the "earthly city," in which there neither is nor can be anything eternal, with the "City of God" was eventually given a political interpretation justifying the universal dominion of the Church as a counterbalance to the "sinful" power of the worldly state.

Soloviev's last treatment of the theocratic conception was presented in artistic form as the "Short Tale of the Antichrist" in the *Three Conversations about War, Progress, and the End of World History*. There is little doubt that Soloviev's theocratic attitudes had changed in the final period of his life, but there are two bodies of opinion on the nature of the change. Opponents of Soloviev's conception (and, it must be suggested, of the idea of theocracy as such) see in the philosopher's final works, and in particular in the *Three Conversations*, the "collapse of theocracy." This position has been most thoroughly expounded by E. Trubetskoi, whose influence on subsequent critics of Soloviev regarding this issue has been tremendous not only by virtue of his reputation for philosophical scholarship but also because of the credibility Trubetskoi's monumental study of Soloviev gains due to their long friendship. Proceeding from his own disagreement in principle with the possibility of bringing about the Kingdom of God on earth, Trubetskoi seeks to prove that by the end of his life Soloviev essentially supported his (Trubetskoi's) position and in the "Short Tale of the Antichrist" represented universal theocracy in the form of a satanic parody.[20] Yet even Trubetskoi must admit that "even here we shall not find a direct renunciation of theocracy."[21] His evidence for the "collapse of theocracy" is constructed either *a contrario* (Soloviev did not make an explicit defense of theocracy, therefore he had not stayed with his former point of view) or on the basis of a contrast between Soloviev's former expectations concerning Russia's role in world political reforms and the unification of churches, on the one hand, and the apocalyptic picture portrayed in the *Three Conversations,* on the other.[22] As a result, Trubetskoi arrives at the categorical conclusion that "in the 1880s . . . theocracy expressed for him [Soloviev] the very essence of his own views and the Kingdom of God itself was understood by him as 'true theocracy.' On the contrary, by 1899 his idea of the Kingdom of God had freed itself of this temporary historical admixture, theocracy had fallen away like a broken shell, and Soloviev had come to regard it as an 'external scheme,' an inessential appendage to his views which could be separated from them without doing them any damage." This is followed by a statement more surprising than convincing: "Generally speaking, Soloviev underestimated the significance of the change that had taken place in him, and for this reason his own assessment cannot be of binding significance for us."[23]

The more positive assessment of Soloviev's theocratic crisis was characterized by Trubetskoi himself in his argument against it: "Soloviev grew disappointed with the realizability of the theocratic ideal, but never with the ideal itself."[24] This point of view, with certain qualifications, seems more sensible. In Soloviev's theocratic conception it is necessary to distinguish the theological and philosophical level of the problem from the realm of the practical reforms on which he pinned his hopes, that is, to distinguish the "abiding" foundation from the "practical action." The philosopher himself was fully aware of the separateness of the two sides of theocratic doctrine. Even in his first approaches to this doctrine in the *Critique of Abstract Principles,* when defining free theocracy as an all-embracing and all-uniting social order founded on love and truth, he asks, "Is this desirable ideal at the same time possible in reality?"[25] Moreover, he leaves this question "entirely open." But recognition of the distance separating the "desirable" from the "realizable" did not put a stop to Soloviev's search for ways to synthesize them. His constant efforts to organize a theocratic society were in essence an attempt to achieve utopian results by practical means. However, his honorable aspiration cannot be disregarded as simply "utopian." As Losev puts it, "this sort of romanticism and utopia must be pondered deeply and should not be approached only politically."[26]

Of course, Soloviev himself saw the theocratic aim not as utopian but as ideal, and consequently as real, since for him reality was not contrary to the ideal but rather oriented toward it. It appears that the very concept of the "utopian" did not have for him the generally accepted fantastic, fairy-tale connotations. Although according to Nikolai Berdiaev, the most frightening thing about a utopia is that it might become reality, in a Solovievian world this is precisely what is beautiful about it. Everything depends on whether the realization occurs "in Thy name" or "in its own name." The philosopher's disappointment in later years stemmed not from any awareness of a collapse of the ideal but from a sense of the inadequacy of the methods for realizing it. "About my French books [his theocratic works]," he wrote in a letter dating from the early 1890s, "I can tell you nothing. Their fate is of little interest to me. Though they contain nothing contrary to objective truth, still I have already outlived that subjective mood, the feelings and hopes with which I wrote."[27] This "subjective mood" he characterized in passing in 1897 as "a keen passion for the theocratic idea in its ecclesiastical form."[28] The clarification "in its ecclesiastical form" is noteworthy and speaks for itself.

Soloviev speaks in still greater detail about the changes he went through in his foreword to an 1899 edition of *Plato's Works*: "As I accumulated life experience without any change in the essence of my convictions, I came more and more to doubt the usefulness and feasibility of those external designs to which my so-called best years were devoted. To be disappointed with this meant to return to philosophical pursuits, which for a time had been pushed far aside."[29] If, ignoring Trubetskoi's advice, we accept Soloviev's self-appraisal, we must acknowledge that the philosopher became disappointed with "external designs," that is, with a historiosophic utopia, but not with the philosophical ideal of a theocratic conception, an ideal which, in the words of the philosopher's nephew Sergei Soloviev, "captivates by the pure gold of radiant and immutable truth."[30] As is aptly noted in a countercriticism to E. Trubetskoi, to part with his dream of theocracy for Soloviev was as impossible "as it was to part with Christianity itself."[31]

One of the arguments usually advanced to support the supposition that Soloviev rejected the very idea of theocracy is the opinion that the kingdom of the Antichrist depicted in the *Three Conversations* is a parody of free theocracy, implying that the author, by dint of the act itself, testifies to his own negative attitude toward the object of parody. "Soloviev not only despaired of theocracy," claims Trubetskoi, "he *felt it to be a lie*."[32] But if one agrees that according to the author's intention the kingdom of the Antichrist is a parody of universal theocracy, it would then be logical to assume that the Antichrist himself represents a parody of Christ. Yet the description of the Impostor-Antichrist in an *artistic* work does not prompt anyone to doubt Soloviev's spiritual loyalty to Christ as a believing Christian or his intellectual loyalty to Him as a philosopher.

Of course, labeling a work as parody would almost necessarily require interpretation of the term, since there is no universally accepted definition.[33] It would appear that Soloviev's critics were proceeding from a notion of parody given once by Mikhail Bakhtin, that parody "is the creation of a *decrowning double [razvenchivaushchii dvoinik]*."[34] Using Bakhtin's image, one can say that Soloviev's Antichrist is not a "decrowning double" of Christ; rather, he represents His falsification, "a kind of photographic negative of Christ."[35] Therefore, the depiction of the kingdom of the Antichrist likewise could not have been for Soloviev a parodying of free theocracy but rather appeared as a "photographic negative" of the Kingdom of God, an *anti*-theocracy, the collapse of which signals the beginning of Christ's reign for a thousand years.[36] It is interesting that Trubetskoi is puzzled by "the final words in the *Three Conversations*" about the thousand years of the Kingdom of Christ. "The Kingdom of Christ," he writes, "in which the dead are brought back to life, is a realm lying *outside the bounds* of world history; consequently, the words about the *thousand years* of its duration sound like a contradiction."[37] But Trubetskoi fails to notice the weakness of his own argument: the precedent for the resurrection of the dead had already taken place during the First Coming of Christ, which occurred *within the bounds* of world history. As one scholar has rightly noted, "in the 'Short Tale of the Antichrist' Soloviev boldly appeals to the Apocalypse of John the Divine and speaks not about the end of history as such, but about the beginning of the history of the chiliastic kingdom, which, according to Apocalypse, is the rule of Christ and the priesthood (Rev. 20:6)."[38]

This does not mean, of course, that the millennial Kingdom of Christ should be viewed as a period of the same nature as the entire foregoing history of mankind. Nikolai Berdiaev is right in claiming that the chiliasm of the "Short Tale of the Antichrist" is transcendent and not immanent to history.[39] In the preface to the *Three Conversations*, Soloviev expounded and defined in great detail the subjects of the "conversations" and the tasks he had set for himself "in writing this little book." To show "the world-embracing rule of the Antichrist, who 'will speak loud and lofty words,' and will cast the radiant veil of goodness and truth upon the mystery of extreme lawlessness at the moment of its final appearance, . . . to show beforehand that deceptive mask beneath which hides the evil abyss"—this was Soloviev's "supreme design."[40] The "Tale" contains not a parody of universal theocracy but an artistic illustration of the Apocalypse, in which the historical and eschatological perspectives converge at a single point. The thousand-year reign of Christ commences "on the historical threshold of metahistory."[41] Rather than renouncing theocracy, Soloviev returns to its canonical pre-figuration: "And I saw thrones, and they sat upon them, and judgment was given unto them: and I saw the souls of them that were beheaded for the witness of Jesus, and for the word of God, and which had not worshipped the beast, neither his image, neither had received his mark upon their foreheads, or in their hands; and they lived and reigned with Christ a thousand years" (Rev. 20:4). Thus Soloviev's true mission in creating the *Three Conversations* was not the bitter acknowledgment of "the collapse of his own theocratic hopes"[42] but *"the disclosure of an actual deception."*[43] His sight was set not on the "deceptive errors" of his own past but on the approaching *actual deception* which is to be realized in the form of a full and symmetrical falsification of free theocracy.

A NICE LITTLE FAMILY AND A THEOCRATIC BROTHERHOOD

In Dostoevsky's work the theocratic idea was reflected in its purest form in his final novel. As I have already shown, *The Brothers Karamazov* has many lines of connection with the personality of Vladimir Soloviev, and this connection shows through very clearly in the novel's treatment of theocracy. At the very beginning of the narrative, as he is introducing his characters to the reader, Dostoevsky tells us that, after graduating from the university, "Ivan Fedorovich suddenly published in one of the big newspapers a strange article that attracted the attention even of non-experts, and above all on a subject apparently altogether foreign to him, since he had graduated in natural science. This article dealt with the issue of ecclesiastical courts, which was then being raised everywhere."[44] Though Ivan Karamazov's article itself does not play as significant a role in the plot of the novel as did an essay written by another student, Raskolnikov in *Crime and Punishment*, the range of problems that grow out of the article's relatively local subject touches upon the problematics of the entire work. The question of judicial structure is viewed by Dostoevsky from the ontological perspective of grace, not law. Such an understanding of the issue reflects the depth of the writer's affinity to the cultural worldview of ancient Rus'. In light of this connection, it has been remarked that for Dostoevsky "a citizen is not a subject for the law but a moral personality rooted in the religious and cultural-historical soil of the nation."[45] From this it naturally follows that a society founded not on judicial law but on the law of love can only arise as the result of a special kind of transformation.

In the chapter "So Be It! So Be It!" it turns out that Ivan's reflections concern precisely such a transformation, which he sees as the transformation of the state into the Church: "The Church should contain in itself the whole state and not merely occupy a certain corner of it, and . . . if for some reason that is impossible now, then in the essence of things it undoubtedly should be posited as the direct and chief aim of the whole further development of Christian society."[46] Ivan's article is a response to the book of a certain "churchman," who, asserting the rightfulness of the separation of Church and state, bases himself on the position that "the Church is a kingdom not of this world." In essence, this is the same argument employed by Trubetskoi and other opponents of Soloviev, who perceive in his theocratic idea not only a utopia but, strictly speaking, a heresy. The answering argument, which Dostoevsky places in the mouth of Father Paisii, as well as Ivan's subsequent words, are very close to Soloviev's line of thought. "If it is not of this world, it follows that it cannot exist on earth at all," says Father Paisii. "In the Holy Gospel, the words 'not of this world' are used in a different sense. To play with such words is impossible. Our Lord Jesus Christ came precisely to establish the Church on earth. The Kingdom of Heaven, of course, is not of this world but in heaven, but it is entered in no other way than through the Church that is founded and established on earth. . . . The Church is indeed a kingdom and appointed to reign, and in the end must undoubtedly be revealed as a kingdom over all the earth — for which we have a covenant."[47] After these words Ivan joins in: "The whole point of my article is that in ancient times, during its first three centuries, Christianity was revealed on earth only by the Church, and was only the Church. But when the pagan Roman state desired to become Christian, it inevitably so happened that, having become Christian, it merely included the Church in itself, but itself continued to be, as before, a pagan state in a great many of its functions."[48]

We find a remarkably similar statement in the first chapter of Soloviev's *Philosophical Principles of Integral Knowledge*: "Christianity, as it manifests itself in the consciousness of its first preachers, did not aspire to any sort of social revolution whatsoever; its entire mission consisted in the religious and moral rebirth of individual people in view of the approaching end of the world. . . . The Roman-Byzantine state preserved a completely pagan character; it experienced absolutely no essential change. . . . The Church joined with it, but did so only mechanically."[49] Soloviev analyzes the historical aspect of the theocratic idea in an analogous way in the *Critique of Abstract*

Principles, which, incidentally, was published at the same time and in the same journal, *Russkii vestnik,* as *The Brothers Karamazov:*

> If it is said, Render unto God the things that are God's, and unto Caesar the things which are Caesar's, we must not forget that Caesar (that is, the power of the state) was indeed *outside* the Kingdom of God, Caesar was a representative not of the worldly element only, but of the pagan element, and consequently the unconditional separation of the realms of Church and state is in this case completely natural and necessary, for what concord hath Christ with Belial?[50] But when Caesar enters into the Kingdom of God and acknowledges himself to be its servant, then the situation obviously changes — within the single Kingdom of God there obviously cannot be two separate and equally unconditional powers. It is precisely for this reason that the Kingdom of God is not of this world, but above it, and it must subordinate to itself this world as something lower, for it was Christ who said: "I have overcome the world."[51]

Soloviev goes on to note: "Someone who does not recognize the divine element at all has no reason to give any place whatsoever to a mystical union in human society; for him the Church is in general but a remnant of old superstitions, which must disappear with the progress of mankind."[52] The same point is made by Father Paisii: "According to certain theories, which have become only too clear in our nineteenth century, the Church ought to be transforming itself into the state, from a lower to a higher species, so as to disappear into it eventually, making way for science, the spirit of the age, and civilization."[53]

The comparisons could be continued, but the kinship between the two thinkers on the theocratic question requires no special proof. "The connection between the theocratic ideas of Soloviev and Dostoevsky is unquestionable, and precedence in time belongs to Soloviev," writes S. Levitskii. "Of course, this idea is close in spirit to the Orthodox messianism of Dostoevsky, so that Soloviev, as it were, expressed that which followed from the views of Dostoevsky himself and which the latter experienced and expressed deeply in his own way. What is more, closeness of spiritual experience prevails here over the category of 'influence.' Therefore the term 'influence' is here best replaced by the word 'reflection.'"[54] Robert Belknap, in his comments on the relations between Dostoevsky and Soloviev, comes to a similar conclusion, emphasizing at the same time Soloviev's critical role in the creation of *The Brothers Karamazov:* "The closeness of these two major figures has made it particularly difficult for scholars — and quite possibly for the authors themselves — to specify which direction the influences were flowing, but there can be no question that the religious discussions and the picture of the monastery itself in *The Brothers Karamazov* would have been very different if

Dostoevsky had not been reading Soloviev and seeing the religious world at least in part through his eyes."[55] Although the "precedence problem" is of secondary importance in an attempt to get to the heart of Soloviev's and Dostoevsky's philosophical ideas, it cannot be completely ignored, since it inevitably arises in almost all comparative analyses of the two writers, particularly when the discussion turns to theocracy. As an illustration, we can cite the opinion of D. Strémooukhoff, who in turn is arguing against S. I. Gessen's study "The Conflict of Utopia and the Autonomy of the Good in the Worldview of F. M. Dostoevsky and Vl. Soloviev":

> One can assert that if in the *Lectures on God-manhood* there exists a certain duality in the Catholic Church, which Soloviev sometimes defends against the attacks of the Orthodox and about which he sometimes, on the contrary, writes that it is seduced by the third temptation, then these latter ideas are due to the influence of Dostoevsky. But do the positive ideas of Soloviev manifest a Dosto-evskian influence? S. I. Gessen thinks that the ideal of free theocracy as it was to be set forth in the *Lectures,* and particularly in the *Critique of Abstract Principles,* is developed under the central influence of the novelist. We believe this to be exaggerated, since the idea of theocracy seems to appear in Soloviev's writings for the first time after his trip abroad, which seems to preclude the possibility of a Dostoevskian influence. The idea of theocracy is already developed in the preface to the *Principles [The Philosophical Principles of Integral Knowledge],* and the *Critique [of Abstract Principles]* only further develops an already existing idea. It is therefore not in the theoretical realm that one must seek Dostoevsky's influence on Soloviev; it seems, however, to be more obvious in a realm which can be viewed as the emotional.[56]

According to Soloviev, the central idea of *The Brothers Karamazov* was to be "the Church as the positive social ideal."[57] Although one might object that the artistic and philosophical ideatic complex of the novel is broader than this definition, Soloviev's assertion unquestionably has basis in fact, not only because Dostoevsky himself imparted his "main idea" to Soloviev during their trip to Optina Pustyn, but also because the very notion of "the Church" encompasses an all-embracing philosophical spectrum and is bound up with fundamental questions posed in the novel. The Church is the form of the Kingdom of God. In Soloviev's words: "The religious life of Christian humanity, like all of life, requires a definite form and it finds this form in the *Church*."[58] To substantiate his doctrine of the Church, he appeals to three interconnected images from Holy Scripture: the Rock, the Body, and the Bride. "First, the Church must *exist* on a real foundation; second, it must *live* and develop; third, it must become *perfect*. From the standpoint of its real existence the Church is conceived as an *edifice* created by Christ, and, accordingly, as the City of God, the New Jerusalem. From the standpoint of its life the Church is conceived as the living *body* of Christ. Finally, from the standpoint of its perfection the Church is presented as the chaste *Bride of Christ*."[59] Thus, by accepting Soloviev's argument, we can arrive at the following formulation: the Church is the form (the edifice) of perfect (the Bride) life (the body). From this it naturally follows that the form of imperfect life, the state, must, like other imperfect forms, strive to be transformed into the perfect.

The enormous gulf that exists between reality and the ideal should not cloud our perception of the potential for the perfect form of life, even within the monstrous and wretched reality of Skotoprigonevsk—the fictional district town in which *The Brothers Karamazov* is set.[60] It is in the light of this potential that Dostoevsky says, "So be it, so be it!" And just as the society of the district town, and with it the whole of Russia and, more widely still, mankind, are the material (indeed, the only possible material) from which the Church or theocratic society is to be formed, so the Karamazov brothers are the potential bearers of theocratic unity.

According to Soloviev's doctrine of theocracy, Christ's absolute power is divided in human society among priests, warriors, and prophets. The priests possess, first and foremost, "the keys of the past"; they are the witnesses of tradition, the custodians of God's law. The warriors (or kings) possess "the keys of the present"; they actively implement Christian principles in the real life of nations. Finally, the prophets, "the possessors of the keys of the future," are the adherents of the perfect life, of the absolute ideal.[61] Surprisingly, the Karamazov brothers fit this scheme, each reflecting a corresponding hypostasis in the theocratic ideal.

Alesha (who is named for St. Aleksii, "the man of God"), a novice in a monastery and "an early lover of mankind," who possesses "in his very nature . . . the gift of awakening a special love for himself," sees in the priestly path the "ideal way out for his soul struggling from darkness to light."[62] More than other men, he is imbued with hope in the Kingdom of God, with faith in "the power that will finally establish the truth on earth, and all will be holy and will love one another, and there will be neither rich nor poor, neither exalted nor humiliated, but all will be like the children of God, and the true kingdom of Christ will come."[63] The elder Zosima, parting with Alesha before his death, says to him: "Thus I think of you: you will go forth from these walls, but you will sojourn in the world like a monk. You will have many opponents, but your very enemies will love you. Life will bring you many misfortunes, but through them you will be happy, and you will bless life and cause others to bless it—which is the important thing."[64] Toward the end of the fourth part of the novel, Alesha, the elder's spiritual heir, says "suddenly for some reason" the same thing to Kolia Krasotkin: "By the way, you are going to be a very unhappy man in your life. . . . But on the whole you will bless life all the same."[65] He thus passes the elder's intimate word on to the youngster, becoming, as it were, the successor to the priestly tradition that extends back into the *past*. The inner link between Alesha and Christ (the first high priest of Christianity) is emphasized by Dostoevsky in the epilogue, with its allusion to the twelve apostles: the boys "had been waiting impatiently for him and were glad that he had come at last. There were about twelve boys altogether."[66]

Dmitrii is "a recently retired military man." For all the vivid individuality of his character, his portrait bears the typical and even hackneyed traits of the army officer: "He wore a moustache and still shaved his beard. His dark brown hair was cut short and combed somehow forward on his temples. He had a long, resolute military stride."[67] "He had had a disorderly adolescence and youth: he never finished high school; later he landed in some military school, then turned up in the Caucasus, was promoted, fought a duel, was broken to the ranks, promoted again, led a wild life, and spent, comparatively, a great deal of money."[68] Dmitrii Karamazov's symbolic affiliation with the class of warrior-kings is also revealed in his position within the family hierarchy: he is the eldest son and, formally, the heir. His impetuous temperament, reflected in the dynamics of decision and action, demands the urgency of the *present*. "Let me finish here and now with loving," Dmitrii implores God as he flies along in the troika toward his "queen of queens" (a designation that he repeatedly bestows on Grushenka, and which indirectly links him as well to the "kingly title"). Moreover, he bears the name of one of the most renowned warriors in Russian history—Grand Duke Dmitrii Donskoi, hero of the battle of Kulikovo, of whom "the chronicles say there had never before been one such as he in Rus'."[69] The Kulikovo victory is viewed by some Russian historians as the event that completed the task of saving Christian Europe from the Asiatic invasion, as the "sign of the triumph of Europe over Asia,"[70] a fact that bears directly on the novel's historical and philosophical problematics.

Finally, there is Ivan, who conforms in type to "the category of people of all ages, sexes, and conditions who have anticipated man's future."[71] His prophecy about the future of mankind in his poem on the "Grand Inquisitor" is in essence a counterapocalypse. Through the Grand Inquisitor, Ivan "corrects" not only the deed of Christ but also the Revelation of the "great prophet" John the Divine, whose name he shares. Ivan's composition is literally permeated with quotations from the Apocalypse—one of Dostoevsky's favorite books. At the same time, it is precisely through him that Dostoevsky advances theocratic ideas aimed at a social transformation in the name of the *future*. Also serving as a prophecy is Ivan's early "little poem" entitled "Geological Cataclysm," with its prediction of a future humanity diametrically opposed to the theocratic ideal: "People will come together in order to take from life all that it can give, but, of course, for happiness and joy in this world only. Man will be exalted with the spirit of divine, titanic pride, and the man-god will appear."[72]

Ivan Karamazov has no aversion even to everyday predictions of the future. Thus he describes in detail for Rakitin—a somewhat cynical and corrupt character in the novel—what awaits the latter: the criticism section in "some thick journal," money in the bank, "a big town house in Petersburg," to which he can transfer his editorial office, "while renting out the rest of the floor to tenants." Ivan has even chosen the spot for this house: "by the New Stone Bridge over the Neva, which they say is being planned in Petersburg to connect the Liteiny Prospect with the Vyborg side." Alesha, hearing of the prediction for Rakitin, exclaims: "Ah, Misha, maybe it will all be just as he says, to the last word!"[73] Ivan even foresees the crime that will take place in the home of Fedor Pavlovich Karamazov, though this "prophecy" is, of course, complicated by many attendant moments. It is also interesting to note that, through Ivan, Dostoevsky imperceptibly introduces an element of foresight or, if one likes, prophecy concerning the dénouement of the entire work: the action of *The Brothers Karamazov* virtually begins with a discussion of Ivan's article about the need for the ecclesiastical courts to replace the existing criminal and civil court system, while the illustration of the inadequacy of the jury that brings in an unjust verdict against Dmitrii Karamazov concludes the "fourth and last part" of the novel.[74]

As Vladimir Soloviev repeatedly emphasizes, the basic connecting principle in theocracy is love. The principle of love is the unifying force that Alesha brings into the relations of the Karamazov brothers. "My brothers are destroying themselves. . . . And they're destroying others with them. This is the 'earthy force of the Karamazovs.' . . . Whether the Spirit of God is moving over that force—even that I do not know," he says.[75] For the "force of the Karamazovs" to cease being merely "earthy," absolute love is needed. It is precisely this prospect that Dostoevsky presents to his characters and to the whole of human society. Not for nothing does he place in the prosecutor's mouth the remark: "Certain basic, general elements of our modern-day educated society shine through, as it were, in the picture of this nice little family." Behind the prosecutor's observations stands a still broader generalization: the Karamazov brothers symbolize that very society in which, for all its imperfection, has been placed the potential for realizing the "positive social ideal." "The process is not finished in you," writes Dostoevsky in his "Summarium of Zosima's Words Addressed to Ivan."[76] Nor is the process finished in Dmitrii, or in Alesha, or in "modern-day educated society," or in mankind. It is for this reason that the Karamazov brothers can be viewed as potential bearers of theocratic unity. "Without brothers there is no brotherhood."[77]

Dostoevsky frequently addressed hypothetical versions of societal organization. For example, "The Dream of a Ridiculous Man" is traditionally viewed as "the culmination in the development of one of the central, constant motifs of Dostoevsky's work—the golden age."[78] At the same time, the social model depicted in this story possesses undeniable features of a theocratic organization of mankind.[79] Formally speaking, the people on the beautiful planet where the "ridiculous man" finds himself exist, as it were, outside Christianity, but in essence their life passes only beyond *historical* Christianity. According to one apt observation, "there is no Christ on the planet but God is love, and, following the dogma about the equipotency of the persons in the Trinity, the word 'love' can be replaced by the word 'Christ.'"[80] With spiritual perspicacity, Dostoevsky leaves his sinless mankind without Christ the *Redeemer* (for with the absence of sin there is no need for the redemption), while stressing the constant presence of Christ as *Love*: "This was an earth that had not been defiled by sin. . . . Their whole lives were devoted only to admiring one another. It was a kind of complete, all-encompassing devotion to one another."[81] On the undefiled planet, mankind lives in accordance with the basic principle of Christian theocracy, in which "the complete union of all in unconditional love prevails."[82] For all that, the organization of an ideal society as such is not an end in itself; it serves only as the means for attaining the absolute ideal: "They had no temples, but they did have a kind of essential, living, and continuous union with the Totality of the universe; they had no religion; instead they had a certain knowledge that when their earthly joy had fulfilled itself to its limits there would ensue—both for the living and for the dead—an even broader contact with the Totality of the universe."[83]

What Dostoevsky calls "the Totality of the universe" essentially corresponds to what Soloviev calls the "unitotality," while the "primordially unitotal" implies God.[84] Incidentally, as authoritative a theologian as Georges Florovsky asserts that "The Dream of a Ridiculous Man"—with two exceptions (the existence of death in the vision of paradise and "the astonishing statement that 'the *only source* of almost every sin of our human race' is sensuality")—"is profoundly Christian."[85] Without a doubt, this work (along with Dostoevsky's other utopian visions, for example, the dreams of Stavrogin and Versilov)[86] continues the tradition of the golden age in European literature, but at the same time the particular atmosphere of love, described by the author as the principle of "the communion with the Whole of the universe," provides grounds to call Dostoevsky's "fantastic story" a theocratic utopia. This is not entirely evident if theocracy is understood only as a religious-political organization of society, yet the proposed interpretation proceeds from the broader perspective formulated by Soloviev: "The whole of this religious politics about which we have had and will have to speak, represents in the affairs of God but a path and means of a partly pedagogical, partly therapeutic nature. In considering all this, we have never forgotten and would not wish to let our readers forget that the supreme good and the true aim of theocracy lies in the perfect reciprocity of a free divine-human union—not in absolute power but in absolute love."[87]

Dostoevsky also provides depictions of human social life which are antipodal to the "golden age," and in which a totalitarian oligarchy imitates precisely the religious-political aspect of the theocratic structure. Although the distance between Shigalev—the paranoid propagandist of ultraradical political theories in *The Devils*—and the Grand Inquisitor is considerable, their programs are nevertheless constructed according to the same corrupted version of the theocratic form of social organization. Shigalev proposes "as a final solution of the question the division of mankind into two unequal parts. One-tenth enjoys absolute liberty and unbounded power over the other nine-tenths. The others have to give up all individuality and become, so to speak, a herd, and, through boundless submission, will by a series of regenerations attain primeval innocence, something like the Garden of Eden. They'll have to work, however."[88] The primitive plan of "Mister [*Gospodin*] Shigalev" (as the "lame man" calls him, stressing a latent sense in the everyday form of address, the desire to rule [*gospodstvovat'*]) is, in principle, based on the same idea as the refined model of the Grand Inquisitor. "What I propose is not villainy; it's paradise, an earthly paradise, and there can be no other on earth," says Shigalev, who, like the protagonist of Ivan's poem, is "somewhat fanatical in his love for humanity."[89]

Dostoevsky, while depicting various versions of social unity, placed his faith in the triumph of the theocratic ideal. He viewed as the aim and culmination of Russian "socialism" a general and universal Church realized on earth, "insofar as the earth is capable of containing it." "It is not in communism, not in mechanical forms that we find the socialism of the Russian People: they believe that salvation is ultimately to be found only in *worldwide union in the name of Christ.*"[90] Thus did Dostoevsky express his hope in the final issue of the *Diary*.

THE EARTHLY TEMPTATIONS: RELIGION AND POLITICS

If the theological and metahistorical foundation of the theocratic idea has the value of "immutable truth," its religious and political grounds contain both the contradictions and the virtues of dynamic phenomena. The concrete application of the theocratic idea to historical practice is quite naturally linked, in both Soloviev and Dostoevsky, to their evaluation of Russia's role in the prospect and the retrospect of the ongoing world process. On this issue both the intersections and the divergences in the views of the two thinkers are great. In mentioning this, it is necessary, of course, to take account of the chronological factor: both Dostoevsky and, even to a greater degree, Soloviev passed through various periods in their respective understandings of Russia's religious and historical tasks, and of the ecclesiastical and social means of achieving them. These tasks, to a large degree, took shape within the framework of the Slavophile tradition. However, Soloviev's attitude toward Slavophilism changed along with the changes in Slavophilism itself. Soloviev felt a kinship with many aspects of the first, "classical" stage of Slavophilism. During its second stage, the Slavophiles, in Soloviev's opinion, began "idolatrizing the Russian people, instead of their earlier doctrine about the Russian people being the receptacle of God's Truth." By its third stage Slavophilism was already worshipping the historical and social anomalies of the Russian people. Speaking about "worship of the people" in the final article in his cycle *The National Question in Russia*, "Idols and Ideals," Soloviev writes: "Making true religion an attribute of nationality can, of course, only be done by people who in essence lack religious interest. . . . Now people no longer say to us, 'Believe as the peasants do,' but simply, 'Live as the peasants do.' This new demand has, of course, the advantage of being easy to carry out."[91] Not without reason does Anatolii Koni, who cites Soloviev's division of Slavophilism into three stages, note that the second and third stages prompted the philosopher to write "extremely severe, indignant lines"[92]—as illustrated by an excerpt from a letter Soloviev wrote in 1883: "And now patriots are suddenly popping up and demanding that, for example, the Church question be resolved not *ad majorem Dei* but *ad majorem Russiae gloriam,* not on a religious and theological basis but on the basis of national conceit. In this case you may remember that 'patriot' rhymes with 'idiot.'"[93]

The belief that the Christian ideal must be realized in all areas of social life, which constitutes the basis of Soloviev's theocratic idea, was organically close to the beliefs of the old Slavophiles: Aleksei Khomiakov, Ivan Kireevskii, Konstantin Aksakov, and Iurii Samarin. The ideal of "life in the Church" also inspired the "younger" Ivan Aksakov, and it was precisely after Soloviev first published an exposition of his theocratic doctrine in the *Critique of Abstract Principles* that he began contributing to Aksakov's journal *Rus'*. In 1877, on the eve of the Russo-Turkish War, Soloviev gave his speech "Three Forces," which was published in *Pravoslavnoe obozrenie*. In this work the young philosopher, besides contrasting Russia to the West and the Muslim East, called for an awakening of "the positive consciousness of the Russian people," pinning his hopes on their capacity "to give life and wholeness to a broken and benumbed humanity by uniting it with the eternal divine element."[94] Distinctly visible in such a statement of the theme is not only the characteristic and paramount feature of a Russian self-awareness born under the sign of the East-West problem, not only a view of this problem as religious first and foremost, a view inseparable from Slavophilism, but also a version of Soloviev's main idea—the attainment of unitotality in Christian God-manhood.

In distinguishing the three forces in the history of human development, Soloviev correlates them with the three world cultures. The first force, in its extreme expression, is "one master and a dead mass of slaves"; the second is "universal egoism and anarchy, a plurality of separate individuals with no inner connection"; the third force "reconciles the unity of the higher element with the free plurality of individual forms and elements, thus creating the wholeness of an organism common to all mankind."[95] Although complete realization of the first two forces is impossible owing to their exclusivity, Soloviev sees each to be predominant in the Muslim East and in Western civilization, respectively. To the despotism of the Muslim "inhuman god" and the self-assertion of the Western "godless man," the philosopher counterposes the higher conciliatory element, the force of the revelation of the Divine world. "The nation through which this force is to manifest itself must be only an *intermediary* between mankind and that world, a free, conscious instrument of the latter."[96] By virtue of "national character" and "historical conditions," it is, in the author's opinion, for the Russian people to be such an intermediary.

It is interesting to underscore two specific features reflected in Soloviev's construction. First, the idea expressed here of the nation's mediation between mankind and the divine world is constructed according to the same principle as the idea that underlies the conception of God-manhood: man is the intermediary between God and material existence, that is, the bearer of unitotality. Second, while seeing Russia's great mission as "a religious mission in the highest sense of the word," Soloviev argues his view with reference to national character and historical conditions, without appealing, as one might expect in such an essay, to Orthodoxy directly. In essence, behind these examples, which could easily be multiplied, lies Soloviev's universalism; his historical method is bound up with a universalized image of the Russian people, while his messianic vision of Russia is bound up with the universal feeling of the Unitotal. As can be seen, even in this article, written in a patriotic spirit close to the Slavophiles, we can already distinguish the coming transformation within Slavophilism itself and in Soloviev's attitude toward it.

Although the philosopher's principal works on Russia's ecclesiastical and political missions (and thereby on the fulfillment of Russia's theocratic mission) date from the 1880s, when Dostoevsky was no longer among the living, Soloviev had already expressed many of his essential views on the problem of East and West during the writer's lifetime.[97] Thus, for example, in the *Critique of Abstract Principles* Soloviev attacks the "abstract mind" and postulates that by affirming the divine element outside the human and natural element, it begets the principle of abstract clericalism or false theocracy. "Understood in this way, the divine element has to aspire to the complete absorption and destruction of elements alien tait, and if it is satisfied instead with their subordination and enslavement, if instead of destroying it simply suppresses, then this is mere charity or grace, and, logically speaking—an inconsistency. And indeed, abstract clericalism has precisely this attitude toward the human and natural element, in personal as well as social life." With this, Soloviev remarks that the fullest historical expression of abstract clericalism "we find in the Western Catholic Church, though it is not alien to other institutions of this sort as well."[98]

Though the censure of Catholicism is expressed here in a balanced tone, it is obvious that the philosopher's attitude toward the Western Church, which in his eyes embodies the principle of false theocracy, is distinctly negative. The brief description of the character of abstract clericalism defines, if only schematically, the foundations upon which any pseudotheocratic construction rests, including the worldly kingdom of the Grand Inquisitor: enforced theocracy suppresses the rational and natural elements in man's personal life as well as in the social sphere, where it seeks to subordinate the civil and economic realm to itself in an external fashion; it seeks "not only to dictate the general goals but also to define the private means of social activity of mankind—to govern and manage in all areas of human society."[99]

In the concluding lecture on God-manhood, Soloviev gives a deep and artistically rich critique of the West in the context of the three temptations of Christ. This context allows for a detailed comparison with Dostoevsky's views on related matters, expressed in his meditation on the three temptations. Soloviev brings against the West an accusation that has given some scholars grounds to speak of Soloviev's philosophical and artistic influence on the conception of the "Legend of the Grand Inquisitor," and others grounds to dispute this assertion.[100] The West, says Soloviev, has created an anti-Christian culture by succumbing to the three temptations of the evil principle. Proceeding from the view that both mankind and individual man embody three elements—the spirit, the intellect, and the sensual soul—the philosopher sees the temptation of evil for the whole of mankind as likewise threefold. He calls the first temptation the abuse of the truth man received in Christ's revelation, in the name of this very truth. This adoption of evil in the name of good displays the sin of the spirit, the expression of which is the aspiration to subjugate *by force* the world which lies in evil to Christ and His Church. "It is to this temptation of the lust for religious power that the part of the Church governed by the Roman hierarchy fell, carrying with it the majority of Western mankind in the first great period of its historical existence—the Middle Ages. The essential falseness of this path consists in the hidden lack of faith that lies at its root."[101]

According to the Gospel of Saint Matthew, the temptation by power was the last temptation of Christ. Dostoevsky, in the "Legend," preserves this canonical order: the "third counsel of the mighty spirit" is aimed at the fulfillment of "all that man seeks on earth, that is: someone to bow down to, someone to take over his conscience, and a means for uniting everyone at last into a common, concordant, and incontestable anthill—for the need for universal union is the third and last torment of man." In essence, the Grand Inquisitor, speaking about the need of mankind toward which the seduction by power is oriented, reveals the inner nature of this need completely in the spirit and even the terminology of Soloviev: "Great conquerors, Tamerlanes and Genghis Khans, swept over the earth like a whirlwind, yearning to conquer the cosmos, but they, too, expressed, albeit unconsciously, the same great need of mankind for universal and general union."[102] However, while recognizing the "great need" of mankind for unitotality, the Inquisitor "abuses" this truth; he makes it the foundation of *his own* universal kingdom, the foundation of a happy and submissive anthill.

Soloviev's interpretation of the second temptation diverges quite distinctly from that of Dostoevsky in the "Legend." The second temptation, that of the intellect, leads to the intellectual sin of pride. Historically, according to Soloviev, mankind succumbed to this temptation both in the rise of Protestantism and in the rationalism that issued from it. Protestantism, by assigning primary importance to personal faith without mediation by the traditional Church, holds fidelity to Holy Scripture as the sole criterion of truth. But to arrive at the correct understanding of Scripture one needs to exercise individual reason, which thus proves to be the actual source of religious truth. It is from this enthronement of individual intellect that Soloviev deduces the aspiration of rationalism to explain the entire content of knowledge by reason alone. Having succumbed to the second temptation, the West developed a self-assertive reason, which in the theoretical realm resulted in the construction of a system of abstract concepts, while in the practical sphere it was expressed in the violence and chaos of the French Revolution. If Soloviev and Dostoevsky alike view the temptation by power as corresponding to the third temptation of Christ in the Gospel of Saint Matthew, the second temptation (which occurs in the same place in each sequence) is perceived differently in the "Legend" and in the *Lectures*. Generally speaking, Soloviev constructs a more consistent and more accurately organized interpretation of the Gospel account (which is not to judge its accuracy as theological interpretation) and its symbolic reflection in the history of the West. Dostoevsky, on the other hand, achieves his tremendous cogency less by force of logic than through consummate artistic mastery. This illustrates, in a straightforward fashion, a dissimilarity in the character of their genius, just as the genres of the two works are dissimilar.

In contrast to Soloviev's historical interpretation, Dostoevsky sees the second temptation as a metaphysical contemplation of freedom. In Dostoevsky "the dread and wise spirit" tempts Christ to prove that He is the Son of God, which corresponds to the sense of the Gospel text: "If thou be the Son of God, cast thyself down: for it is written, He shall give his angels charge concerning thee: and into their hands they shall bear thee up, lest at any time thou dash thy foot against a stone" (Matt. 4:6). Yet the interpretation of this passage requires "a dash of insight": to succumb to the devil's temptations means committing two sins, not one. The first sin lies in the very act of tempting God, to which Christ indeed responds, "Thou shalt not tempt the Lord thy God" (Matt. 4:7). The second sin lies in daring to demonstrate one's exclusivity, to assert oneself. Christ, by not succumbing to the temptation of the first sin, that of doubt, thereby avoids that of the second, that of pride. Therefore, while Soloviev has every reason to see the second temptation leading to the sin of intellectual pride, a sin into which Western humanity has fallen, Dostoevsky views the second temptation as posing the problem of freedom. If he mentions pride, it is only within the context of this fundamental problem—pride as an aspect of free self-expression: "It is the pride of a child and a schoolboy! They are little children, who rebel in class and drive out the teacher."[103]

In their interpretations of the temptation of the flesh (the first temptation in the Gospel and in the "Legend," the third in the *Lectures*), Dostoevsky and Soloviev differ little. Soloviev sees the destiny of mankind—which has not followed Christ's words, "Man shall not live by bread alone, but by every word that proceedeth out of the mouth of God" (Matt. 4:4)—in materialist socialism. Dostoevsky, once again linking the problematics of the three temptations to the category of freedom, foresees a society whose obedience is bought with bread: "Better that you enslave us, but feed us."[104]

In addition, Dostoevsky has a "fourth temptation" of Christ, that to which He is subjected by the Grand Inquisitor. This is the temptation by love. The Grand Inquisitor tests the faithfulness of Christ's love for mankind just as the "dread and wise spirit," of whom the Inquisitor is a disciple, tested Christ's faithfulness to the Lord God. "I swear, man is created weaker and baser than you thought him! . . . Respecting him less, you would have demanded less of him, and that would be closer to love, for his burden would be lighter," the Inquisitor suggests.[105] The spirit in the wilderness tested the God-man by tempting His divine nature: "If thou be the Son of God, cast thyself down" (Matt. 4:6). The Inquisitor tests Him by tempting His human nature: If thou be the Son of Man, the Inquisitor says in effect, act according to thy human nature, give men the kind of love that we give them, an unburdensome *human* love; not a love whose "burden" is "light" (Matt. 11:30), but one with no burden at all. The Grand Inquisitor calls into question not Christ's divinity but His humanity. For precisely this reason, Christ's reply to the "fourth temptation" is human, that is, tangible materially, with the flesh. His kiss signifies not forgiveness, not even understanding, but love—that mystical love which the Inquisitor does "not want," since he himself does "not love" Christ.[106] This is why in the scene with the kiss the Inquisitor five times in a row is called *starik*, "old man," which identifies him with the very mankind toward which he had tried to elicit Christ's sympathy in a temptation of love.

THE RUSSIAN IDEA AND THE THEOCRATIC IDEAL

Indisputably, the interpretation of the temptations of Christ has in both Dostoevsky and Soloviev a twofold orientation—reflecting both the universally Christian sense of the Gospel account and its historical application. Although the similarity of the two interpretations extends in both directions, they differ in the precise way they accuse the West of anti-Christianity. Soloviev's criticism of the West can be called, to use his own terminology, primarily positive, whereas Dostoevsky pursues on the whole a negative criticism. Even during the period of his greatest closeness to the messianic hopes of Slavophilism, Soloviev discerned in Western Christianity "the truth of God, though wearing incongruous clothing,"[107] and in accord with the creative spirit of his philosophical system of unitotality, he later arrived logically at the ecumenical idea of the union of churches. Significant from the standpoint of Christian ethics is the philosopher's initial position, which reflects one of the basic principles of his program for a universal Church: "Owing to historical conditions Catholicism has always been the worst enemy of our people and our Church, but it is precisely for this reason that we should be fair to it."[108] As a friend once said of Soloviev: "He was not so much a politician as a man of lofty spirit, which is not always suitable in politics."[109] The loftiness of Soloviev's spiritual aspirations, his truly universal perspective on the tasks he set, his universal approach to their resolution — everything that could be called manifestations of the philosopher's spiritual farsightedness — at the same time made for a certain shortsightedness in his practical approach to the "Russian idea." Therefore, while seeing the problem of East and West as that of "uniting two unilateral truths in a higher fullness, as a mutual complementation," and Russia's great mission as overcoming "through love and the renunciation of sin a thousand years of strife,"[110] he failed to notice the full complexity of the problem, ignoring the many confessional and political differences between Western and Eastern Christianity.

The basic historical and philosophical motifs of Soloviev's and Dostoevsky's criticism of the West frequently coincide, revealing their common foundation in the theocratic idea. Thus, in Dostoevsky's notes from 1880-81 we read: *"The state is the Church*. Our difference from Europe. The state is above all a Christian society and strives to become the Church [*khristianin-krest'ianin*, Christian-peasant]. *In Europe it's the opposite* (one of our profound differences from Europe)."[111] Dostoevsky is virtually repeating what he had already expressed in *The Brothers Karamazov*: "According to the Russian understanding and hope, it is not the Church that needs to be transformed into the state, as from a lower type to a higher type, but, on the contrary, the state should end by being accounted worthy of becoming only the Church alone, and nothing else but that."[112] But in comparison to this exposition of the idea, in his notebook Dostoevsky sets Russia off against Europe far more distinctly and adds a particular argument. If the novelistic version in no way differs in spirit from Soloviev's construction of the question, the version in the diary entry has that nuance which, becoming a tendency, identifies Orthodoxy and nationality (*narodnost'*)—a conception attractive to Dostoevsky and utterly alien to Soloviev.

Another essential intersection of ideas on the same subject is clearly evident in the January 1877 issue of *The Diary of a Writer*. There, under the subheading "Three Ideas," Dostoevsky arrives at conclusions very close to those Soloviev expounded, partly in his "Three Forces" (published that same January in *Pravoslavnoe obozrenie*) and partly in his analysis of the three temptations in the *Lectures on God-manhood*. "Three ideas rise up before the world . . . ," writes Dostoevsky.

> On one side, at the edge of Europe, there is the Catholic idea—condemned and waiting in great torment and perplexity: Is it to be or not to be? Is it still to live or has its end come? . . . In that sense, for instance, France over the ages has seemed to be the most complete incarnation of the Catholic idea. . . . This France, who developed from the ideas of 1789 her own particular French socialism—i.e., the pacification and organization of human society without Christ and outside of Christ, . . . is and continues to be in the highest degree a Catholic nation wholly and entirely, completely contaminated by the spirit and the letter of Catholicism. . . . For French socialism is nothing other than the *compulsory* union of humanity, an idea that derived from ancient Rome and that was subsequently preserved completely in Catholicism. . . . On the other side rises up the old Protestantism. . . . This is the German. . . . Through his entire history he dreamed only of and longed only for his unification so he could proclaim his own proud idea.[113] . . . And meanwhile, in the East, the third world idea—the Slavic idea, a new idea that is coming into being—has truly caught ablaze and has begun to cast a light that has never before been seen; it is, perhaps, the third future possibility for settling the destinies of Europe and of humanity.[114]

Though Dostoevsky distinguishes the Catholic idea from the Protestant, fundamentally they remain closely interwoven: Protestantism is a faith "of protest and of mere *denial*, and as soon as Catholicism disappears from the world, Protestantism will also disappear right after it because it will have nothing to protest against; it will be transformed into straight atheism and thus will it end."[115] Thus, behind the three ideas lie the same two ideas—West and East. Counterposed to the Western, Roman idea of a false theocracy, of a "compulsory unity of humanity," is the Russian idea based on inner freedom in the name of a true and free theocracy. Of course, in the theoretical aspect of this position Dostoevsky is in agreement not only with Soloviev but also with all the representatives of Slavophilism, who were convinced that truth would shine forth out of the East. But his attitude toward the West is even more contradictory than that of the Slavophiles.

Berdiaev wrote of Dostoevsky that "on the one hand, he is a firm universalist; for him the Russian is the universal man [*vsechelovek*], Russia's mission is a world mission, and Russia is not a closed and self-contained world. . . . On the other hand, Dostoevsky displays genuine xenophobia, he cannot stand Jews, Poles, or the French, and he has a tendency toward nationalism."[116] An illustration of this paradox in Dostoevsky's universalist views can be found in a telling passage from his Pushkin speech: "With friendship and complete love that we accepted the genius of other nations into our soul, . . . we revealed . . . our readiness and our inclination for the general reunification of all people of all the tribes of the great *Aryan* races" (my italics).[117] However, Dostoevsky's remark is not exceptional for his time and accords with the Eurocentrist point of view shared then by many historians, including Sergei Soloviev.

The questions and themes associated with the "Russian idea" run through Dostoevsky's entire work. Yet there is a distinction between how Dostoevsky the novelist and Dostoevsky the essayist develop this subject: "where the publicist declaims, the artist probes beneath the surface."[118] The straightforward and frequently banal conservatism with which he expresses his views in *The Diary of a Writer* is replaced in his fictional works by a profound enthusiasm that expresses not only the author's position but also the multiplex individuality of his characters. Within the framework of artistic reality, Dostoevsky approaches the same questions that trouble him on national and religious politics in a dialectic rather than dogmatic manner, although his ideological aims remain unchanged. Recalling Soloviev's division of Slavophilism into three stages, one could say that Dostoevsky's work reflects, to a certain degree, all three perspectives simultaneously: from universalism to nationalism and chauvinism. The nationalistic perspective shows through most distinctly in the essayist. Very likely, the writer's intuition played no small role in such a placement of emphasis: a declarative statement of ideological extremism is harmful to the aesthetics of artistic prose, unless it is employed with ironic intent.

Those "wonderful words about Western Europe," cited unfailingly by all who write about Dostoevsky's attitude to the West, are frequently called upon to serve as evidence of his universalism. Indeed, the poetry of the pages devoted to the "land of holy miracles" in *The Raw Youth, The Brothers Karamazov,* and *The Diary of a Writer* is permeated with heartfelt emotion.[119] Generically, however, this "poetry" is closest of all in spirit to the funeral elegy. In speaking of Europe, Dostoevsky always appeals to the past, denying Europe not only a future but even a present. This feature is expressed most succinctly by Ivan Karamazov: "I want to go to Europe. . . . Of course I know that I will only be going to a graveyard, but to the most precious graveyard, that's the thing! The precious dead lie there, each stone over them speaks of such an ardent past life, of such passionate faith in their deeds, their truth, their struggle, and their science, that I—this I know beforehand—will fall to the ground and kiss those stones and weep over them—being wholeheartedly convinced, at the same time, that it has all long been a graveyard and nothing more."[120]

Usually, citations of this passage stop here. But Ivan continues: "And I will not weep from despair, but simply because I will be happy in my shed tears. I will be drunk with my own tenderness." This declaration, one may suggest, reflects Dostoevsky's own ambiguous love of Europe. The very idea of being moved to tenderness by one's own tears over a grave contains something unbearably false: here love for an object (if it even exists) is superseded by the self-love of the subject. In fact, national self-love is constantly admixed to Dostoevsky's declarations of love for Europe and his expressions of universalist aspirations: "Only to the Russian, even in our day, has been vouchsafed the capacity to become most of all Russian when he is most European, and this is true even in our day, that is, long before the millennium has been reached. That is the most essential difference between us Russians and all the rest, and in that respect the position in Russia is as nowhere else. In France I am a Frenchman, with a German I am a German. with the ancient Greeks I am a Greek, and by that very fact I am most typically a Russian."[121]

This is one of the Dostoevsky's favorite ideas; it is already reflected in his critical articles of the 1860s ("the Russian ideal is all-wholeness, all-reconciliation, all-humanity" [*vsetselost', vseprimirimost', vsechelovechnost'*])[122] and passes, with few changes, through his work to its culminating expression in his Pushkin speech. The beauty of this vision veils the paradox hidden within it. Lev Karsavin, noting "several incompatible ideas" in Dostoevsky's discussion of this subject, comments: "Declaring the Russian people to be the messiah-nation, Dostoevsky unwittingly identifies their universal humanity with their nationality, dissolving the latter in the former."[123] Indeed, Dostoevsky sees the very capacity for universal humanity as an exclusive trait of the Russian people. The contradiction, rightly noted by Karsavin, can be explained (but not done away with) only from Dostoevsky's own position. For him, Russian is a synonym for Orthodox ("A man who is not Orthodox cannot be Russian," he says through the mouth of Shatov),[124] while Orthodox is a synonym for Christian ("Catholicism is as good as an unchristian religion," proclaims Prince Myshkin—"Prince Christ").[125] For the Christian, in turn, "there is neither Hellene, nor Jew" (Rom. 10:12). This is why the

Russian (that is, Christian) can be a Frenchman, a German, or even an ancient Greek, or "Hellene," thereby following his own national (Christian) nature. Thus ecumenicity, as a Christian quality, becomes a purely Russian quality.

Such an identification of the national element with the religious has as its basis not universalism but nationalism, though "from the other end" (*s drugogo kontsa*), as Ivan Karamazov would say. This point of view also helps to elucidate the famous words on humility from the Pushkin speech—"Humble thyself, O haughty man; first curb thy pride"[126]—as well as the definition of "the Slavic idea in its highest sense" as sacrifice, "the necessity of sacrifice."[127] On the one hand, a genuinely Christian spirit is present here, but on the other hand, following this Christian spirit is regarded as the fulfillment of "the great Orthodox duty" which gives one the exclusive *right,* through humility and sacrifice, to take on the role of Christ, the role of the savior of mankind. The spiritual attractiveness and nobility of this aim are combined with an essentially blasphemous desire: to affirm in Christ's name a new messiah—the Russian people. As Nikolai Berdiaev writes, "such an exclusively messianic consciousness cannot be called a humble consciousness." Dostoevsky "considered the Russian people the most humble people in the world. Yet he was proud of this humility."[128] The paradox, or rather the sin, of the Christian consciousness—pride in humility—may symbolize most remarkably the contradictions in Dostoevsky's "Russian idea," which reveal themselves, however, not only Christologically but also methodologically.

In this light, it is interesting to note a striking peculiarity in the character of Dostoevsky's love for Europe. Speaking of "the land of holy miracles," where "every stone is cherished and dear," he has in mind primarily its secular culture (to the extent that it is at all possible to separate the secular and religious aspects of European culture). He calls precious "the treasures of their arts and sciences"[129] or, still more abstractly, the "passionate faith in their deeds, their truth, their struggle, and their science,"[130] without mentioning the spiritual strength of the Catholic saints or the religious life of the European peoples. But when Dostoevsky addresses the values of the Russian people, the category of culture drops away completely from his argument— only religious values are at issue. Thus he regards Europe and Russia from deliberately different perspectives.

The ideological grounds for the position he has chosen must be viewed through the complexity of the concept of culture in Russian thought. Thus according to Soloviev's early definition: "The East never succumbed to the three temptations of the evil principle—it preserved Christ's truth; but while preserving this truth in the *soul* of its people, the Eastern Church did not implement it in external reality, did not give it a real expression, did not create a *Christian culture* as the West created anti-Christian culture."[131] Berdiaev later makes a still more radical generalization: "The Russian idea is not an idea of culture."[132] It can be no accident that in all his panegyrics on "the land of holy miracles," Dostoevsky uses the name "Europe," a name associated with the values of culture, whereas in addressing the spiritual opposition between the "Roman" and the "Russian" ideas, he resorts to the appellation "West," symbolizing the religious essence of Europe.

The first stage of Slavophilism, in which its universalist aspect stands most prominently, was therefore well expressed in Dostoevsky's writings. Following Soloviev's classification further, we find the second stage of Slavophilism, that of the idolization of the Russian people, no less well represented. In Dostoevsky's novels, this motif acquired its most striking embodiment in the personality of the monomaniac Shatov from *The Devils*. Shatov is obsessed by the idea that "only one nation is 'god-bearing,' that's the Russian people."[133] Dostoevsky "bestowed" upon Shatov many of his own pet views, and much of what Shatov says in the famous dialogue with Stavrogin is reminiscent of statements in *The Diary of a Writer* and in Dostoevsky's letters and notebooks. But what is most significant in this dialogue is not so much the development of Shatov's thought, in itself very interesting and characteristic, as the turns in the conversation which expose its "unsteadiness" [*shatkost'*]. In response to Shatov's sermon, at the center of which stands the phrase "God is the synthetic personality of the whole people," Stavrogin first offers the common objection of opponents to Slavophilism: "You reduce God to a simple attribute of nationality."[134] But then he deals him a fatal blow: "'Do you believe in God, yourself?' 'I believe in Russia, I believe in her Orthodoxy. I believe in the body of Christ. I believe that the new advent will take place in Russia. I believe,' Shatov muttered frantically. 'And in God? In God?' 'I. I will believe in God.'"[135] In this conversation from *The Devils*, the breadth and universalism of Dostoevsky's views are displayed, perhaps, in a purer form than in his double-faced though profoundly attractive words about the ecumenicity of the Russian people. Here, as Berdiaev observes, Dostoevsky "himself exposes the lie of religious nationalism, of religious nation-worship, exposes the danger of a national messianic consciousness."[136]

The myth of a "nation god-bearer" entails two possible attitudes toward other nations. The first, as I have said, consists in one nation taking upon itself the mission of saving all other nations. Despite the ambiguity of such a claim, this attitude is based, if not on love, then at least on a distinctive ethical conception. The other possible attitude excludes any and all good feeling with respect to "alien" nations and inevitably leads to a declaration of hatred. "The image of the nation-god is postulated—and at the other pole arises the nation-devil," writes a contemporary.[137] Dostoevsky, who always penetrated to the very depths where paradox is born, also appreciated this double potential of Slavophilism. According to Radlov, he "not only worshipped his people and their creed, he also considered all others to be false. His legitimate feeling of national pride passes into false nationalism, and this is easy to trace in a two-fold manner—religious and political."[138]

Dostoevsky examines questions of national politics in Russia almost exclusively from a chauvinistic point of view. One could cite myriad examples of his coarse anti-Semitic, anti-Polish, anti-French, and anti-Turkish statements. Suffice it to quote one passage touching upon Russia's geopolitical situation:

> Germany *needs* us even more than we think. And she needs us not for a temporary political alliance, but *forever*. The idea of a reunited Germany is a broad, majestic one with roots in ages gone by. What can Germany share with us? Her object is the whole of Western humanity. She has assigned herself the Western world of Europe, to instill there her principles in place of the Roman and Romanic ones and eventually to become its leader, leaving the East to Russia. Two great peoples, thus, have been destined to change the face of this world. These are not some fanciful inventions of the mind or of ambition: this is the way the world is composing itself.[139]

"Dostoevsky had a prophetic gift," writes Berdiaev. "this gift has been justified by history. . . . But it is mainly Dostoevsky's negative rather than positive prophecies that have come true."[140] Undoubtedly, Dostoevsky deemed his prophecy about Germany and Russia a positive one for mankind as a whole, for "this world." Soloviev's intuition similarly failed to predict Germany's fateful historical role in the coming century. In 1900 he saw Germany as a natural and reliable ally of Russia in the creation of the Christian coalition against the Asiatic "yellow threat."

If for Dostoevsky the question of the religious superiority of the Russian people became also a question of Russia's political superiority, with a nationalism verging on imperialism, for Soloviev the religious role of Russia always remained a religious one, in the full sense of the word (*religio*, "bond"). He believed that in the dispute between East and West Russia should not represent one of the disputing parties, that it has a mediatory and conciliatory duty and should be in the highest sense the arbiter in this dispute. Soloviev sees in the Russia transformed by Peter the Great a purely external and formal union with the West, only "the preparing of ways and external methods for true reconciliation. And this reconciliation," he says, "inevitably lies in store for Russia: without it she cannot serve the cause of God on earth. The task of Russia is a Christian task, and Russian politics must be Christian politics."[141]

Expounding his political views in the early 1880s, Soloviev reduced the whole of Russian politics, foreign and domestic, to three questions: the Polish (or Catholic), the Eastern, and the Jewish. But what is essential for an analysis of this aspect of his worldview is not so much the historical context of the questions raised as the solution Soloviev posits. He sets as the main condition for resolving the first question reconciliation with the Church of Rome—an intolerable notion for many of his contemporaries. Anticipating their objections, he writes with irony in *The Great Dispute and Christian Politics*: "I do not dare to address myself to *present-day* Christians, for whom the Pope is simply the Antichrist, condemned to an evil downfall; I do not dare to speak to sinless and unsullied men who can only cast stones at the whore of Babylon. But I am certain that in Orthodox Russia one can also find not a few people who, conscious of their own imperfections and sins and their own endless falling away from the Christian ideal, will open up the spring of just and benevolent feelings even for the 'Antichrist' and the 'whore of Babylon.'"[142] If Soloviev defines the moral principle for the worldwide rapprochement of nations by quite naturally extending Christ's commandment to international relations—"Love all other peoples as your own"[143]—he sees the theological basis for the rapprochement of the Eastern and Western Churches, and later their union and, in the end, the worldwide theocratic unity, in the very nature of the Church. "The life of the Church as the *divine-human* body is in its essence made up of two elements: the received truth of God and the human reality conformable to it."[144] In a historical sense, the Christian Church "represents the reconciliation of two constituent principles: the Eastern, which consists of passive devotion to the Divinity, and the Western, which asserts man's independent action. For the Church, both the one and the other are equally necessary."[145]

With the issue formulated thus, the division of churches looks like a distortion and a violation of the very ontological essence of the Church. One must not forget that the correlation of positive and negative elements in Soloviev's philosophical system always occurs under the badge of unitotality, understood as a teleological principle. "The eternal and divine world," says Soloviev in the *Lectures on God-manhood*, "as the ideal plenitude of everything and the realization of good, truth, and beauty, appears to the reason as that which in and of itself must be, what is *normal*."[146] Therefore, the violation of the norm "is only another, improper, *interrelation* of the very same elements which also make up the existence of the divine world."[147]

Though Soloviev says this apropos of the existence of the natural world, the same approach is evident in his justification of the basis for the reunification of churches in a universal Church. That Soloviev attached tremendous importance to a union of churches is understandable. For him it was the necessary first step on the road to the realization of the *norm*. "In Soloviev's eyes the unity of churches," as Trubetskoi writes, "is the beginning not only of a world-historical revolution but also of a cosmic revolution: for with the unification of the whole of Christianity in Christ begins the world transformation of mankind, which in turn, according to the apostle, is to be the beginning of the transformation of the whole of creation—the universal liberation from 'the slavery of decay.'"[148] The philosopher's ecumenical activities can justifiably be called a struggle. Failing to gain support in his fatherland, in either official Church or social circles, he managed to find people of like mind among Catholics, particularly in Croatia. Carried away by his ideas, Canon Racki and Bishop Strossmayer, who called Soloviev "a pure soul, pious and indeed holy,"[149] responded to the philosopher's plan with both spiritual support and practical assistance.[150]

The resolution of the Eastern question, which had grown particularly acute in light of the Russo-Turkish war, was also seen by Soloviev to be possible only through the reconciliation of Russia with the West. It was precisely from this perspective that he analyzed the political situation: "When our war against Turkey turns into a struggle against the Western powers, when Vienna proves to be between us and Constantinople, when Polish Catholics enter the Turkish ranks against the Russian army and Orthodox Serbs in Bosnia unite with Muslims against Catholic Austria, then it becomes fairly clear that the chief dispute here is not between Christianity and Islam, nor between Slavs and Turks, but between the European, primarily Catholic West and Orthodox Russia."[151] To the Slavophiles' dream of Constantinople ("*Constantinople must be ours*, even if only in the next century!" wrote Dostoevsky in 1877), Soloviev responded not as an Orthodox politician but as a Christian historian: "The fate of Russia depends not on Constantinople or anything of the kind, but on the outcome of the inner moral struggle between the elements of light and dark within herself. . . . Let Russia, even without Constantinople, even within her present boundaries, become a Christian realm in the full sense of the word—a realm of justice and mercy—and then all the rest—it is certain—will come to her."[152]

Finally, with regards to the Jewish question, Soloviev also envisioned only a religious solution, believing in a future union of Jews with Orthodox and Catholic Christianity on a common theocratic soil. Soloviev had shown a profound interest in Judaism as far back as his early years of philosophical study, when he had spent his time exploring the Cabbala and other mystical doctrines in the library of the British Museum. In 1884 he began studying Hebrew and within two years was already reading the Torah, the books of the Prophets, and the Psalms in the original. According to Sergei Trubetskoi, just before Soloviev passed away, already in a half-conscious state, he prayed for the Jewish people and read psalms in Hebrew.

Soloviev's attraction to the Jews was an organic manifestation of his world-view.[153] In Judaism Soloviev saw and honored the environment that gave rise to Christianity. As early as the *Lectures on God-manhood*, he speaks of how only on the soil of Judaic monotheism, which offered for the first time the concept of the living God, could the incarnation of the Divinity occur. For this reason, all the problems associated with the situation of the Jews in Russia, all the accusations and reproaches hurled against them, Soloviev regards as but local phenomena, compared to the metahistorical background linking the biblical past and the theocratic future of Judaism and Christianity. Moreover, the path to the resolution of the Jewish question, as with the Eastern question, lies through the resolution of the "Christian" question, that is, through the unification of the Eastern and Western Churches. In his 1884 essay "The Jews and the Christian question," Soloviev writes: "The more fully the Christian world may express the Christian idea of spiritual and universal theocracy, . . . the more possible and nearer may become the conversion of the Jews. Thus, *the Jewish question is a Christian question.*"[154]

To sum up, one can say that the idea of theocracy, extremely important to Soloviev, was inwardly close to Dostoevsky as well. But Dostoevsky, to paraphrase his own character Ivan Karamazov, accepts the idea of theocracy without accepting the world of theocracy. In order to implement the ideal in real life, as Soloviev remarked in his article "The Russian National Ideal," Dostoevsky "would have had to relinquish a host of deep-rooted prejudices, preconceived ideas, and elemental national instincts which were within in him and which he expressed in his works without noticing their contradiction with the universal ideal he proclaimed."[155] Desiring to soften this judgment of Dostoevsky, the philosopher finds an excuse for his "prejudices" in the fact that "in the realm of ideas he was more a sage and an artist than a strictly logical, consistent thinker."[156]

This comment is less an illustration of Dostoevsky's "inconsistency" than an expression of Soloviev's loyalty toward his late friend. For in the final analysis there is no doubt that Dostoevsky, for all the complexity of his views, passionately and sincerely believed in Christian social principles which made theocracy the social ideal both for him and for Soloviev.

5

Justification of Good versus Justification of Evil

Only when I absolutely choose myself do I infinitize myself absolutely, . . . and this absolute choice of myself is my freedom, and only when I have absolutely chosen myself have I posited an absolute difference, the difference, that is to say, between good and evil.
— *Søren Kierkegaard*

APPROACHES TO ETHICS

"If good, as such, must without fail be true, then it is clear that truth, in its essence, cannot be something that is contradictory or alien to good," wrote Soloviev in his treatise *Theoretical Philosophy*.[1] From this definition it naturally follows that for him philosophical ethics was inseparable from, and indeed coincides with, knowledge as a whole, in all its forms; that is, to use Soloviev's terminology, ethics must be resolved within the framework of "integral knowledge." Though moral philosophy is the special focus of one of Soloviev's late writings, his monumental study *The Justification of the Good* (1894–97), ethical problems are in one way or another associated with the philosopher's entire oeuvre, beginning with *The Crisis of Western Philosophy*. Already in this study Soloviev points out the unsoundness of rationalistic as well as empiricist ethics. "Consistent rationalism," he writes, "in the person of Hegel flatly negates the very principle of practical, or moral, philosophy."[2] In its turn empiricism, which produced a semblance of ethics in utilitarianism, when taken to its logical extreme is likewise equivalent to a complete negation of moral philosophy, since the notion of empirical benefit is too relative to serve as the basis for any sort of integral or normative doctrine; as a result, individual preference becomes the practical norm.

According to Soloviev, the relation of rationalism and empiricism to ethics is conditioned by a principal proposition common to both tendencies of Western philosophy—the raising of reason and experience, which possess only partial value, to the status of absolute sources of knowledge, thereby ignoring metaphysical perception, otherwise known as faith. In the first case, metaphysics disappears in absolute logic (Hegel); in the second, in empirical psychology (Mill). Soloviev is most interested in those moral doctrines which correspond to the transitional moment in the development of both tendencies: Kant's doctrine of moral formalism and the development of a philosophy of immediate feeling or common sense in the Anglo-Scottish philosophical school. Yet here too the absoluteness of the moral sense is destroyed by the relativity of the premises. The categorical imperative of Kant, which requires that all individual actions be founded on a recognition of man and mankind as the end rather than the means, inevitably conceives of this end as the benefit of mankind, thereby acquiring a material meaning Kant did not intend. In turn, the guidance of common sense in choosing the moral over the immoral can find no criterion for such a preference other than in the universal benefit of the former in comparison with the latter, which transforms the morality of immediate feeling into its opposite—the morality of calculated utilitarianism. A qualitatively different character is possessed, from Soloviev's point of view, by the moral doctrine of Schopenhauer, based to a large extent on the feeling of compassion, which, however, differs from the compassion of empiricism by proceeding from the metaphysical essence, which Schopenhauer believed to lie in the substantial identity of beings. Thus the moral sense, according to Schopenhauer, expresses and reflects the unity of world life or a united world will. Though this ethical position has in Soloviev's eyes objective value, he notes that the metaphysical principle does not save Schopenhauer's moral philosophy from contradictions, owing to the imperfection of his metaphysics itself.

In his subsequent writings, Soloviev analyzes what he sees as both the positive and the negative aspects of the various ethical trends within the framework of the basic currents of Western philosophy. In particular, many of the tenets of Schopenhauer's moral doctrine are subjected to critical reinterpretation by Soloviev (as, for example, in chapter 3 of the first part of *The Justification of the Good*). But in his master's thesis he continues by affirming the need for a universal synthesis of science, philosophy, and religion, the attainment of which would require logically perfect Western forms to be united with the spiritual content of Eastern contemplations. For all its brevity and even sketchiness of exposition, *The Crisis of Western Philosophy* expresses Soloviev's principal ethical view, which would subsequently become more profound and refined at all levels while remaining essentially unchanged: that the absolute basis of morality is of a metaphysical nature. "In perfect inner agreement with the Supreme Will, recognizing the absolute significance or value of all other wills, so long as they also contain the image and likeness of God, participate as fully as possible in the task of the perfection of yourself and of all for the sake of the ultimate revelation of the Kingdom of God in the world."[3]

However, in order to treat Soloviev's ethics in a sound fashion, one must define one's own position with respect to an essential problem which only arose later as a result of criticism of *The Justification of the Good*. The fundamental reproach directed against the philosopher held that in his ethical treatise, in contradiction to his earlier writings, he allegedly defended the independence of ethics from religion and metaphysics. The most vocal proponent of this view was E. Trubetskoi, who devoted nearly the entire second volume of his *Soloviev's Worldview* to a critique of *The Justification of the Good*, thereby laying the foundation for a debate which continues to this day.[4] Both in the analysis of his friend's theocratic position and in the critique of his ethics, Trubetskoi, naturally, attacks the philosopher primarily from the point of view of his own interpretation of Soloviev's ideas. The problem is that Trubetskoi's very interpretation often is more a reflection of his polemics with Soloviev than an impartial analysis of his friend's philosophy. While Trubetskoi's charges cannot be seen as completely unfounded, since formally Soloviev's stated intention was to set up "moral philosophy as an independent science," Trubetskoi never takes into account that when Soloviev separates ethics from metaphysics, he has in mind the division of two *scholarly* disciplines, referring not to their transcendental essence but to their theoretical exposition. In other words, Soloviev is making his object the study of ethics as a philosophical category, irrespective of the other philosophical category of metaphysics, yet without denying what he sees as the self-evident connection of ethics with religion. "By its very essence moral philosophy has a very close connection with religion," writes Soloviev, "and,

in the way it achieves cognition, with theoretical philosophy."[5] Trubetskoi's
failure to recognize this explains another charge he brings against the author
of *The Justification of the Good*: inconsistency. In the critic's opinion,
Soloviev, having proclaimed the independence of moral philosophy, continues to appeal, unjustifiably, to religion and metaphysics. In fact, there is
nothing contradictory in the methodology of Soloviev's treatise. On the contrary: the division of metaphysics and ethics is purely methodological in
nature and serves the task Soloviev has set, the justification of the good as a
moral category.

In comparing the approaches of Soloviev and Dostoevsky to various aspects of ethics, one needs to consider—besides the basic difference that the
philosopher is obliged to answer questions, whereas it is enough for the writer
merely to raise them—the major distinction between Dostoevsky's and
Soloviev's respective attitudes to the problem of good and evil. Even though
both make ethics dependent on metaphysics,[6] the metaphysical premises that
form the foundation of moral philosophy are correlated somewhat differently
by the two thinkers. The main difference lies in the fact that in Dostoevsky
the correlation of the categories of good and evil have, so to speak, an air of
Manichaeism, in which these categories are declared to be two absolutely
independent primordial elements,[7] whereas Soloviev (similarly to Schelling,
who in turn continues the tradition of Saint Augustine) regards evil as a falling
away from good, although he grants it objective status. Of course, neither's
views can be reduced to these general tendencies. Thus, the notion of evil as
a falling away from good can be clearly traced in Dostoevsky's work, for
example, in the distinction between *obraz* (image) and *bezobrazie* (literally,
that which is "without image"), as elaborated by Robert Jackson, in the
moral-aesthetic spectrum of Dostoevsky. This in turn is deducible from the
absolute significance for the Christian consciousness of the image of Christ
and, consequently, of the perception of evil as the absence of His image.[8]

For Soloviev's part, despite the presence of determinism in his conception
of good, "no one will ever suspect him of obliterating the *borders* between
good and evil."[9] In his essay "The Meaning of Poetry in the Verse of Pushkin," Soloviev writes: "Both good and evil are subject to beauty, since they
both exist; but what can never exist and which, therefore, cannot take the
form of beauty, is the nondistinction between good and evil, such that one
might be regarded as the other."[10] All the same, Trubetskoi is justified in
saying that Soloviev "lacked that sense of the sinful abyss which is so powerful in the work of Dostoevsky." "It is," he writes, "precisely because
Soloviev was allowed to approach so near to the Divine in his contemplation
that he had an insufficient sense of how far it yet was from our reality."[11]

Since the problem of evil is directly dependent on the question of freedom, there is also a distinctive nuance in the two thinkers' development of this question. "The good," says Soloviev in *The Justification of the Good,* "determines my choice in its favor by the full infinity of its positive content and being; consequently, this choice is *infinitely* determined, its necessity was absolute, and there is in it no arbitrariness *whatsoever*; on the contrary, in the choice of evil there is no determining basis, no necessity *whatsoever,* and consequently endless arbitrariness."[12] This view has allowed critics of the philosopher to speak of Soloviev's supposed "metaphysical dualism," inferable from the fact that "if with regard to evil in man he allots significant place to the element of freedom, with respect to the paths of good, determinism remains in force."[13] If one compares Soloviev's and Dostoevsky's approaches to freedom of choice from this point of view, the divergence between them proves fairly substantial. Indeed, for Dostoevsky, who lays bare the irrational heart of human nature where the unceasing struggle of good and evil is waged, a deterministic conception of good would deprive this struggle of metaphysical meaning, conditioned by the principle of freedom. But Soloviev, in speaking about human freedom, draws a distinction between moral freedom, which is an ethical *fact,* and unconditional freedom of choice (that is, freedom of will), which is a metaphysical *question*. With the problem stated thus, Dostoevsky's interpretation of the category of freedom occurs within parameters similar to those in Soloviev's. In the "Legend of the Grand Inquisitor," he addresses both the ethical *fact* and the metaphysical *question*. "You desired the free love of man, that he should follow you freely," the Inquisitor tells Christ. "Instead of the firm ancient law, man had henceforth to decide for himself, with a free heart, what is good and what is evil, *having only your image before him as a guide*" (my italics).[14] It is this addition that brings Dostoevsky's thought nearer to Soloviev's assertion that the idea of good can, with full inner necessity, determine man's conscious choice in its favor.[15] That is, the idea of good (the image) guides choice, although, as the Grand Inquisitor continues, freedom of will presupposes the possibility of disputing "even your image and your truth." This next step on the paths of freedom, leading as it seems to the depth of the metaphysical question, turns on a logical dead-end: since man's freedom, as follows from the Grand Inquisitor's accusations, is a gift from God, from Christ, using it to dispute its own source creates the effect of a *contradictio in adjecto*.

In essence, on the question of freedom both Dostoevsky and Soloviev follow more or less the division of freedom into a lower and higher, as in Saint Augustine's conception. Dostoevsky is basically analyzing the freedom of man that manifests itself in the choice between good and evil, that is, a dynamic freedom on the path to an absolute, static freedom. Soloviev, on the other hand, sees first and foremost the freedom that is realized in the Absolute, that is, a static freedom in God, which is implied in Soloviev's famous line: "Nepodvizhno lish' solntse liubvi" (Only the sun of love is motionless). Synthesizing the two approaches, one can conclude that the struggle of good *and* evil in the world process is at the same time the struggle of good *with* evil. It is precisely within such a dialectics of good and evil that the metaphysical heart of Dostoevsky's moral search is exposed. And it is to the same dialectics that Soloviev arrived in the *Three Conversations*, where he offers his final answer to the question of good and evil:

> Indeed, evil exists, and it is expressed not in the absence of good alone, but in the positive opposition and preponderance of lower qualities over higher in all spheres of being. . . . We know that the struggle of good with evil is carried out not in the soul only and in society but, more profoundly, in the physical world. And it is here that we have already known in the past one victory of the good basis of life—in the personal resurrection of the One—and that we await future victories in the collective resurrection of all. And then evil obtains its sense or the definitive explanation for its existence in the fact that it serves the ever greater celebration, realization, and strengthening of good: if death is more powerful than mortal life, resurrection into eternal life is more powerful than both. . . . The true victory over evil is in true resurrection.[16]

On this issue the positions of Soloviev and Dostoevsky obviously coincide. "On earth there is *but one* sublime idea," writes Dostoevsky in *The Diary of a Writer*, "namely, the idea of the immortality of man's soul—since all the other 'sublime' ideas of life which make man live are *merely derived from this one idea*."[17] There is no doubt that in speaking of "the idea of the immortality of man's soul," Dostoevsky, like any Christian, is also implying the idea of resurrection. ("Soloviev and I . . . believe in an actual, literal, personal resurrection."[18]) Thus only the "sublime idea" of resurrection into eternal life can serve as the foundation for all other ideas, including the ethical.

Dostoevsky's artistic depiction and ethical criticism embrace the broadest spectrum of all possible moral theories, not only those that had been established or proclaimed by the second half of the nineteenth century but also others that were just coming into being or were even foreseen by the writer. One of Dostoevsky's first statements "against positivism" appeared in *Notes from Underground*, where, according to Vasilii Rozanov, the idea of "the impossibility of organizing human nature rationally" is expressed in dialectical terms.[19] "Oh, tell me, who was it first announced, who was it first proclaimed, that man only does nasty things because he does not know his own interests; and that if he were enlightened, if his eyes were opened to his real normal interests, man would at once cease to do nasty things, would at once become good and noble because, being enlightened and understanding his real advantage, he would see his own advantage in the good and nothing else, and we all know that not one man can, consciously, act against his own interests, consequently, so to say, through necessity, he would be doing good? Oh the babe! Oh the pure, innocent child!"—thus with irony speaks the Underground Man, ideologically repelled by the "stone wall" of rationalism and, in the present instance, of utilitarianism.[20]

Dostoevsky juxtaposes the naïve but by no means innocent idea of man's moral dependence on his enlightenment and understanding of his own advantage, which is proclaimed by utilitarianism, not with a metaphysical recognition of the category of the good, which by definition can find no direct expression in the existential worldview of a "paradoxalist," but with the statement of a fundamental philosophical problem—the theme of freedom. Thus, demolishing the utilitarian conception of ethics, he transfers the solution to the moral question over into the metaphysical realm. "Reason is nothing but reason and satisfies only the rational side of man's nature, while will is a manifestation of a whole life, that is, of a whole human life including reason and all man's head scratching."[21] Dostoevsky's response to the Underground Man's rejection of the "advantageous good" becomes not the proposal of another ethical alternative but an indication, mediated through the issue of freedom, of where to look for one.

It is not difficult to see that each of Dostoevsky's novels contains some refutation of rationalistic morality in all its forms. But it is interesting to note as well the various ways the rationalistic and metaphysical elements are correlated by Dostoevsky, how he pits the justification of evil against the justification of the good within the specific philosophical atmosphere of each of his works. Once again, Dostoevsky's four great novels provide us with an opportunity to step into the writer's laboratory and discern how his creative mind conducts a particular intellectual experiment under various conditions within the framework of four different settings.

EVIL AS GOOD AND/OR JUSTIFICATION OF NAPOLEON

There is no doubt that Raskolnikov, theorizing about the right to commit crime, knows that killing is wrong. Otherwise, what would be the point of all his attempts to persuade himself to the contrary? But it is noteworthy that in committing his crime, that is, the act of evil, he is guided by speculative, rationalistic justification, whereas he performs his good actions by proceeding, as if unconsciously, from certain absolute principles of morality. In *Crime and Punishment* it is the rationalistic justification of evil rather than its metaphysical nature that is examined. At the same time, it is precisely metaphysically, outside rational reasoning, that good is justified in the novel. Raskolnikov's idea, for all its "originality," has taken shape in his consciousness not without the influence of the latest trends of the day, and specifically of positivistic theories. "*The very same ideas*" occur not to him alone.[22] If the motives of murder "for oneself" (which were examined above) make Raskolnikov's crime unique in its way, the justification of crime in the name of "the common good" is, in the author's opinion, not original at all: "It was all the most ordinary and the most often heard . . . youthful talk and thought," observes Dostoevsky, referring to a conversation between an officer and a student early in the novel.

Yet Dostoevsky at once sets up a boundary between the theory and practice of utilitarian and positivistic morality—one that implies another, nonrationalistic morality. "You are talking and speechifying away, but tell me, would you kill the old woman *yourself*?" asks the officer. "Of course not! I was only arguing the justice of it. . . ." "But I think, if you would not do it yourself, there's no justice about it." Raskolnikov shifts this boundary but does not abolish it. The theory and the practice of crime unite along one side of the boundary, occupying the rational space in Raskolnikov's mental life, while the manifestations of extrarational good, half-deliberate in their motivation, are found in that space which, in proportion to its distance from the boundary, passes into a metaphysical perspective. Of course, the extrarational moral element as such cannot be called entirely mystical or metaphysical; for Raskolnikov it has rather an empirical character, which manifests itself almost exclusively in the feeling of compassion. But compassion, while being the empirical basis for morality, is nevertheless, in Soloviev's phrase, "none other than the insight into the great mystery of the unity of world life,"[23] that is, in essence, a metaphysical insight. Regardless of the application of this statement to a number of diverse philosophical and religious moral doctrines, there is no doubt that for Dostoevsky compassion to a large degree represents the very foundation of metaphysical ethics as it exists in Christianity. The writer even makes the categorical declaration in the notes to *The Idiot* that "compassion is the whole of Christianity."[24] Therefore, it is compassion that becomes the litmus test for Raskolnikov's ethical position.

One of the first signs of the split between Raskolnikov's mind and his soul, or, to put it another way, between the rational and the extrarational in his consciousness, is the episode on the boulevard from the fourth chapter of the novel.[25] Feeling compassion for a deceived young girl whom he has chanced to notice and wishing to protect her from a new depraver, Raskolnikov, with little thought, summons a policemen, gives him his last twenty kopecks for a cab to take her home, and goes to great pains on her behalf. Then suddenly, with everything nearly settled, he pulls himself up sharp: "In an instant he seemed to be turned upside down. . . . 'Hey, here!' he shouted after the policeman. . . . 'Let them be! What is it to do with you! Let her go! Let him amuse himself.' He pointed at the dandy. 'What is it to do with you?'" His consciousness, "turned upside down," begins to operate "dialectically": "And why did I want to interfere? Is it for me to help? Have I any right to help? Let them devour each other alive—what is it to me?" And then his "aimless thoughts" begin to wander between compassion for the girl, for all such girls, and vulgarly positivistic arguments about an inevitable "percentage," arguments that he himself views with irony: "Poor girl! . . . She will come to herself and weep, and then her mother will find out. She will give her a beating, a horrible, shameful beating and then maybe turn her out of doors. And even if she does not, the Daria Frantsovnas will get wind of it, and the girl will soon be slipping out on the sly here and there. . . . But what does it matter? That's as it should be, they tell us. A certain percentage, they tell us, must every year go . . . that way . . . to the devil, I suppose, so that the rest may remain fresh, and not be interfered with."[26] Despite his "But what does it matter?" Raskolnikov understands full well the impropriety of applying such a "percentage" principle to the girl, but he does not wish at all to see the impropriety of that same "arithmetic" being applied to the old pawnbroker whom he has decided to kill.[27]

Raskolnikov's attitude toward the old woman is based firmly in the realm of speculative ideas. He progressively reduces her to a purely rational level, calling her "old crone" (*starushonka*)—still an animate image, but already belittled in human terms; then "louse" (*vosh'*)—no longer a human image, but still a living creature; and, finally, "principle"—a completely abstract and inanimate image. It is natural that, given such a distortion of the human image, there is no room for compassion. Yet at the same time this chain of substitutions, which Raskolnikov has probably constructed unconsciously, indicates that he is not morally hopeless: were he to assign the "louse" and "principle" the place in his consciousness which she holds metaphysically by right of birth—the place of a human being—his attitude toward her would by definition be conditioned by the metaphysical feeling of compassion. This is supported by all of Raskolnikov's extrarational moral actions.[28]

Thus, having seen Marmeladov home after their chance encounter, Raskolnikov, "unnoticed," places on the windowsill of the destitute family's room some copper coins "he had received as change for his ruble in the tavern." He does this unconsciously, obeying an instinctive moral impulse. But once he has assessed his action rationally, he plunges into self-criticism: "What a stupid thing I've done, they have Sonia and I need the money myself." And at this point, as in the episode with the young girl on the boulevard, his rational reasoning turns cynical: "Sonia wants make-up, too—such smartness costs money."[29] These words, Raskolnikov "caustically" recalls, had been said not long before by Sonia's fool-playing father. But Marmeladov also says something else; "positively inspired," he declaims a hymn to compassion, a true sermon in the spirit of Origen, if one should seek to correlate it with the Christian theological tradition: "Why am I to be pitied, you say? Yes! There's nothing to pity me for! I ought to be crucified, crucified on a cross, not pitied! Crucify me, oh judge, crucify me but have pity! . . . But He will pity us Who has had pity on all men, Who has understood all men and all things, He is the One, He too is the judge. . . . And He will judge and will forgive all, the good and the evil, the wise and the meek."[30] This image of mystical compassion, the idea of superhuman pity, has nothing in common with the "arithmetic" of justice that Raskolnikov accepts speculatively, yet rejects intuitively.

Also unaccountable from a speculative point of view is Raskolnikov's early love. Razumikhin, the positive personification of rational good, is puzzled over Raskolnikov's dead fiancée: "She must have had some good qualities or it's quite inexplicable."[31] Even Raskolnikov himself does not understand his infatuation: "She was such a sickly girl, quite an invalid. . . . She was an ugly little thing. I really don't know what drew me to her then—I think it was because she was always ill. If she had been lame or hunchback, I believe I should have liked her better still. Yes, it was a sort of spring delirium."[32] It is obvious that manifestations of good and of love occur in Raskolnikov almost unconsciously, whereas manifestations of evil require rationalistic justification. Dostoevsky offers yet another slice from his character's existence, one that in current terminology is usually called the subconscious: Raskolnikov's famous dream of the slain horse reveals not only his moral potential but also his inner moral connection with all living things through compassion—that is, in religious terms, a mystical connection.

The profound nature of the split that has taken place with Raskolnikov can be illustrated by a significant exclamation that Dostoevsky places in his character's mouth: "My life has not yet died with that old woman! The kingdom [*tsarstvo*] of Heaven to her—and now enough, madam, leave me in peace! Now for the reign [*tsarstvo*] of reason and light, and of will, and of strength, and now we will see!"[33] The Kingdom of Heaven, mentioned as if unconsciously, is actually in opposition to the reign of reason. The metaphysical element is cut off from the rational element. Reunification begins only at the end of the novel (or at the beginning of the "new story"). "Life had stepped into the place of dialectics and something quite different would work itself out in his mind," says Dostoevsky.[34] There can be no doubt that the new life here arises together with a new moral where, using Soloviev's reasoning, the rational, empirical, and religious (mystical) elements must be joined in an organic synthesis.

GOOD AS GOOD: A PORTRAIT OF A "TRULY BEAUTIFUL PERSON"

Dostoevsky continued his polemic with rationalism (in its positivistic version) in *The Idiot,* in a secondary plot-line associated with Ippolit Terent'ev, Burdovskii, and their company. But the main moral conflict of the work has to do less with a critique of positivistic ethics than with an analysis of the metaphysical nature of both good and evil. The tragic triangle that forms the gravitational center of all the other lines in *The Idiot* consists of good, evil, and beauty. Schematic though such a framework may seem, it is precisely these categories that Prince Myshkin, Rogozhin, and Nastasia Filippovna symbolize.[35] But, if Nastasia Filippovna is aware that she possesses beauty, neither Myshkin nor Rogozhin recognizes his fateful connection to the element of good or evil hidden with him. Neither of them understands his own nature—the prince through innocence, Rogozhin through ignorance. They are both utterly devoid of the rational element. They both exist within the same extrarational space; in this lies their kinship, their fraternity, sealed first by an exchange of crosses and later by blood and the mutual madness that overtakes them in the presence of Nastasia Filippovna's dead body—a liberation from *ratio* in the literal sense. ("They are both insane," as Dostoevsky noted in his sketches for the novel.)[36]

Prince Myshkin really performs not a single act of good in the novel: he does not drag "two small children from a burning apartment during a fire in the middle of the night," like Raskolnikov; he does not save helpless orphans from certain poverty and death, like Svidrigailov; he does not make efforts on behalf of an unknown provincial, like Ippolit Terent'ev. It is easy to wheedle out of him now twenty-five rubles, now ten thousand, but this willingness to give money away to drunkards and swindlers can scarcely be called a good deed. Yet of all Dostoevsky's characters, it is Myshkin who personifies the idea of the good, as far as it can be approximated within the bounds of human life. While for all the others doing good is essential for the conscious or unconscious assertion of a moral element in their lives, Myshkin by his very existence asserts less morality than unmediated good, since existence as such cannot be called a moral act. For this reason Dostoevsky's "Prince Christ" symbolizes the metaphysical rather than the ethical-practical embodiment of the good. This specific feature, reflected in the figure of Myshkin, finds an analogy in the parable of Martha and Mary (Luke 10:38–42), where ethical service to good is contrasted with a metaphysical partaking of good.

The essence of the good inherent in Myshkin is not conveyed in the form of an epithet (a good man), but rather as an absolute element that defines, ideally, the phenomenon of man, a level of abstraction introduced by the symbolic treatment of the prince: "You are the first man I have seen in my life!" Nastasia Filippovna tells him.[37] The Gospel association is emphasized further when Ippolit declares, "I say good-bye to Man."[38] Set against the metaphysical perspective of the concept of "man" presented in *The Idiot*, the semantic degradation of this concept that Dostoevsky plays on early in the novel appears especially ironic. The prince's casual conversation with the Epanchin's valet in the hall of their home is characterized as "incongruous," since to carry on such a conversation "is perfectly suitable between man and man but utterly unsuitable between guest and *man* [*chelovek*, "manservant"]."[39] This short introductory episode serves not only to display the goodness of the prince but also his love. It is not enough to say of him that he is good to people—he loves them. "I do not understand," he marvels, "how one can . . . talk to a man and not be happy in loving him."[40] Good is the prince's nature, and love its manifestation. Myshkin's love for people is in no way connected to democratism or (depending on one's taste) aristocratism; if one is to speak in such terms, it reflects his universalism. "We are such different people on the face of it, for many reasons, that perhaps there can be no points in common between us," he tells General Epanchin, "but, you know, I myself do not believe this. . . . People size each other up by eye and so can't find anything in common."[41] The universalism of Myshkin's attitude toward people is based in the compassion he accepts as "the chief and perhaps only law of all human existence."[42]

If one compares the first reaction of each character in the novel to man (that is, man *in general*), the defining component in the psychology of their relations both with people and with the world stands immediately exposed. When Rogozhin, warmly dressed "in a full, black, sheepskin-lined overcoat," encounters in a train compartment a chance fellow traveler, Myshkin, "blue with cold," he observes him for a long while until finally, "with that indelicate smile in which satisfaction at the misfortunes of one's neighbor is sometimes so unceremoniously and casually expressed," he asks: "Chilly?"[43] This expressive picture of Rogozhin provides a glimpse not only of the malicious joy coloring his attitude toward his "neighbor," but also of the level on which he perceives the other man—the physical. The detailed depiction of his sheepskin coat with the help of four adjectives (*shirokii merlushichii chernyi krytyi tulup*) allows us to feel the material density of Rogozhin's "satisfaction" as he observes the stranger suffering from the cold. True, by the end of the encounter he declares that he has "taken to" the prince and once again materially corroborates his favorable disposition: "We'll put you into a first-class fur coat, I'll get you a first-class dress-coat, a white waistcoat, or whatever you like, I'll fill your pockets with money."[44] But this change in Rogozhin's mood is explained not so much by any sudden impulse toward goodness on his part as by the irresistible influence of the good emanating from Myshkin.

No less revealing is Nastasia Filippovna's reaction to man. The first words uttered by her in the novel are addressed (almost as with the prince, who straight from the train finds himself in the Epanchins' entrance hall) to a servant: "If you are too lazy to mend the bell, you might at least be in the hall when people knock. Now he's dropped my coat, the duffer. . . . They ought to turn you off. Go along and announce me."[45] Of course, her "annoyance" and "irritation" at the sluggish servant are explicable and, perhaps, even excusable. Her reaction is "natural" for a temperamental, glamorous woman of society circles. The irony of the situation lies in the fact that the "servant" is actually the prince, who has happened to open the door. And from the common perspective of that particular milieu it is precisely Myshkin's own conversation with the valet, as from man to man, that is unnatural and unsuitable. One cannot say that Nastasia Filippovna is not good to people in the everyday sense of the word—she is on kind terms with her maids and looks after a few old men; yet she is good, like most people, selectively. In contrast, the good which determines the prince's attitude toward man is not selective; it is independent of objective causes. It is this type of good, native to him, that Myshkin longs to see in Nastasia Filippovna's face as he gazes for the first time at her portrait: "It's a proud face, awfully proud, but is she good? Ah, if she were! Then all would be saved!"[46] Considerably less philosophical significance is usually attached to these words than to a famous apothegm also given to the prince by Dostoevsky: "Beauty will save the world." Early in the novel the prince responds to a comment Adelaida makes to him by saying: "I am really a philosopher perhaps, and—who knows?—perhaps I really have a notion of instructing. That's possible, truly."

Philosophical instruction, in the sense it is applied to Myshkin, does not always include explanation. The prince himself offers no interpretation of his words about beauty. But Ippolit, in whom cynicism has blended with a metaphysical terror in the face of death, indirectly comments on this idea: "'Gentlemen!' he shouted loudly, addressing the whole company, 'the prince asserts that beauty will redeem the world! But I assert that the reason he has such playful ideas is that he is in love. . . . Don't blush, prince, it makes me sorry for you. What sort of beauty will save the world? . . . Are you a zealous Christian?'"[47] Ippolit certainly understands that the prince's idea is not "playful" but "zealously" Christian. But in the Christian worldview, beauty in accord with good and truth reflects the ultimate unity of that triangle; moreover, good (*dobro* or *blago*), as Soloviev asserts, "by its essence comes before truth and beauty, since the spirit necessarily comes before the intellect and the soul."[48] Beauty without good cannot have the completeness of an absolute positive element. Equally incomplete is truth without good: "You have no tenderness, nothing but truth, and so you judge unfairly," says Aglaia, expressing an idea that the prince calls "very clever."[49] Therefore—"beauty will save the world," but "is it good? Ah if it were! Then all would be saved!" Outside such a unity of concepts, the profound thought is only a "playful idea."

Opening the novel with a descriptive portrait of Rogozhin and Myshkin, Dostoevsky was not afraid of using a somewhat traditional symbol to depict the outward appearance of his main characters: Rogozhin has "almost black hair," while Myshkin has "very fair hair." Throughout nearly the entire first chapter, until their names are revealed and even for some time thereafter, the young men are described as "dark" and "fair." But lying behind these epithets is not simply the traditional portrayal of a "positive" and a "negative" personality; this is the characterization (though also a traditional one) of light and dark forces, of good and evil. Just as in Myshkin the element of good means more than the notion of a "good man," so in Rogozhin the element of evil cannot be designated by the definition "evil man." The concept of personal morality or personal immorality cannot fully correspond to the scale of the opposing forces in the novel. As one scholar reminds us, "the distinction between good and evil is not the comfortable distinction between right and wrong."[50] The evil of which Rogozhin is the repository is by its essence extrapersonal; it is a metaphysical evil, whose name is death. Of course, the realistic level of the narrative demands a realistic representation of the descriptive features in the character's personality. Describing Rogozhin on this level, Dostoevsky consistently employs various derivatives of the word "evil" (*zlo*): "zlobnaia ulibka,"[51] "zlobno posmotrel,"[52] "s zlobnoi ulybkoi,"[53] "zlobno,"[54] "s kakoi-to otkrovennoi zloboi,"[55] "vsia zloba moia,"[56] "zlobno zasmeialsia,"[57] "litso ego iskrivilos' v zlobnuiu nasmeshku,"[58] "tvoiu liubov' ot zlosti ne otlichish'" (the prince's words to Rogozhin: "There's no distinguishing your love from hate"),[59] "chto-to zlobnoe . . . zagorelos' v litse ego,"[60] "s zlobnoiu dosadoi,"[61] and so on to the very end of the novel. This list alone is enough for us to see the dominating trait in Rogozhin's psychological portrait. But alongside the realistic level of the author's description of Rogozhin exists the surrealistic level of his perception by the other characters. And on this level evil begins to lose the individual traits of a single gloomy man—the dark (in every sense) merchant Rogozhin—and reveals its mystical nature.

Thus the theme of eyes emerges. Rogozhin's eyes, as if separate from Rogozhin himself, begin to haunt first Myshkin and later Nastasia Filippovna. "'As I got out of the train this morning, I saw two eyes that looked at me just as you did now from behind.' 'You don't say so! Whose eyes were they?' Rogozhin muttered suspiciously. Myshkin fancied that he shuddered. 'I don't know; I think I must have imagined it all in the crowd. I am beginning to see things.'"[62]

"Why that shiver again, that cold sweat, that darkness and chill in his soul?" the "weak, suffering, agitated" prince later asks himself. "Was it because he had once more seen those *eyes*?"[63]

Nastasia Filippovna speaks of the same thing: "I have almost ceased to exist and I know it. God knows what lives within me in my place. I read that every day in two terrible eyes which are always gazing at me, even when they are not before me. Those eyes are *silent* now (they are always silent), but I know their secret."[64]

Myshkin, with his natural faculty for insights, sees in Rogozhin the fatal, destructive element of evil from the very beginning: to Gania's question whether Rogozhin would marry Nastasia Filippovna, he replies, "I dare say he'd marry her and in a week perhaps murder her."[65] But at the same time the prince does not *believe* what he knows: "Parfion, I don't believe it!" he cries, even as he sees with his own eyes the gleaming knife above him.[66] The prince believes in *man* and therefore does not believe in death, the ultimate evil. It is not by chance that Dostoevsky places in Rogozhin's home a copy of Holbein's painting *The Dead Christ*.[67] It is interesting, moreover, that it is Rogozhin himself who draws the prince's attention to the picture.

Myshkin glanced at it as though recalling something, but he was about to pass through the door without stopping. . . . But Rogozhin suddenly stopped before the picture. "All these pictures here were bought for a ruble or two by my father at auctions," he said. "A man who knows about paintings looked at all of them. They're rubbish, he said, but this one— . . . is of value. . . . I've kept it for myself." . . . Rogozhin suddenly turned away from the picture and went on. . . . "And by the way, Lev Nikolaevich, I've long meant to ask you, do you believe in God or not?" said Rogozhin suddenly after having gone a few steps. "How strangely you question me—and look at me!" Myshkin could not help observing. "I like looking at that picture," Rogozhin muttered after a pause, seeming again to have forgotten his question. "At that picture!" cried Myshkin, struck by a sudden thought. "At that picture! Why, that picture might make some people lose their faith." "That's what it is doing," Rogozhin assented unexpectedly.[68]

This brief conversation concerning the picture has a special significance in the novel, the symbolic level of which is revealed in Ippolit's "explanation."

The picture represented Christ who has only just been taken down from the cross. . . . Artists usually paint Christ, both on the cross and after He has been taken from the cross, still with extraordinary beauty of face. They strive to preserve that beauty even in His most terrible agonies. In Rogozhin's picture there's no trace of beauty. It is in every detail the corpse of man. . . . Looking at such a picture, one conceives of nature in the shape of an immense, merciless, dumb beast, or . . . in the form of a huge machine of the most modern construction which, dull and insensible, has aimlessly clutched, crushed and swallowed up a great priceless Being, a Being worth all nature and all laws, worth the whole earth, which was created perhaps solely for the sake of the advent of that Being! This picture expresses and unconsciously suggests to one the conception of such a dark, insolent, unreasoning and eternal Power to which everything is in subjection.[69]

This "dark Power" assumes in Ippolit's delirium the shape of "a huge and loathsome spider" which is replaced by Rogozhin: "Rogozhin put his elbows on the little table and began to stare at me without speaking. . . . I felt a cold chill at my spine and my knees trembled. At that very instant, as though guessing that I was afraid, Rogozhin moved away the hand on which he was leaning, drew himself up, and his lips began to part, as though he were going to laugh; he stared at me persistently."[70] The deliberate association of Rogozhin with death is underscored later in the brief naturalistic description of another of Ippolit's dreams: "I dreamt last night that I was smothered with a wet cloth by . . . a man . . . well, I'll tell you who it was—Rogozhin! What do you think of that?"[71] If the prince's and Nastasia Filippovna's forebodings of disaster are explicable by their fateful proximity to Rogozhin, for Ippolit he is a stranger and, objectively, represents no threat to him whatever. Yet the "positivist," who in his will has left his skeleton to the Medical Academy "for the benefit of science," already stands on the brink of the metaphysical abyss; for this reason, probably, he perceives both the "Man" in Prince Myshkin and the "merciless and dumb beast," the "huge machine" "parting its lips," in Rogozhin.

EVIL AS EVIL: EVIL CHILDREN OF GOOD FATHERS

If in *The Idiot* the nature of good and evil is most strikingly visible in their metaphysical aspect, in *The Devils* these categories are examined in terms of a rationalistic experiment. Although this experimental process is traced in diverse forms through the actions of the individual characters in the novel, its dimensions are defined by a collective rather than a personal consciousness. The attempt of an individual rationalistic justification of evil, which with Raskolnikov still clashes with the extrarational justification of the good, has been already realized in *The Devils,* as a phenomenon existing in society. Moreover, the "devils" do not even see the need for a justification of evil, since they have completely lost the criterion for defining moral concepts. In the chapter entitled "A Meeting" Dostoevsky, in a satirical tone, presents an array of popular nihilistic ideas, according to which "the superstition about God came from thunder and lightning" and "there's no such thing as moral or immoral." Though the intentionally primitive formulation of such statements exaggerates the rationalistic rectilinearity of the revolutionary "organizers of the future society," the nature of their worldview is reflected with the utmost clarity. Showing the ethical distortion and absurdity of the "devils'" ideology, Dostoevsky feels no doubt as to the historical and philosophical roots of the idea of an "earthly paradise" conditioned by "unlimited despotism." Rationalistic evil is born of rationalistic good. In essence, Dostoevsky's ethical system views the rationalization of good as an ambiguous phenomenon fraught with the transformation of the true good into its opposite, by virtue of the a priori limited nature of the rational method: "Reason has never had the power to define good and evil, or even to distinguish between good and evil, even approximately."[72]

Stepan Trofimovich Verkhovenskii, a "master liberal" with "an extremely gentle and unresentful heart," is portrayed by Dostoevsky with ruthless irony. But at the same time his description of Stepan Trofimovich shows flashes of the same affectionately condescending tone that sounds so distinctly in the description of Kolia Krasotkin—a teenage character in *The Brothers Karamazov*. This authorial intonation, among other things, points to the shared trait that links these very different characters: ideological infantilism. In both instances the character's worldview is presented as immature, though for different reasons—youthful naveté in Kolia's case, archaic naveté in Stepan Trofimovich's. The senior Verkhovenskii's ideas are viewed by Dostoevsky as a stage that has already been passed; they are essentially temporary ideas with no currency. One can only remain under the charm of Stepan Trofimovich's style of reasoning for a certain time, but sooner or later there will come illumination. At the very beginning of the novel the narrator establishes a definitively retrospective tone: "Alas! We could do nothing but assent. We applauded our teacher and with what warmth, indeed! And, after all, my friends, don't we still hear to-day, every hour, at every step, the same 'charming,' 'clever,' 'liberal,' old Russian non-sense?"[73] Stepan Trofimovich's symbolic role in the novel is quite apparent: he is Petr Verkhovenskii's father, Stavrogin's tutor, and the "teacher" of a local circle of young men who will later form the diabolical circus. But at the same time, as is perfectly clear, he is bound by ties of friendship to the Chronicler, who possesses the vague yet appreciable advantage of objective moral appraisal as joint character and narrator. Stepan Trofimovich has tu-tored not only Stavrogin but also Liza and Dasha, the two main female characters of the novel, and he has been granted one trait which Dostoevsky bestows as a rare privilege on his characters: "It was wonderful how children took to him!"[74]

It is impossible to call the senior Verkhovenskii's personal influence defi-nitely immoral; the potential harm of such an influence is rooted in the ethical ambivalence of rational humanism and is revealed not in terms of the popular notions of "bad" and "good" but in the heart of the metaphysical foundation of ethics. Not without reason is Stepan Trofimovich "merely" Petr's father, and his influence on his son not formative (indeed, until the events related in the novel they have only seen each other twice) but, as it were, genetic. In this way Dostoevsky points to nihilism's hidden, "genetic" link to liberalism and rationalistic humanism, of which liberalism is a dif-fused expression. The irony of the "master liberal's" position lies in the fact that he is himself horrified by the nihilistic transformation of humanistic principles. "I agree that the author's fundamental idea is a true one," he says, referring to Chernyshevskii's *What Is to Be Done?* — "but that only makes it more awful. It's just our idea, exactly ours; we sowed the first seed, nurtured it, prepared the way, and indeed, what could they say new, after us? But, heavens! how it's all expressed, distorted, mutilated! . . . Were these the conclusions we were striving for? Who can understand the original idea in this?"[75]

Stepan Trofimovich's credo rests on an amorphously deistic idea à la Hegel: "I believe in God, *mais distinguons*, I believe in him as a Being who is conscious of Himself in me only. . . . As for Christianity, for all my genuine respect for it, I'm not a Christian. I am more of an antique pagan, like the real Goethe, or like an ancient Greek."[76] It is not surprising, therefore, that the senior Verkhovenskii is "passionately" fond of the "civic role." In the Hegelian system, drawn from the idea of pure reason, the civic society is proclaimed to be one of the degrees of manifestation of the moral substance with which the subject recognizes his own solidarity. The two other de-grees—the family and the state—are not as dear to Stepan Trofimovich's heart, but Dostoevsky never intended to make of him a consistent Hegelian. It is precisely the civic sphere that turns out to be the soil in which Stepan Trofimovich's self-awareness is awakened and faces the eternal ideas of truth, beauty, and good. Moreover, the enlightenment to which the author leads him at the end of the novel occurs gradually, as though touching each of the categories of this triad in turn.

Stepan Trofimovich's address during the rowdy party in Lembke's home begins with an exposure of the stupidity of those whom he himself would later call "devils": "Ladies and gentlemen, I've solved the whole mystery. The whole secret of their effect lies in their stupidity! Yes, gentlemen, if this stupidity were intentional, pretended and calculated, oh, that would be a stroke of genius! But we must do them justice: they don't pretend anything. . . . If it were expressed ever so little more cleverly, everyone would see at once the poverty of this shallow stupidity. But as it is, everyone is left wondering; no one can believe that it is such elementary stupidity."[77] But, having discerned the particular forgery, Stepan Trofimovich does not yet see the falseness of the whole ideological system, inimical to him on the surface but native at heart. Contrasting two ideological branches within the same rationalistic worldview, he is defending values which are in turn devalued when compared with a cardinally different value system—the metaphysical.

But this realization does not come to him until just before his death. In his muddled speech at the party he still clings to the hope that a liberal reconciliation with the "devils" within the framework of humanistic ideals will bring about the desired harmony: "Messieurs, the last word in this business— is forgiveness. . . . The enthusiasm of the youth of today is as pure and bright as in our age. All that has happened is a change of aim, the replacing of one beauty by another! The whole difficulty lies in the question which is more beautiful, Shakespeare or boots, Raphael or petroleum?" In his opinion the young generation "is coming to grief through being deceived only in the forms of beauty." This assertion seems utterly bizarre: why might "boots" and "pe-troleum" be forms of beauty, and on what basis is one form preferable to another? But, as Catteau observes, "Dostoevsky's contemporary reader would immediately recognise the symbols as part of an ideological contest in which the arms (the images) and the battleground (Russia in 1870) were quite familiar."[78] And Stepan Trofimovich's ultimate statement, which he makes "at the utmost pitch of excitement," delivers to the "battleground" one of Dostoevsky's favorite ideas, that without beauty life is impossible: "for there would be nothing left in the world. That's the secret at the bottom of everything, that's what history teaches! Even science would not exist a moment without beauty. . . . it would sink into bondage, you couldn't invent a nail even!"[79]

In Dostoevsky, beauty is never merely aesthetic form but always presupposes a spiritual dimension. This view is deeply rooted in Russian Christian tradition, most evidently in the Orthodox perception of the icon, where a phenomenon's aesthetic value is inseparable from its religious context. In the case of Dostoevsky, Jackson's concept of *obraz* and *bezobrazie*, which could be applied to a broad spectrum of issues, is also key to understanding the writer's idea of beauty. "Obraz, for Dostoevsky, is the axis of beauty in the Russian language. It is aesthetic form, and it is also the iconographic image, or icon, the visible symbol of the beauty of God."[80] *Obraz* is the antipode to *bezobrazie*, which means ugliness, or more literally, without image, without form, and, implicitly, without icon. Stepan Trofimovich's declaration of the place of beauty in the world exhibits the spiritual perspective that will be fully revealed only in the description of his final days. As a whole, his story, which both begins and concludes *The Devils,* not only serves as a logical frame, pointing to the importance of Stepan Trofimovich's biography for the narrative, but ultimately, with the aid of a direct appeal to the New Testament, acquires the meaning of a parable that elucidates the philosophical scheme of the whole novel. Dostoevsky's letter to Maikov, written shortly after the publication of the first part of the novel, leaves no doubt about the author's intentions. "Stepan Trofimovich is a secondary character; the novel won't be at all about him; but his story is closely linked to other events (main ones) in the novel, and therefore I've taken him as a kind of cornerstone for everything."[81]

The first Gospel text offers an interpretation of the causes that have ensured the conditions for the activation of evil; the second speaks of present effects and predicts future ones. With words from the Apocalypse, Dostoevsky illustrates the relativism of the rationalistic good represented in *The Devils* through the senior Verkhovenskii, its unreliable nature, and the absence of clear-cut criteria for definition: "And to the angel of the church in Laodicea write: The words of the Amen, the faithful and true witness, the beginning of God's creation. I know your works: you are neither cold nor hot! Would that you were cold or hot! So, because you are lukewarm, and neither cold nor hot, I will spew you out of my mouth. For you say, I am rich, I have prospered, and I need nothing; not knowing that you are wretched, pitiable, poor, blind, and naked."[82] (Dostoevsky first quotes these same lines in the chapter "At Tikhon's," but within Stavrogin's problematics they have a more particular and limited application.) The second Gospel quotation defines the cardinal idea of *The Devils,* being the same passage that Dostoevsky set as an epigraph to the entire chronicle. Thanks to this parable from the Gospel of Saint Luke, Stepan Trofimovich perceives the direct connection between himself and the "devils": "Those devils that come out of the sick man and enter into the swine—they are all the sores, all the foul contagions, all the impurities, all the devils great and small that have multiplied in that great invalid, our beloved Russia, in the course of ages and ages. . . . They are us, us and them, and Petrusha and *les autres avec lui,* and me perhaps at the head of them, and we shall cast ourselves down, possessed and raving from the rocks into the sea, and we shall be drowned—and a good thing too, for that is all we are fit for. But the sick man will be healed and 'will sit at the feet of Jesus' and all will look upon him with astonishment."[83]

After leading Stepan Trofimovich through a multitude of travails, Dostoevsky grants him the healing he hopes will be the lot of the whole of Russia. The "few words" spoken by Stepan Trofimovich before his death express a cathartic culmination to the basic philosophical problems of the novel. Having started from a conception of God as Being who is conscious of Himself in the subject only, Stepan Trofimovich discovers the God who is love, that is, the Christian God: "Love is higher than existence, love is the crown of existence; and how is it possible that existence should not be under its dominance?"[84] He arrives at conclusions which are directly contrary to "many of his former convictions." "If there is a God, then I am immortal," he says, concluding a sequence of similar polemic utterances in *The Devils,* such as the old captain's "If there's no God, how can I be a captain then?"[85] and Kirillov's "If there is no God, then I am God."[86] By showing the spiritual transformation of Stepan Trofimovich, Dostoevsky places a choice before the humanistic consciousness: to transform rationalistic good into metaphysical good, or else to surrender to its inevitable mutation into rationalistic evil. As Nikolai Berdiaev remarked, "humanism is the realm of the middle," and after Dostoevsky a return to the old rationalistic humanism is no longer possible.[87]

GOOD AS EVIL: CHRIST IN THE COURT OF IVAN KARAMAZOV

In his final novel Dostoevsky offers an unparalleled dialectical analysis of ethical problems. In the person of Ivan Karamazov, a rationalistic conception of the good is exhibited with a high degree of philosophical sophistication. Yet the thrust of Ivan's moral position lies not in the assertion of any logically complete system of ethics but in a paradoxical denial of the very conclusions he has reached through the rational logic he has chosen on principle. Sergei Gessen draws attention to how the dialectics of good is revealed in *The Brothers Karamazov* through the female personages. He finds that "the moral essence of Katia corresponds precisely to good as it is represented by the personality of Ivan," that is, arising from " frigid, burdensome duty."[88] It is easy to see how the abstract formalism of such a moral conception might be philosophically close to Kantian ethics, whose ultimate expression, the categorical imperative, is a universal principle based on the consciousness of moral duty. In Kant the categorical imperative affects the organization of the world, including even its theological aspect, since Kant deduces God from morality. Accordingly, Kant bases religion on morality, and the existence of God, which is not possible to prove on the basis of theoretical reason, is postulated through the moral principle in the realm of pure practical reason.

The connection between the philosophical problematics of Dostoevsky's final novel and Kant's fundamental conclusions has not eluded scholars. Iakov Golosovker, the author of small but very intriguing book *Dostoevsky and Kant*, asserts that the unnamed main characters in the novel are thesis and antithesis, that is the formative components of Kant's famous antinomies of pure reason by which Kant seeks to ground the impossibility of metaphysics as objective cognition, within the framework of his transcendental dialectics in the *Critique of Pure Reason*. Golosovker cites many examples from *The Brothers Karamazov*, mostly concerning Ivan, which provide clear responses to many of Kant's philosophical propositions. Moreover, he illustrates what he perceives to be an intellectual duel between Dostoevsky and Kant, in which the latter appears as the Devil, "the clown philosopher."[89] Nevertheless, in calling Ivan "the dialectical hero of Kant's antinomies" and Kant "the Devil," who has caught Ivan in this intellectual hell, Golosovker is essentially attacking Kant's method. At the same time, however, Golosovker undermines Kant's ultimate goal, which was to destroy what he considered to be false metaphysics and create a true one in its stead. Kant's antithetics are to serve as the means to achieve the first part of this task, since, showing the impossibility of proving the truth of both thesis and antithesis, antithetics allowed Kant to critique the ability of pure reason to resolve metaphysical questions.

Dostoevsky was in no way opposed to Kant in this central point. It is precisely the limitations of theoretical reason that Ivan means when he calls his mind "Euclidean." Moreover, Ivan's subsequent intellectual development continues in the same direction as Kant's philosophy: answers to questions of metaphysics are to be found in the sphere of ethics. However, it is here that the cardinal divergence between Dostoevsky and Kant occurs. Kant's ethical science, wittily termed "moral chemistry" by Soloviev, is fundamentally distinct from Dostoevsky's moral teaching. And Ivan's intellectual torments demonstrate this difference with perfect clarity. Kant rejects the confines of pure theoretical reason as insufficient for obtaining real knowledge, while Ivan's covetous mind is striving to break the limits of "Euclidean" reason, because it prevents him from "loving life." Kant's ideal is the realm of practical reason where man's actions must be governed by understanding the rules of moral duty. Dostoevsky's ideal is the realm of Christian love.[90]

While examining the Dostoevsky-Kant connection in *The Brothers Kara-mazov,* it is necessary at least to touch upon Vladimir Soloviev's attitude toward Kant, since, as I have suggested, Ivan's intellectual characteristics were to some degree inspired by the young philosopher. A. F. Losev maintains that "in the history of philosophy there have probably never been two philosophers so opposed in their thinking as Vladimir Soloviev and Kant"[91] As a contrast to the metaphysical dualism that arises in Kant because of the contradiction within reason itself, which is treated as the exclusive capacity of the cognizant subject (that is, man), Soloviev posits a dialectical monism, conditioned by the recognition of an objectively existing universal intellect whose thought is completely independent from the consciousness of the empirical subject. In his article on Kant, Soloviev extends the Kantian conception of the phenomenal world as representation by correlating it with the idea that the individual intellect formally coincides with the transcendental intellect. Therefore, while in both the ethical realm and the sphere of cognition man as empirical subject is subordinated to the existing moral order of the phenomenal world, this world in turn is created as a representation of man's own intellect, only as supreme reason, which operates and is revealed in man. From this point of view, the abyss posited by Kant between the moral and the physical worlds disappears (in principle). Between man's position in the two worlds there turns out to be not merely a correlation but a direct inner connection. "Truth," writes Soloviev, "is known by the empirical mind only formally, just as moral good exists for the empirical, heteronomous will only in the form of duty."[92]

It is not difficult to see that Soloviev's "point of view" in no way coincides with the point of view—or, rather, the absence of one—in Ivan Karamazov, who, as Golosovker puts it, "was swinging on a rocker arm of antinomies" above the Kantian abyss. In no way does this occur because

Ivan lacks a mastery of the art of dialectical proofs. The chief reason is that his potentialities of cognition are defined by the limitations of rational-empirical experience and not oriented toward the organic unity of "integral knowledge." "His mind is held captive," Alesha says of Ivan.[93] Using the parameters of Soloviev's theory of cognition, one can say that the absolute inner knowledge inherent in man as metaphysical being shows itself in Ivan's consciousness, as in any phenomenal consciousness, only partially. The comprehension of reality is achieved in three ways: material reality is comprehended through empirical science, ideal reality through abstract philosophy, and spiritual reality through intuitive experience. Complete truth is revealed in a proper synthesis of the mystical and natural elements through the instrumentality of the rational element. However, if Dostoevsky the philosopher, like his character, "needs to resolve his thought," for Dostoevsky the artist the most important thing of all is not truth itself but rather the search for truth; it is important "to love life more than the idea of it."

These pros and contras in the problematics of *The Brothers Karamazov* are resolved by the very plot of the novel, where Ivan Karamazov's life appears as a search for truth. The tragic paradox is that Ivan wants precisely a Christian truth, yet one founded on proof rather than faith. It is clear that his intellectual efforts are not founded on the idea of a harmony of faith and reason in the spirit of Thomas Aquinas (if one should seek an analogy in the history of philosophical thought), nor even on the transformed version of this idea in Neothomism, which marries Aquinas's system to Kant's philosophy. On this point Ivan's position is, perhaps, comparable to the doctrines of some medieval scholastics, and above all to the rationalization of faith by the "knight of dialectics," Peter Abelard, whose work *Sic et non* uses essentially the same method of "pros and contras" to question Church dogma and authority.

But for Ivan the chief obstacle to a proof of Christian truth becomes the problem of theodicy, that is, justification of God. One can say that Ivan's "theodicy" actually amounts to a justification not so much of God as of his own lack of faith in Him, since Ivan presents a claim to a God in whom he does not believe.[94] In positing the direct dependence of the metaphysical question on the ethical, Ivan would seem to be following the principle of Kant. But Dostoevsky's character actually violates the logic of the categorical imperative by doubting above all the very moral element that is supposed to prove the existence of God in Kant's system. Ivan doubts the presence of good in God. What is remarkable, however, is that he thus indirectly seeks to escape from the "false circle" of Kant's reasoning, where, as Soloviev

writes, "God and the immortal soul are inferred from morality, while morality itself is conditioned by God and the immortal soul."[95] But his final break
with "Euclidean," empirical reason occurs not in his adherence to metaphysical good but in his clash with metaphysical evil per se. Regardless of the
interpretation of the figure of the Devil in the plot structure of *The Brothers
Karamazov,* his actual appearance in the pages of the novel signifies a personification of metaphysical evil no less real than Goethe's Mephistopheles
or Mikhail Bulgakov's Woland.

According to Leibniz's classification, "evil may be taken metaphysically,
physically, and morally. Metaphysical evil consists in mere imperfection,
physical evil in suffering, and moral evil in sin."[96] Using this classification,
which was widely accepted in European philosophy, one can say that in
providing the grounds for his "rebellion," Ivan proceeds from a rejection
precisely of physical evil. He cites examples of the monstrous cruelty of
adults toward children, examples of the unheard-of sufferings specifically of
children, "so as to make it more obvious." (Incidentally, one of these stories,
describing the sadistic killing by Turks of nursing infants before their
mothers' eyes, is repeated almost verbatim by the General in Soloviev's
Three Conversations.) This staggering list of evil deeds is offered by Ivan as
support for his renunciation of the "future harmony": "If the suffering of
children goes to make up the sum of suffering needed to buy truth, then I
assert beforehand that the whole of truth is not worth such a price."[97] He
"does not want harmony for love of mankind." But he does not want *theoretical* harmony for his *theoretical* love of mankind, and he has taken "children only" not just "to make it more obvious" but also because it is for them
that he makes an exception in his *lack of love* for humanity. It is not without
reason that Dostoevsky begins the chapter "Rebellion" with Ivan's admission:
"I never could understand how it's possible to love one's neighbors."[98] Dostoevsky's words from *The Diary of a Writer* may serve as a commentary on
Ivan's bewilderment: "Love for humanity is even entirely unthinkable, incomprehensible, and *utterly impossible without faith in the immortality of
the human soul to go along with it*."[99]

Does Ivan possess such a belief? When Fedor Pavlovich Karamazov asks
him, "And is there immortality, Ivan? At least some kind, at least a little, a
teeny-tiny one?"—Ivan replies categorically: "There is no immortality either."[100] Therefore, Ivan's love for people is akin to that of the Grand Inquisitor whom Ivan has "made up." "They both" fail to understand the full
essence of God's love for humanity: "Christ's love for people is in its kind a
miracle impossible on earth."[101] But at the same time, while considering
people unworthy of God's love, Ivan also considers God's love insufficient,

since it does not deliver human life from suffering. The methodological root of Ivan's failure to comprehend God's love, that is, His goodness, lies in the fact that even as he is proceeding from the empirical experience of physical evil, he attempts to understand the nature of metaphysical Good.[102] Leading Christ to a court of rationalist morality, Ivan denies Him ethical justification, declaring that Good is thus evil. And only by passing through the recognition of moral evil—his own sin—and coming into contact with metaphysical evil—"mere imperfection" (as Leibniz put it, with scientific accuracy) in the form of a "Russian gentleman" who dreams of becoming incarnate in a "fat, two-hundred-and-fifty-pound merchant's wife"—does Ivan approach (but only approach) a justification of the Good, that is, the main question of theodicy.

"This question," writes Sergei Bulgakov, "has been answered by theologians, for whom it is formulated as the problem of God's design, and by philosophers—both optimists, like Leibniz, and pessimists, like his vicious critic Voltaire, or Schopenhauer and Hartmann, spiritualists and materialists, deists and atheists. . . . Every philosopher, or rather, every thinking and therefore philosophizing person must resolve this question at his own peril and expense, not with reason, not with logic only, but with his whole being."[103] At the beginning of the novel Ivan poses this question logically, and just as logically answers it with his intention "to return the ticket." But at the end of the novel Ivan resolves this question "with his whole being." The responsibility for evil, which he had placed entirely on God, turns out to be also his, Ivan's, responsibility. He may never have found his own "rational" answer to the eternal question of theodicy, but it is precisely through Ivan that the answer given by the elder Zosima finds its corroboration: "Each one of us is guilty on behalf of all and for all on earth."[104] And obviously this famous statement serves not only as a formula of ethical responsibility but also as a formula of unity.[105]

The methodological approach Soloviev applied to the problem of good and evil in *The Justification of the Good* corresponds to the array of formulations in Dostoevsky. In his treatise Soloviev chooses a method of analysis basically similar to that which guides Ivan Karamazov, yet in contrast to Ivan, Soloviev examines not the Good (with a capital G) but the good; in other words, he is judging not God but human morality, as indicated by the title: *The Justification of the Good: A Moral Philosophy.* Thus the method of rational analysis, with which both Ivan and Soloviev operate, forces the former down a philosophical dead-end while steadily leading the latter toward his goal. Ivan, demanding a rational meaning for life, strives in the spirit of the tradition of theodicy to subject metaphysical Good to purely rational analysis. The hopelessness of his attempt leads him to revolt—that is, to a condemnation, not a justification, of the Good. Soloviev makes his goal not the justification of the Good, which for him is a given truth, but the justification of the good, as a subject of moral philosophy. At the same time, his methodologically rational analysis of ethical elements bears an inner connection to metaphysics, though not as a philosophical discipline but rather as its transcendental essence.

As stated above, the observations of Soloviev's critics concerning the insufficiently metaphysical character of the ethical system in *The Justification of the Good* and, most important, the separation of ethics from metaphysics, while formally correct, were employed unjustly to reproach the author, since he purposely was not conducting a metaphysical investigation into the Divine Being and the origin of evil in the world.[106] Even so, Soloviev's metaphysical views are revealed in *The Justification of the Good* with perfect clarity. "The individual human personality is infinite: this is the axiom of moral philosophy," he declares.[107] The very organization of the treatise shows that in constructing his moral philosophy, Soloviev has followed the same metaphysical and logical principle as he did in building his conception of the God-man. The work is divided into three parts: "Good in human nature," "Good from God," and "Good through the history of mankind." The first part examines the question of natural human morality, that is, organic and imperfect, the second part discusses the perfection of good in God, and the third part is devoted to the process of perfection (or the concordance of the imperfection in human nature with the perfection on God) as the goal of life. Thus *The Justification of the Good* contains not only the philosopher's ethical theory but also his ethical program, which is directly tied to the metaphysical program he presented in the *Lectures on God-manhood*.

"Every single person, as an individual, possesses the possibility of perfection, or of positive infinity," writes Soloviev.[108] If the achievement of perfection is regarded by Soloviev as a potential, then perfection itself (in its absolute expression) is accepted by him as a given. Therefore, in his ethical treatise metaphysical Good appears as a religious *fact* and not a philosophical *question,* which obviously deprives the problem of theodicy of most of its relevance. Herein lies the chief distinction of Soloviev's work from customary philosophical and theological treatments, where the question of theodicy is a necessary condition for the analysis of ethical problems.

For Dostoevsky as for Soloviev, moral good is justified by the existence of metaphysical Good. Moreover, it is justified by the absoluteness and, "finally," determinedness of metaphysical Good: "I know that I will finally be reconciled, that I, too, will finish my quadrillion and be let in on the

secret," the Devil acknowledges in *The Brothers Karamazov*.[109] For Dostoevsky the writer, the important thing is not the "secret" but the "quadrillion":
he confronts, combines, and experiments with various manifestations of good
and evil, letting us listen to the arguments and justifications of the one and
the other, thereby blazing the "quadrillion-long" trail to metaphysical Good,
which, for all its mystery, is no "secret" at all.

Conclusion

The Art of Integral Vision

Nothing in the world is intelligible except in and starting from the whole.
—*Pierre Teilhard de Chardin*

The theme of unity underlies the argument of this book. Both Soloviev and Dostoevsky, thanks to their mastery of the art of integral vision, succeeded in exploring this theme on many levels: it manifests itself in their writings as a *structural pattern* and as a *philosophical conception,* as an *artistic principle* and as a *religious postulate.*

Dostoevsky's novels consistently exhibit a certain intrinsic unity, serving as a *structural* constituent and permitting those novels to be interpreted as a cycle. As early as in 1911, Viacheslav Ivanov wrote: "Dostoevsky's labyrinth was a novel, or rather a cycle of novels. . . . It is for good reason that Annenskii attempted to draw a kind of schematic sketch, determining the psychological and almost biographical connection between the various characters of the single action Dostoevsky depicted over the course of several novels."[1]

As an *artistic* dimension of Dostoevsky's novels, the principle of unity has become the subject of elaborate studies, among which Mikhail Bakhtin's work occupies a special place. According to Bakhtin, the idea of unity manifests itself in Dostoevsky polyphonically, that is, as unity in diversity, a "unity of a higher order." One may say that Dostoevsky's polyphonism performs the same function with respect to unity as universalism in Soloviev. Nonuniversal or nonpolyphonic unity is deprived of freedom; it is authoritarian and (in Bakhtin's terms) monological. Polyphonism is the artistic expression of philosophical universalism. Thus Dostoevsky's polyphonism and Soloviev's universalism stand as main characteristics of their common *conception* of unity.

Finally, in Soloviev and Dostoevsky the idea of unity advances as a *religious postulate* of the Christian worldview. The notions of unity and plurality are among the most important in defining the relationship between humanity and Christ. In Soloviev's view, Christ's "divine organism" embodies unity of the "first kind," that is, a creative unity that draws the plurality of the elements into itself as the One. The unity of the "second kind," the phenomenal unity of the creation, is realized in ideal, or "normative," mankind. Perfect plurality drawn into unity is denoted as God-manhood.

In this respect, the choice between the God-man and the man-god may be viewed as the choice between a unity inclusive of plurality and a unity exclusive of it. Thus what seems a mere quantitative nuance in terms of one system, in qualitative terms betrays an abyss dividing two opposite systems. Dostoevsky's characters are placed on the edge of this abyss, endowed with both the right and the opportunity to choose.

Similar correlations are discernible in the two authors' attitudes to theocracy. The societal form of human unity, achieved through the consolidation of power in the hands of ecclesiastical and state institutions, cannot be called true theocracy. A unity that autocratically suppresses plurality symbolizes not theocracy but totalitarianism. Only the ideal balance of plurality in unity is able to guarantee the ideal theocratic society, based on the inspirational force of love. Even though this interpretation eliminates neither the practical nor even the theoretical difficulties addressed in the book, at least it properly poses the theocratic question.

Within the discussion of the ethical teachings of Soloviev and Dostoevsky, the idea of unity is implied as a decisive factor in the discourse about the autonomy of the good. The good as a moral category is always correlated to the metaphysical Good, which is the absolute unity.

The unity of all things is the most prominent theme of modern Russian religious thought, and there is no doubt that Soloviev's metaphysics remains the most influential model of this idea. However, as such the idea of unity is so all-inclusive that, away from its concrete expressions, it becomes evasively abstract. This is why in speaking each time about unity, one means perforce the reflection of it in a particular notion. In truth, the entire dynamics of human consciousness and existence arises from the collision of multifarious views on unity and plurality. This is not surprising: after all, oppositions such as the individual and the collective, integration and fragmentation, cosmos and chaos, which are relevant to any discourse, from political to poetic, are reducible to the basic philosophical dichotomy of *one and many*. All this reflects on the relationship of unity and diversity in human culture. As T. S. Eliot observed: "Excess of unity may be due to barbarism and may lead to tyranny; excess of division may be due to decadence and may also lead to tyranny: either excess will prevent further development in culture. The proper degree of unity and of diversity cannot be determined for all people at all times."[2]

The contemporary mindset, however, reacts to the idea of unity at best with ambivalence, and at worst by rejecting it. Frightened by the encroachment of totalitarianism in this century, modern thought at the same time has lost the sense of harmony as a value. As a result, the idea of unity, which intimately pertains to the notions of both harmony and totalitarianism, has discredited itself. It has begun to connote either threatening reality or an unattainable utopia, or a combination of both.[3] The contemporary approach to the idea of unity can be analyzed in terms of various disciplines and theories. I will mention only a few.

The twentieth century has seen semiotics become one of the most influential fields in the humanities. Arising out of two scholarly traditions, the American philosophy of pragmatism and the European science of linguistics, this discipline offers an extremely productive approach and flexible methods for the study of every aspect of culture. Proceeding from the simplest datum and analyzing all the subsequent data in terms of similarity and difference, semiotics provides a sui generis example of the relationship between unity and plurality. On the one hand, the notion of "sign" determines the unity and interconnection of all signs within the system. On the other hand, the number of systems is by no means limited, thus implying their infinite plurality. Intrasystemic unity therefore becomes an isolated phenomenon that relates to the plurality of systems as a mere methodological principle. This accounts for the limitations of semiotic thinking. Its logic follows from the particular to plurality, but it is unable to supply the procedures leading from plurality to unity. This dilemma is not lost on semioticians: as Yuri Lotman observed, "the complex object is reduced to the sum of the simple ones. Heuristic expediency (the convenience of analysis) begins to be perceived as the ontological faculty of the object."[4]

Furthermore, the very principle of intrasystemic unity is fraught with the danger of "semiotic totalitarianism." This fitting term was coined as a warning against "the assumption that everything has a meaning relating to the seamless whole, a meaning one could discover if one only had the code."[5] One may observe that this assumption is rooted in various deterministic theories in science and philosophy, paralleling, for instance, the argument which holds that any description of the state of the universe stumbles upon our insufficient knowledge of its initial conditions. In terms of the Bakhtinian philosophical discourse, "the seamless whole" stands for an example of "monological," that is, imperfect unity, while the true "polyphonic" unity is fulfilled in diversity.

The recognition of the hidden flaws of semiotics led to the revision of some of its basic concepts. Thus the Russian school of semiotics introduced the notion of "semiosphere." With the help of this notion the entire semiotic space began to be treated as one mechanism, and the emphasis radically shifted: not a sign as such but the semiosphere as a whole became the starting point of semiotic analysis. This signifies the eventual adaptation on the part of semioticians to the philosophical principle of unity in diversity.

Early in the century Soloviev's friend, the philosopher Ernst Radlov, defined harmony precisely as a notion which implies "unity in diversity." "In music," he writes, "it means consonance of many sounds in one whole, and the Pythagoreans took this from music for their teaching on the harmony of spheres."[6]

It is clear that, by abolishing the idea of harmony, the postmodern consciousness has also abolished the idea of unity. According to the clear-cut statement of one contemporary German philosopher, the general characteristic of postmodernity is reducible to the following formulation: "Postmodernism begins where the whole ends. . . . It positively exploits the end of the whole and unity, attempting to enhance and develop the manifest plurality in its legitimacy and originality."[7] Postmodernism, in other words, is a celebration of diversity without unity, instead of unity in diversity. As a result, the cultural criterion is determined in terms not of unity but of plurality. Tradition is replaced by vogue, the author by readers, and message by the "system of opinions." Human life, as well as human history, are perceived as a sequence of fragments and episodes. In the account of Alasdair MacIntyre, this tendency to partition each life into a variety of segments, each with its own norms and modes of behavior—the tendency to think atomistically about human action and to analyze complex actions and transactions in terms of simple components—makes the unity of human life invisible to us.[8] It must be said that Dostoevsky, a born paradoxicalist, offered radical insights into the psychology of modern man, exploring the hidden dissonance of existence and, consequently, crucially contributing to the development of modernism. Yet, despite Dostoevsky's apparent "modernism," he was capable of looking beyond man's state into his essence.

In the realm of natural science, the idea of unity has always exercised a powerful impact. Darwin's evolutionary theory, Mendeleev's periodic table, Newton's laws and theory of gravitation reflect the idea of unity, respectively, in biology, chemistry, and physics. At the threshold of a new millennium, the centrality of this idea as regards various branches of sciences cannot be doubted. Furthermore, it is becoming clear that sciences themselves form the increasing order of unity, an indication of their tendency to function as unity in diversity. This does not mean to deduce one science from another, but to discover the deeper principles operating beyond the confines of the given discipline. Thus molecular biology rests upon chemistry, and chemistry on quantum physics. Finally, the quest for the "theory of everything" is pivotal as regards the contemporary dispute within fundamental physics itself. Is it possible to create a unified theory not deducible from any ulterior theory which would prove that absolute unity does exist? Steven Weinberg, winner of the Nobel Prize in physics, whose views are shared by many leading physicists, has written: "Of course a final theory would not end scientific research, not even pure scientific research, nor even pure research in physics. . . . A final theory will be final in only one sense—it will bring to an end a certain sort of science, the ancient search for those principles that cannot be explained in terms of deeper principles."[9] It is understandable why among present-day physicists, regardless of their individual religious beliefs, it has become a widespread metaphor to refer to the final laws of nature as "the mind of God." However, it would be naïve (and vulgar) to use this fact as a basis for far-reaching conclusions: the task of physics cannot be mixed with that of metaphysics. In this respect, as in general, any analogies between science and the humanities should be made with caution and an awareness of the subtle difference between mixture and unity.

The concept of unity may reveal itself as the philosophical foundation of a scientific search or as a source of aesthetic harmony, as a philosophical idea in religious formulation or as religious truth in philosophical interpretation. Unity can be used as a method and can be established as an end in itself. Soloviev's teaching reflects all these nuances most comprehensively. His philosophy, in the words of Sergei Bulgakov, "answers the most profound and elevated needs of the human spirit: the aspiration to an integral worldview that would be not only theoretical but also practical."[10] It would be an exaggeration to suggest that Dostoevsky implemented and, at the same time, pursued the idea of unity with the equal thoroughness. Nevertheless, the artistic form and philosophical substance of his work unmistakably communicate this idea. Moreover, the unity and wholeness of his "integral knowledge" arise from the very nature of his genius. As Soloviev pointed out, Dostoevsky "was at once a mystic, a humanist, and a naturalist. He commanded a vital feeling of inner connection with the suprahuman, and was in this sense a mystic; it was in this very feeling that he located human freedom and power. He knew all human evil but still believed in all human good and was, by general admission, a true humanist. But his faith in man was free from any onesided idealism or spiritualism: he took man in all his fullness and reality."[11] In 1838, the young Dostoevsky wrote to his brother: "The poet, in a transport of inspiration, comprehends God. Consequently, he fulfills the purpose of philosophy."[12] Soloviev and Dostoevsky shared a single higher aim, a single vision of their purpose, and each of them in his "comprehension of God" was both a poet *and* a philosopher.

No single photograph portrays Dostoevsky and Soloviev together. But we could easily imagine both of them in the same picture: two very different men, thirty years apart in age; one an ex-revolutionary, ex-convict, an expert on human psychology, who knew firsthand both spiritual inspiration and the power of temptation; the other, a young prodigy from a prominent intellectual family, a university professor, whose deepest emotions were provoked by unique mystical experience and passion for philosophical inquiry. The great Russian writer and the great Russian philosopher united by the Christian vision of unity.

Notes

INTRODUCTION

1 Robert Belknap, *The Genesis of "The Brothers Karamazov,"* 21.
2 Lopatin, "Filosovskoe mirosozertsanie V. S. Solov'eva," 54.
3 Levitskii, "Vl. Solov'ev i Dostoevskii," 209.
4 D., 14:288; *The Brothers Karamazov,* 318.
5 As defined by Andrzej Walicki, *narodnost'* "means both nationality and the German *Volkstum,* and was not only intended to convey a certain nationalistic trend, but also reflected the effort of the autocratic regime to expand its social base, to rely *directly* on the 'people' in the broad sense of the word." See Walicki, *The Slavophile Controversy,* 46.
6 Novikov, *Izbrannye sochineniia,* 387–93.
7 S., 3:121.
8 Odoevskii, *Sochineniia,* 1:41.
9 Ibid., 202.
10 Ibid., 298.
11 Chereiskii, *Pushkin i ego okruzhenie,* 483.
12 Pushkin, *Polnoe sobranie sochinenii,* 12:303.
13 Chaadaev's "exclusion" from the cultural fabric of nineteenth-century Russia is

comparable to the banishment of free philosophical inquiry from Russian culture during the Soviet period: in both cases the continuity of the creative cultural process was violated (although the scales of these violations are, of course, incommensurable).

14 Zen'kovskii, *Istoriia russkoi filosofii*, 1:162. It should be noted that the "Russocentrist" interpretation of Chaadaev continues to find advocates. Thus Walicki considers the problem of Russia "the starting point and central issue of Chaadaev's philosophy" and cites with approval the Soviet author M. Grigorian, who in an article on Chaadaev (see *Iz istorii russkoi filosofii*) criticizes Zen'kovskii's emphasis on Chaadaev's "purely metaphysical and theological conceptions" (Walicki, *The Slavophile Controversy*, 87). For a recent survey of the ongoing dispute about the foundation of Chaadaev's philosophy, see the commentary to *Philosophical Works of Peter Chaadaev*, ed. Raymond T. McNally and Richard Tempest, 260.

15 Chaadaev, *Polnoe sobranie sochinenii i izbrannye pis'ma*, 1:381, 383.

16 Soloviev's father, the famous historian Sergei M. Soloviev, was personally acquainted with Chaadaev and saw him socially in the 1850s. See ibid., 2:616.

17 *Letters*, 3:248.

18 From the verb *sobirat'* (to put together, to unite) and the noun *sobor* (meaning both "council," the organ of Holy Spirit, and "cathedral").

19 Kireevskii, *Polnoe sobranie sochinenii*, 1:275.

20 See Khomiakov, *Polnoe sobranie sochinenii*, 1:148; and Raeff, *Russian Intellectual History*, 212 f.

21 In this connection, one entry from Kireevskii's archive is not without interest: "I. V. Kireevskii in 1834 married Miss Natalia Petrovna Arbenina, who was brought up according to the strict rules of Christian piety. . . . Some time later they started to read Schelling together, and when they would come to great, luminous thoughts, and I. V. Kireevskii demanded that his wife marvel, she at first responded that these thoughts were known to her from the writings of the Church Fathers. She repeatedly demonstrated this to him in the works of the Church Fathers, which sometimes compelled Kireevskii to read page after page. He was displeased to recognize that indeed there was in the Church Fathers much that he had admired in Schelling. He did not like to admit this, but used to take the books secretly from his wife, and read them with fascination" (Kireevskii, *Polnoe sobranie sochinenii*, 1:285 f.).

22 For more on this subject, see Chap. 4.

23 S., 1:151; Kireevskii, *Polnoe sobranie sochinenii*, 1:264.

24 Kireevskii, *Polnoe sobranie sochinenii*, 1:252; S., 1:151. It is interesting that they both metaphorically personify philosophy.

25 As Walicki essentially does in *The Slavophile Controversy*, chap. 15.

26 In fact, the analytical approach is much more prominent in another of Kireevskii's essays, one not mentioned by Walicki, "A Review of the Present-day Condition of Literature" (*Polnoe sobranie sochinenii*, 1:121 ff.), which Soloviev seems to have had in mind when he refers in his dissertation to "the correct, albeit too

general critique of philosophical rationalism . . . in several articles by Khomiakov and I. Kireevskii" (S., 1:58).

27 Kireevskii, *Polnoe sobranie sochinenii*, 1:243.

28 In his youth, Kireevskii was a member of the Wisdom-lovers' circle.

29 Kireevskii, *Polnoe sobranie sochinenii*, 1:264.

30 S., 1:151.

31 Walicki's examination of Soloviev's relationship with the Slavophiles is primarily concerned with the influence of the latter on the former. Following Evgenii Trubetskoi's somewhat artificial periodization of Soloviev's creative life, Walicki regards the whole first "preparatory" period (that is, up to 1881) as the "Slavophile stage of his intellectual evolution," thereby obscuring all other philosophical influences on the young Soloviev and, more important, the originality of his own outlook.

32 Tolstoi, *Polnoe sobranie sochinenii*, 62:128.

33 See Soloviev's articles under the general heading "The National Question in Russia."

34 Vl. Solov'ev, *Sochineniia v dvukh tomakh*, 2:289.

35 Bakhtin, *Problems of Dostoevsky's Poetics*, 296.

36 Soloviev's influence on Bakhtin, though increasingly an object of study, has still not been dealt with thoroughly. In touching upon this question here, if only tangentially, I feel it necessary to point out that among the scores of Russian thinkers who have been influenced by Soloviev, Bakhtin stands out for his phenomenological approach to Soloviev's religious and philosophical concepts. This is, in part, one of the reasons that Bakhtin's development of Soloviev's ideas lacks the aura of mystical idealism characteristic, for example, of the Solovievian echoes in Viacheslav Ivanov. Further comments on the reflections of Soloviev's ideas in Bakhtin can be found in Chap. 1. For a stimulating discussion of the Soloviev-Bakhtin connection, see B. Groys, "Problema avtorstva u Bakhtina i russkaia filosofskaia traditsiia," *Russian Literature* 26 (1989): 113–30; and C. Emerson, "Russian Orthodoxy and the Early Bakhtin," *Religion and Literature* 22, nos. 2–3 (1990): 109–32.

37 Bakhtin, *Problems of Dostoevsky's Poetics*, 289. On Bakhtin's conception of unity in Dostoevsky, see Morson and Emerson, *Mikhail Bakhtin: Creation of a Prosaics*, chap. 6.

38 Bakhtin, *Problems of Dostoevsky's Poetics*, 3.

39 In fact, by calling Dostoevsky the creator of "a new artistic model of the world," Bakhtin assigns him a role similar to that which Soloviev assigned to Dostoevsky, whom he called the herald of a new religious art. (Of course, this analogy is predicated on the comprehensive meaning Soloviev read into the term *religious*.)

40 Bakhtin, *Problems of Dostoevsky's Poetics*, 6; Morson and Emerson, *Mikhail Bakhtin: Creation of a Prosaics*, 240.

41 Bakhtin's rejection of "ideological monologism," which he sees reflected in idealistic philosophy, does not preclude comparison of his interpretation of unity with

Soloviev's, due to the special nature of Soloviev's idealism. In Soloviev, the "affirmation of the unity of existence" is never transformed into the "principle of the unity of the consciousness." (See Bakhtin, *Problems of Dostoevsky's Poetics*, 80.)

42 S., 8:464.

43 Ibid., 2:311.

44 Bakhtin, *Problems of Dostoevsky's Poetics*, 298.

45 S., 1:288.

46 Bakhtin, *Problems of Dostoevsky's Poetics*, 295.

47 Ibid., 43.

48 Ibid., 288.

49 S., 1:349.

50 The religious nature of Bakhtin's worldview remains a subject of debate. Although Morson and Emerson are correct in denying that Bakhtin's works "are really a theology in code," at the same time I consider a purely secular interpretation of Bakhtin's thought unsatisfactory, especially with regard to his works on Dostoevsky. Whether he purposely based himself on theological concepts, or whether theology arose spontaneously from his works, it is clear that this element is present. According to Boris Groys, the "united spirit," standing as a synonym for the Christian God, "recedes into the text, though it does not completely lose a certain eschatological and theological shading" ("Problema avtorstva," 125). How strong is this shading? There can be no precise measure. But if we seek to describe a *possible* correlation of Bakhtin's conception of the polyphonic novel with a Christian model of the world, his method, as I see it, might more accurately be defined not as a code but as literary critical symbolism. See on this question Clark and Holquist, *Mikhail Bakhtin*, 247-52; Introduction to Morson and Emerson, *Rethinking Bakhtin*; Morson and Emerson, *Mikhail Bakhtin: Creation of a Prosaics*, 111, 114; Emerson, "Russian Orthodoxy and the Early Bakhtin"; and Jackson, *Dialogues with Dostoevsky*, 269-92.

51 Sergei Soloviev and Lev Shestov emphasize the differences rather than the affinities between Soloviev and Dostoevsky. See S. Solov'ev, *Zhizn' i tvorcheskaia evoliutsiia Vladimira Solov'eva*, 297-98; Shestov, *Umozrenie i otkrovenie*, 29.

52 The basic edition of Soloviev's writings is the twelve-volume *Sobranie sochinenii Vladimira Solov'eva* (Brussels, 1966, 1970). (Sometimes an additional volume, *Pis'ma i prilozhenie*, is referred to as volume 13.) This edition (with the exception of volumes 11 and 12) is a reprint of the second *Sobranie sochinenii* (St. Petersburg, 1911-14) and of the four volumes of *Pis'ma Vladimira Sergeevicha Solov'eva* (St. Petersburg, 1908, 1909, 1911, 1923).

53 Vl. Solov'ev, *Pis'ma*, 3:80.

54 Konstantin Leontiev, *O Dostoevskom: Sbornik statei*, 17. It must be said that Leontiev, while noting Dostoevsky's "belief in man," is critical in his examination of the character of that belief; see Chap. 1.

55 Shestov's book *Dostoevsky and Nietzsche*, first published in 1902, immediately provoked heated debate in the critical press. Among those who accused Shestov of an "arbitrary interpretation" of Dostoevsky, one should mention Mikhail

Gershenzon (*Nauchnoe slovo* 2 [1904]) and Nikolai Berdiaev ("Tragediia i obydennost'"; see Berdiaev, *Filosofiia tvorchestva, kul'tury i iskusstva*, vol. 2). Berdiaev was quite persistent in his criticism of Shestov's philosophical and religious views. (See, for example, "Iz perepiski N. A. Berdiaeva, S. N. Bulgakova i L. I. Shestova," 258.) However, it would seem that we cannot fully comprehend Shestov's interpretation of Dostoevsky without considering the nature of Shestov's religious thought, which, as Vasilii Zen'kovskii remarked, is not anthropocentric but theocentric (Zen'kovskii, *Istoriia russkoi filosofii*, 2:320). On Nietzsche and Dostoevsky, see also Jackson, *Dialogues with Dostoevsky*, chap. 13.

56 Properly speaking, the definition "religio-philosophical" has a tautological ring in the case of Soloviev and Dostoevsky, since they had no other philosophy than the religious.

57 Vl. Solov'ev, *Pis'ma*, 3:5.

CHAPTER 1

1 See Vl. Solov'ev, *Filosofiia iskusstva i literaturnaia kritika* (1991); *Stikhotvoreniia, estetika, literaturnaia kritika* (1990). [An Address Given at the Grave of F. M. Dostoevsky] was first published by G. Kjetsaa in *Scando-Slavica* 31 (1985): 109–16. The "Note" has two versions, reflecting in the variant reading essential aspects of Soloviev's attitude toward Lev Tolstoi. See the commentary to Vl. Solov'ev, *Stikhotvoreniia, estetika, literaturnaia kritika*, 524; also, the following page contains a brief summary of Soloviev's view of Dostoevsky's religiosity (in a letter to Konstantin Leontiev), a view that requires careful interpretation.

2 A partial summary of the virtually boundless critical material devoted to Dostoevsky can be found in V. Seduro's *Dostoevsky in Russian Literary Criticism, 1846–1956*. I have purposely excluded from my discussion two important books, Lev Shestov's *Dostoevsky and Nietzsche: The Philosophy of Tragedy* (1903) and Nikolai Berdiaev's *Dostoevsky's Worldview* (1923), since both authors approach Dostoevsky's work almost entirely from the vantage point of their own philosophical constructions.

3 See, among others, D., 25: 28–31; Grigorovich, *Literaturnye vospominaniia*; Annenkov, *Literaturnye vospominaniia*; and Panaev, *Literaturnye vospominaniia*.

4 Belinskii, *Sobranie sochinenii*, 8:131.

5 Ibid., 404.

6 Annenkov, *Literaturnye vospominaniia*, 258.

7 Belinskii, *Sobranie sochinenii*, 8:128.

8 In 1898 Soloviev gave a speech about Belinskii, the text of which has not yet been discovered (see Vl. Solov'ev, *Stikhotvoreniia, estetika, literaturnaia kritika*, 489).

9 Dobroliubov, *Literaturnaia kritika*, 2:362.

10 D., 18:84.

11 Ibid., 129.

12 Dobroliubov, *Literaturnaia kritika*, 2:431, 434.

13 Ibid., 440.

14 Ibid., 472.

15 In this connection, see V. Erofeev's interesting essay "Vera i gumanizm Dosto-evskogo," in his *V labirinte prokliatykh voprosov*.

16 Pisarev, *Sochineniia*, 4:316.

17 S., 3:185.

18 Pisarev, *Sochineniia*, 4:351.

19 Ibid., 320.

20 D., 7:141.

21 Merezhkovskii, *Polnoe sobranie sochinenii*, 11:175.

22 See Shestov, *Dostoevskii i Nitsshe*.

23 N. Kotrelev points out an error in various editions tying Mikhailovskii's attack on Soloviev to the second of his "Three Speeches in Memory of Dostoevsky" (see Vl. Solov'ev, *Stikhotvoreniia, estetika, literaturnaia kritika*, 513; cf. Mikhailovskii, *Literaturno-kriticheskie stat'i*, 641).

24 Mikhailovskii, *Literaturno-kriticheskie stat'i*, 184.

25 Ibid., 186.

26 Shestov, *Dostoevskii i Nitsshe*, 88.

27 See below for the Leontiev connection.

28 Erofeev, "Vera i gumanizm Dostoevskogo," 12.

29 Bakhtin, *Problems of Dostoevsky's Poetics*, 54.

30 Vl. Solov'ev, *Stikhotvoreniia, estetika, literaturnaia kritika*, 198.

31 Ibid., 199.

32 From an editorial note by Ivan Aksakov—see ibid., 523.

33 Leont'ev, "O vsemirnoi liubvi," 24.

34 Vl. Solov'ev, *Stikhotvoreniia, estetika, literaturnaia kritika*, 193.

35 Ibid.

36 Leont'ev, "O vsemirnoi liubvi," 17. As Gibson remarks, "Dostoevsky was fasci-nated to the end of his days, with the earthly paradise (after all, Christians do pray: thy will be done on earth as it is in Heaven); he demythologizes hell, and says nothing about the fear of the Lord, which for Leontiev was all-important" (*The Religion of Dostoevsky*, 7).

37 Zen'kovskii, *Istoriia russkoi filosofii*, 1:452.

38 Vl. Solov'ev, *Pis'ma*, 1:21.

39 Radlov, *Vladimir Solov'ev: Zhizn' i uchenie*, 69.

40 Vl. Solov'ev, *Pis'ma*, 2:117.

41 Vl. Solov'ev, *Stikhotvoreniia, estetika, literaturnaia kritika*, 512. The editor of this volume, N. Kotrelev, gives an excellent historical commentary to Soloviev's "Three Speeches."

42 Ibid., 167.

43 Ibid.

44 Mikhailovskii, *Literaturno-kriticheskie stat'i*, 184.

45 Vl. Solov'ev, *Stikhotvoreniia, estetika, literaturnaia kritika*, 168.

46 D., 10:373; *The Possessed (The Devils)*, 416.

47 S., 3:190.

48 In employing here the notions of *synthesis* and *dialectics*, I must point out that Soloviev defines more precisely his own use of these terms in the third chapter of *The Philosophical Principles of Integral Knowledge* (S., 1:341).

49 See Chap. 4.

50 S., 3:190.

51 For instance, assigning a special role in the formation of Christian theology to the Jews, he sees the strength of Israel in a capacity for the materialization of the personal element, because of which, in his opinion, it was precisely in their midst that the incarnation of the Deity occurred, and thanks to which the future Israel will serve as active mediator for the humanization of material life and nature. See "Evreistvo i khristianskii vopros," in S., 4:136–85.

52 Vl. Solov'ev, *Stikhotvoreniia, estetika, literaturnaia kritika,* 168.

53 Ibid., 171.

54 Ibid., 176.

55 Ibid., 178.

56 Losev, *Vladimir Solov'ev i ego vremia,* 509.

57 For more on this, see Chap. 4.

58 S., 3:214.

59 Ibid., 212.

60 Ibid., 214.

61 Losev, *Vladimir Solov'ev i ego vremia,* 513. In fact, Soloviev and Dostoevsky's "intuition for matter" is rooted in the kenotic tradition, with its respect for matter which, in the words of St. John of Damascus, "God has filled with His grace and power. . . . Do not despise matter, for it is not despicable. God has made nothing despicable" (St. John of Damascus, *On the Divine Images,* 23-24).

62 R. Gal'tseva and I. Rodnianskaia consider Soloviev to be in general "the coryphaeus of Russian philosophical criticism, and indeed, its original founder"—see their introduction to Vl. Solov'ev, *Filosofiia iskusstva i literaturnaia kritika,* 10.

63 As the framework of this study does not allow me to trace the full extent of the link between Soloviev's writings and subsequent works in Russian thought devoted to Dostoevsky, I must limit my choice of examples of such a kinship.

64 At the same time, it must be noted that this did not prevent the "irresponsible" Rozanov (as D. Chizhevskii calls him) from speaking of Dostoevsky in the same "abusive" style to which he resorted when discussing his ideological opponents.

65 It was, incidentally, Rozanov who first called Ivan Karamazov's composition a "legend."

66 This view is expressed by Viktor Erofeev, with reference to Viktor Shklovskii, in the introductory essay to the collection of Rozanov's works, *Nesovmestimye kontrasty zhitiia*; cf. Rozanov's own opinion: "In 1876 he [Dostoevsky] began publishing his *Diary of a Writer,* creating with it a new, unique, and beautiful form of literary expression which will surely be destined to play a great role in the future, in all troubled periods" (Rozanov, *Nesovmestimye kontrasty zhitiia,* 42).

67 Ibid., 250.

68 Rozanov called Strakhov, who was friends with many and closely linked with prac-

tically all of the Russian literary figures of the last third of the nineteenth century, his "godfather in literature." Rozanov was not only influenced by Strakhov's ideas, he also owed his first literary success to him: it was Strakhov who persuaded him to publish *The Legend of the Grand Inquisitor* and assumed the expenses incurred. Rozanov's essay in memory of Strakhov goes far beyond the boundaries of official obituary both in scope and in content, and represents a moving testimony of friendship and grief. This essay contains another sort of testimony as well—of Rozanov's contradictory attitude toward Soloviev; this time Rozanov (who elsewhere called Soloviev "a chip off the true 'Adversary of Christ'") said that Soloviev and Tolstoi "were the first and earliest in our numb, frozen land to worship the true God; in a society that did not wish to hear His holy name, they pronounced that name loudly" (see Rozanov, *Literaturnye ocherki,* 274).

69 As René Wellek correctly observes, V. V. Rozanov examined "The Legend of the Grand Inquisitor" almost as a sacred text. See "Literary Criticism of Ivanov" in *Vyacheslav Ivanov: Poet, Critic and Philosopher,* 226. Steven Cassedy discusses the theological style of approaches to literary texts in *The Origin of Modern Literary Criticism and Theory.* He suggests that "much of modern criticism is theological not only in its character but in its origin, too" (12). Moreover, he emphasizes that this is particularly true of Russian literary scholarship, where patterns of theological thought traditionally penetrate studies of literature and language.

70 See, for example, ibid., 121 n. °, where Rozanov, retelling the scene of Christ's resurrection of a seven-year-old girl, writes: "One is struck by the lifelike quality Dostoevsky has instilled in this amazing episode. . . . There are certain events in Dostoevsky's biography which might explain to some degree this strange, inconceivable lifelike quality of a fantastic and supernatural scene." He then supports his idea with the story of the birth and swift death of Dostoevsky's first daughter, whose memory, he surmises, may have influenced the "lifelike quality of the episode." (One may add that Dostoevsky also had another, perhaps even more tragic personal experience that may be linked with the creation of this episode in the "Legend"—the death of his youngest son, Alesha, which occurred precisely during the early period of his work on *The Brothers Karamazov.*)

71 See, for example, Rozanov, *Literaturnye ocherki,* 67 n. °, 134 n. °°°°, or 144 n. °°.

72 See, for example, ibid., 124 n. °.

73 See, for example, ibid., 107 n. °, 108 nn. °, °°.

74 See, for example, ibid., 136 n. °, 138 n. °.

75 See, for example, ibid., 59 n. °°, 187 n. °.

76 Vl. Solov'ev, *Stikhotvoreniia, estetika, literaturnaia kritika,* 171.

77 Rozanov, *Nesovmestimye kontrasty zhitiia,* 71.

78 "How can we not see in the words [of Petr Verkhovenskii] 'I intended to give the world to the Pope' the theme of the activity of the theologian and commentator on current affairs Vladimir Soloviev, with his efforts to give Russia spiritually to the Pope, in order that he might receive the physical instrument, the material

force for the restoration of his dominion over a teetering, disorganized world?" (ibid., 209). See also Soloviev's response to a similar charge by Rozanov in his 1894 essay "The End of Argument": "He [Rozanov] has undoubtedly read *The National Question in Russia,* which, among other things, flatly rejects the absurd notion of the assimilation of the Eastern Church by the Western (Latinization), and it is precisely this absurd notion that he attributes to me!" (S., 6:481).

79 See "On *Crime and Punishment*" (1890); the discussion of Dostoevsky in "On the Reasons for the Decline and on the New Trends in Contemporary Russian Literature" (1893); "The Prophet of the Russian Revolution" (1906).

80 It is possible to see an indirect reference to Soloviev in the quoting of his famous poem "Ex Oriente Lux" and in the fact that Merezhkovskii places Soloviev's lines in the context of Dostoevsky's thought: "There arises the same question that so troubled and tormented Dostoevsky: O Rus', v predviden'e vysokom / Ty mysl'iu gordoi zaniata; / Kakim ty khochesh' byt' Vostokom / Vostokom Kserksa il' Khrista? [O Russia, in lofty foresight you entertain a proud thought; what kind of East do you want to be, the East of Xerxes or of Christ?]" (The quotation is not quite exact: Soloviev has "kakim zhe.") Elsewhere Merezhkovskii uses an all-embracing Solovievian metaphor when he calls Russia the boundary between "Xerxes and Christ," a land "of supreme universal and historical polarity, the land of Peter and Pushkin, Tolstoi and Dostoevsky" (Merezhkovskii, *Polnoe sobranie sochinenii* [1914], 10:26).

81 We should, of course, note that even though Soloviev was indeed one of the first to juxtapose Tolstoi and Dostoevsky, this comparison was historically natural and cannot be regarded as Soloviev's particular innovation.

82 Soloviev's italics. Vl. Solov'ev, *Stikhotvoreniia, estetika, literaturnaia kritika,* 170.

83 Merezhkovskii, *Polnoe sobranie sochinenii* (1914), 10:26.

84 Ibid., 9:115.

85 Ibid., 11:34.

86 Ibid., 18:89–171.

87 S., 9:48–49.

88 According to Sergei Soloviev, Vladimir Soloviev, while clearly disapproving of the *Mir iskusstva* circle, made an exception for Merezhkovskii alone and called him "the only truly honorable one among them" (see S. Solov'ev, "Biografiia Vladimira Sergeevicha Solov'eva," 43).

89 Merezhkovskii, *Polnoe sobranie sochinenii,* 9:xi.

90 This raises a question: Could Merezhkovskii's entire conception have been influenced by the figure of the Prince "Antichrist" in the *Three Conversations,* which was created by Soloviev in his polemic with Leo Tolstoi and definitely had the *Count* as its prototype? The attempt to answer this question might bring interesting results, but that is clearly the stuff of another inquiry.

91 See, René Wellek, "Literary criticism of Ivanov," 226–27

92 Ivanov, "O znachenii Vl. Solov'eva v sud'bakh nashego religioznogo soznaniia," 34, 36.

93 Ivanov, *Sobranie sochinenii,* 2:20.

94 Soloviev's ideas were accepted by Ivanov wholeheartedly as a valid foundation for his own creative quest. It is not my task here, however, to list all the evidence, scattered throughout Ivanov's work, of the role Soloviev played in his life. Much has also been written on this topic by his contemporaries; see, for example, the introduction and commentary by Olga Deschartes to Ivanov, *Sobranie sochinenii*, 1:7-228, 3:746-804. Ivanov's formula *a realibus ad realiora*, central to his thought and traceable back to scholastic theology, means the progression from the "lower" level of reality to a "higher," "more real" (in a metaphysical sense) reality.

95 Published in German in 1932, and in English translation in 1952 (*Freedom and the Tragic Life: A Study in Dostoevsky*, trans. Norman Cameron [New York: Noonday Press). A Russian translation has appeared in volume 4 of Ivanov's *Collected Works*.

96 Bakhtin, *Problems of Dostoevsky's Poetics*, 10.

97 Ivanov, *Sobranie sochinenii*, 2:538.

98 S., 6:85.

99 Vl. Solov'ev, *Stikhotvoreniia, estetika, literaturnaia kritika*, 168 (Soloviev's italics). Though the scope of this study does not permit us to delve deeply into Soloviev's treatment of realism in aesthetics, one may cite the opinion of V. Zen'kovskii: "No one among us has written more about (metaphysical) realism in aesthetics than Vladimir Soloviev" (*Istoriia russkoi filosofii*, 2:231).

100 See Ivan Lapshin, "Problema / 'chuzhogo Ia'v noveishei filosofii," *Zhurnal Ministerstva Narodnogo prosveshcheniia* (1909).

101 S., 1:223.

102 Ibid., 222.

103 Ivanov, *Sobranie sochinenii*, 4:502; *Freedom and the Tragic Life*, 26-27; translation changed.

104 Ivanov, *Sobranie sochinenii*, 4:503; *Freedom and the Tragic Life*, 28.

105 Ivanov, *Sobranie sochinenii*, 4:773; see D., 27:65.

106 Ivanov, *Sobranie sochinenii*, 4:433.

107 Bakhtin, *Problems of Dostoevsky's Poetics*, 11, 165.

108 In the following discussion of Bakhtin, I deal almost exclusively with the material in his book *Problems of Dostoevsky's Poetics*. Any additional material from Bakhtin that might be fruitfully examined falls outside the scope of this chapter. One example for future study of Solovievian roots and analogies in Bakhtin is certainly the thesis, fundamental to both men, of the interdependence of creativity and responsibility, that is, of the aesthetic and ethical aspects of being. In his early work *Author and Hero*, Bakhtin expresses a point of view which in essence agrees with Soloviev's position as argued, in particular, in an essay which even today provokes a controversial reaction: *The Fate of Pushkin*. This point of view consists in the fact that "for Bakhtin, creativity and responsibility were inseparable, both part of the 'task' and work of daily life" (see Morson and Emerson, *Mikhail Bakhtin: Creation of a Prosaics*, 41). Certain aspects of the conformity of Bakhtin's positions to those of Soloviev on the question of the correlation between ethics and aesthetics are observed by K. G. Isupov in his

study "On the Aesthetics of Life and the Aesthetics of History: The Traditions of Russian Philosophy in M. M. Bakhtin," in which Isupov asserts that "the principal feature of Bakhtin's philosophy is the coincidence of art and life, which he recognized from the very start" (*M. M. Bakhtin kak filosof*, 68).

109   Morson and Emerson, *Mikhail Bakhtin: Creation of a Prosaics*, 232–33. A bibliography of recent works on Bakhtin also includes such studies as: Clark and Holquist, *Mikhail Bakhtin*; Morson, *Bakhtin: Essays and Dialogues on His Work*; Morson and Emerson, *Rethinking Bakhtin: Extensions and Challenges*; and Todorov, *Mikhail Bakhtin: The Dialogical Principle*.

110   Bakhtin, *Problems of Dostoevsky's Poetics*, 285. On the interpretation of Bakhtin's "theological" pronouncements, see Introduction, n. 48.

111   Vl. Solov'ev, *Stikhotvoreniia, estetika, literaturnaia kritika*, 168.

112   Ibid., 180.

113   Bakhtin, *Problems of Dostoevsky's Poetics*, 6.

114   Ibid., 13.

115   Ibid., 26.

116   Vl. Solov'ev, *Stikhotvoreniia, estetika, literaturnaia kritika*, 175.

117   Bakhtin, *Problems of Dostoevsky's Poetics*, 166.

118   Ibid., 11.

119   As Boris Groys observes, Bakhtin's works abound in hidden references specifically to the Solovievian tradition. (It is worth noting that this scholar believes that Bakhtin "based his conception of the author and authorship on the conception of the figure of the philosopher which evolved in the philosophy of Soloviev" ("Problema avtorstva," 114–15).

120   "Poeziia Ia. P. Polonskogo," in Vl. Solov'ev, *Stikhotvoreniia, estetika, literaturnaia kritika*, 333.

121   S., 2:354–55.

122   S., 6:85.

123   S., 3:189.

124   Todd, "Vladimir Solov'ev's Pushkin Triptych," 254.

125   In this essay Soloviev underlined an ontological essence of the phenomenon of beauty as a transfigurational force by choosing for the epigraph Dostoevsky's words: "The beauty will save the world."

126   S., 6:39–40.

127   It is worth noting Dostoevsky's reference to a diamond in his attempt to describe the creative process to Maikov in 1869: "A poetic work, I think, appears like a virgin precious stone, a diamond, in the poet soul, all ready, in all its essence, and that is the poet's first business *as a creator and maker*, the first part of his creation. If you please, it is not even he who is the creator, but life, the mighty essence of life, the God living and real, concentrating his power in the diversity of creation *here and there*, and most often in a great heart and in a powerful poet, so that if it is not the poet himself who is a creator . . . then at least his soul is that very same mine that begets diamonds and without which it's impossible to find them anywhere" (D., 29[1]:39; *Letters*, 3:160).

128 West, *Russian Symbolism,* 42.

CHAPTER 2

1 *Neizdannyi Dostoevskii,* 331. This letter, to all appearances, accompanied an article that the author was sending or planned to send to Dostoevsky. R. Galtseva and I. Rodnianskaia believe that Soloviev wanted to call Dostoevsky's attention to the abstract of his dissertation "The Crisis of Western Philosophy (Against the Positivists)." (See "Raskol v konservatorakh" in *Neokonservatizm v stranakh Zapada,* part 2: *Sotsial'no-kul'turnye i filosofskie aspekty* [Moscow, 1982], 239.) However, Soloviev's "small experiment" never appeared in the pages of *Grazhdanin* for reasons that remain unknown. In addition to this letter, the following extant letters from Soloviev to Dostoevsky have thus far been published: 23 Dec. 1873, 12 June 1878, and 26 May 1880—see Vl. Solov'ev, *Filosofiia iskusstva i literaturnaia kritika,* 628-29.
2 See Luk'ianov, *O Solov'eve,* 1:125.
3 See D., 29-1:74, 28-2:353, 499.
4 Ibid., 8:172; *The Idiot,* 195.
5 D., 8:179; *The Idiot,* 202.
6 D., 8:191; *The Idiot,* 217; see also D., 9:369, 440.
7 D., 30-1:212, 237, 238.
8 See Vs. Solov'ev, *Vospominaniia o Dostoevskom,* 8-11. See also a letter to Dostoevsky of 31 Jan. 1878—D., 29-1:259; also *F. M. Dostoevskii,* 424-26.
9 Dostoevskaia, *Vospominaniia Dostoevskoi,* 181-82; *Reminiscences,* 223-24. Anna dates Vladimir Soloviev's appearance at their home to 1873: "That winter [1873-74] Vladimir Sergeyevich Soloviev—then still a very young man, who had just completed his education—began coming to visit us." Soloviev took his candidate examinations in June 1873 (see Luk'ianov, *O Solov'eve,* 1:289). He was in Petersburg from the latter half of November 1873 (ibid., 307, 308). Judging by Soloviev's letter to Dostoevsky of 23 Dec. 1873, they had already met one another: "I was planning to stop by to say goodbye to you today. . . . I still hope we see each other; however, I'll be in Petersburg in the autumn" (Vl. Solov'ev, *Filosofiia iskusstva i literaturnaia kritika,* 628). On the other hand, the cited conversation indicates Soloviev's age as twenty-four—that is, 1877, the year of Soloviev's move to Petersburg. Most likely, in recalling Soloviev's visits, Anna was not concerned with chronology.
10 Dostoevskaia, *Dnevnik,* 19.
11 See *F. M. Dostoevskii,* 359.
12 D., 28-1:55; *Letters,* 1:46.
13 See D., 68-69.
14 Mochul'skii, *Dostoevsky: His Life and Work,* 13.
15 See Alekseev, *Rannii drug Dostoevskogo.*
16 S., 7:77. Interestingly, in 1891, that is, three years before the appearance of the separate chapters of *The Justification of the Good,* Leskov "reports" in a

letter to Leo Tolstoi: "I also do not smoke tobacco, but I drink 'ruby wine' (as the deacon Akhilka used to say) in moderation 'for my stomach's sake and mine frequent ailments." (Vladimir Soloviev says that you authorized him to do this)." (Leskov, *Sobranie sochinenii*, 11:494; "for my stomach's sake . . ." is a paraphrase from 1 Tim. 5:23.) From this joking remark one may conclude that Soloviev discussed the moral aspect of drinking with Leo Tolstoi. Other evidence of their polemics on this question reflects far greater disagreement and less deference: "V pechati trepet i zastoi / I novostiami bedno / Broshiuru izdal Lev Tolstoi / O tom, chto p'ianstvo vredno" (There's trembling and stagnation in the press, and very little news; Leo Tolstoi has published a pamphlet that says drunkenness is harmful: Vl. Solov'ev, *Stikhotvoreniia* [1974]: 167); "Otkazat'sia ot vina— / V etom strashnaia vina; / Smelee peite, khristian, / Ne ver'te staroi obez'iane" (To give up wine is a terrible crime; drink freely, Christians, don't believe the old monkey: ibid., 172). The latter epigram became known from a letter Soloviev wrote to Count D. A. Olsuf'ev, in which he also refers to *Three Conversations* (1898-99), a work that devotes considerable space to a critique of Tolstoyism.

17 Vs. Solov'ev, *Dnevnik*, 424; see also Vs. Solov'ev, *Vospominaniia o Dostoevskom*, 9.
18 D., 14:259; *The Brothers Karamazov*, 258-86. Indeed, this motif occurs repeatedly in Dostoevsky's works. For example, in *The Devils* Kirillov tells the chronicler: "You are like my brother, very much, extremely. . . . He has been dead seven years" (D., 10:94; *The Possessed (The Devils)*, 98).
19 S. Solov'ev, *Zhizn' i tvorcheskaia evoliutsiia Vladimira Solov'eva*, 75; A. V. Amfiteatrov also sees "something Stavroginian" in Vladimir Soloviev—see Amfiteatrov, "Vl. S. Solov'ev. Vstrechi," 6.
20 Luk'ianov, *O Solov'eve*, 1:171.
21 Vl. Solov'ev, *Pis'ma*, 3:294.
22 D., 27:48.
23 Vl. Solov'ev, *Pis'ma*, 3:80.
24 Luk'ianov, *O Solov'eve*, 1:260.
25 Vl. Solov'ev, *Pis'ma*, 3:81.
26 Ibid., 56.
27 Dostoevskaia, *Vospominaniia Dostoevskoi*, 180; *Reminiscences*, 221.
28 See Vl. Solov'ev, *Stikhotvoreniia* (1974), 148, 255.
29 *Grazhdanin* 48 (1874).
30 See Luk'ianov, *O Solov'eve*, 1:427.
31 *Perepiska L. N. Tolstogo i N. N. Strakhova*, 85.
32 Vs. Solov'ev, *Vospominaniia*, 27-29.
33 Luk'ianov, *O Solov'eve*, 1:352.
34 Ibid., 382.
35 Vl. Solov'ev, *Pis'ma*, 2:2.
36 It seems that Katia Romanova had cast a truly romantic spell over her cousins: even Vladimir Soloviev's youngest sister, Poliksena (a poet who later wrote under the pseudonym Allegro), was at some point in love with her. According to the

recollections of family friend Ekaterina Lopatina (El'tsova) about their younger days together, "Sena fell quite deeply in love—with yearning, expectation of meetings, declarations and tears—with her female cousin, the same beauty Katia Romanova with whom Volodia himself was once in love" (*Kniga o Vladimire Solov'eve,* 127).

37 In 1878 Bestuzhev-Riumin founded the famous Higher Courses for Women in Petersburg. In 1880, responding to a request from Bestuzhev-Riumin, Soloviev prepared the curriculum in philosophy for the courses and taught this subject to the female students until his abrupt resignation in 1881.

38 See Vladislavlev's article on Soloviev's dissertation in *Zhurnal Ministerstva narodnogo prosveshcheniia,* January 1875: 247–71.

39 See Nechaeva, *Zhurnal M. M. i F. M. Dostoevskikh "Vremia,"* 66.

40 See letter of 6 Nov. 1872—D., 29-1:255.

41 Later Soloviev came to regard Vladislavlev with open hostility. Objective explanations for this are most easily found in the rejection by the liberal community—and in particular the *Vestnik Evropy* circle, to which Soloviev belonged—of, in the first place, the "obscurantism" Vladislavlev displayed in university politics (especially with the adoption in 1884 of a new antiliberal charter), and in the second place, of Vladislavlev's appointment in 1887 as rector of Petersburg University without faculty approval. What is more, Soloviev, who had never been close to Vladislavlev in philosophical orientation, in the late 1880s called into question the quality of his one-time opponent's scholarly achievements. Judging by the reminiscences of Esper Ukhtomskii, Vladislavlev indeed could not be called an outstanding educator: "Vladislavlev was not sympathetic to students' involvement with philosophy proper, he even discouraged them from studying philosophy. . . . His opinion about the students who had shown enthusiasm for Soloviev was unfavorable" (see *Rossiiskii arkhiv,* 394).

42 For a detailed survey of articles in the press devoted to the defense, see Luk'ianov, *O Solov'eve,* vol. 1, chap. 12.

43 Vs. Solov'ev, *Vospominaniia o Dostoevskom,* 16.

44 Stakheev, "Gruppy i portrety," 86. We have no reason to question the authenticity of this story, but nevertheless Dostoevsky's tone and the use of the familiar *ty* in addressing Soloviev are somewhat bewildering.

45 Vl. Solov'ev, *Pis'ma,* 2:337, 185.

46 Luk'ianov, *O Solov'eve,* 3-1:45.

47 Ibid., 2-3:55.

48 Ibid., 154.

49 Ianzhul, "Vospominaniia," 7–8.

50 Anna Dostoevskaia casts doubt on the reliability of Ianzhul's memoirs (see *Vospominaniia Dostoevskoi,* 295). But this may be the result of her negative attitude toward the memoirist.

51 Luk'ianov, *O Solov'eve,* 2-3:88.

52 Vl. Solov'ev, *Pis'ma,* 2:13.

53 Incidentally, for the title of an 1876 poem written during his return from Egypt

to Russia, Soloviev chose a line directly from *Tabula Smaragdina*: "Vis ejus integra si versa fuerit in terram" (Strength shall be indivisible if it turns to earth: S., 12:28); Soloviev quoted this same phrase (in a slightly changed form) more than twenty years later in *The Justification of the Good* (S., 8:275).

54 Shumaker, *The Occult Science in the Renaissance*, 179. In addition, this aspect of Soloviev's poetics can easily be interpreted within the framework of the literary theory of carnivalization proposed by Mikhail Bakhtin.

55 A characteristically Symbolist survey of the literary tradition behind Soloviev's poem can be found in Andrei Belyi's essay "The Apocalypse in Russian Poetry": "The splendor of Fet's pantheism is for Soloviev a cloth beneath which the tragism of Lermontov, purified by means of religion, manifests a series of universal historical symbols.... By illuminating Lermontov's lyricism with universal consciousness, Soloviev must inevitably rip the half-mask from the face of the Unknown Lady-Friend who appeared to Lermontov" (Belyi, *Simvolizm kak miroponimanie*, 414).

56 D., 25:122; *A Writer's Diary*, 967.

57 D., 25:265.

58 *F. M. Dostoevskii*, 62.

59 D., 25:123; *A Writer's Diary*, 968.

60 Vl. Solov'ev, *Sochineniia v dvukh tomakh*, 2:669.

61 B. S., "Iz nedavnego proshlogo," 455.

62 Dostoevskaia, *Vospominaniia Dostoevskoi*, 230; *Reminiscences*, 290.

63 Leont'ev, *Pis'ma k Rozanovu*, 58.

64 Dostoevskaia, *Vospominaniia Dostoevskoi*, 231; *Vospominaniia* (1971), 393; *Reminiscences*, 291.

65 D., 30-1:14, 15; *Letters*, 5:20, 21..

66 S., 3:122.

67 Fedorov, *Sochineniia*, 85.

68 Vl. Solov'ev, *Pis'ma*, 2:347.

69 Dostoevskaia, *Vospominaniia Dostoevskoi*, 232; *Reminiscences*, 292-93.

70 S., 3:197-98.

71 Ibid.

72 D., 15:472.

73 Ibid.

74 S. Solov'ev, *Zhizn' i tvorcheskaia evoliutsiia Vladimira Solov'eva*, 41.

75 D., 14:214; *The Brothers Karamazov*, 235.

76 Peter Moghila was a seventeenth-century metropolitan of Kiev, famed for his *Orthodox Confession*, compiled along the lines of the various systematic Latin catechisms.

77 Koni, *Vospominaniia o pisateliakh*, 550.

78 One of many illustrations of this can be found in a memoir about Soloviev dating from the 1870s, the years of his friendship with Dostoevsky; see *Kniga o Vladimire Solov'eve*, 284.

79 Leskov, *Sobranie sochinenii*, 11:146.

80 *Perepiska L. N. Tolstogo so N. N. Strakhovym*, 111. In Strakhov's letters to Tolstoi,

the name Vladimir Soloviev comes up repeatedly. Yet despite a certain amount of praise of Soloviev, Strakhov's overall tone is such as to make Soloviev's description of him as "my enemy-friend" understandable (see Vl. Solov'ev, *Pis'ma*, 1:130).

81 Dostoevskaia, *Vospominaniia Dostoevskoi*, 257–58; *Reminiscences*, 325–27.

82 See Luk'ianov, *O Solov'eve*, 3:76.

83 That there was a correspondence there is no doubt: see, for example, the colorful description of Soloviev's ritual of reading the letters from his "intended" in the reminiscences of his sister Mariia Bezobrazova (*Kniga o Solov'eve*, 104); see also Radlov's commentary to his publication, in the second volume of *Pis'ma*, of verses by Soloviev extracted "from the papers of S. P. Khitrovo."

84 Sofiia Petrovna Khitrovo, née Bakhmet'eva, was married to Mikhail Aleksandrovich Khitrovo. As Luk'ianov puts it, he was "a brilliant, interesting man, a stately landowner, a diplomat of the old school, who wrote fine poetry, never gave a thought to tomorrow, and was at the same time a great Don Juan. Sofiia Petrovna married him not so much for love as under pressure from her relatives. The couple lived sometimes together, sometimes apart, now getting along, now separating anew. M. A. Khitrovo died shortly after the marriage of their daughter (Veta) [in 1896]." See "Materialy k biografii Vl. Solov'eva," 401.

85 See K. M. El'tsova, "Sny nezdeshnie," in *Kniga o Solov'eve*, 137.

86 Ibid., 107.

87 Bulgakov, *Tikhie dumy*, 94. Compare this statement with a stanza from Blok, who was profoundly influenced by Soloviev: "I mne, kak vsem, vse tot zhe zhrebii / Mereshchitsia v griadushchei mgle: / Opiat'—liubit' Ee na nebe / I izmenit' ei na zemle" (And for me, as for everyone, the same lot appears in the approaching darkness: once again—to love Her in heaven, and betray her on earth). (Blok, *Sobranie sochinenii*, 3:78.)

88 S., 2:v, vii, viii.

89 Dostoevskaia, *Vospominaniia Dostoevskoi*, 253; *Reminiscences*, 321.

90 Vl. Solov'ev, *Pis'ma*, 2:101.

91 D., 30-1:331.

92 Ibid., 148.

93 S., 2:6.

94 D., 30-1:147; *Letters*, 5:187.

95 D., 153; *Letters*, 5:196.

96 D., 155; *Letters*, 5:197–98.

97 D., 156; *Letters*, 5:199.

98 D., 176; *Letters*, 5:226.

99 D., 26:129–31; *A Writer's Diary*, 1271–73.

100 D., 26:148; *A Writer's Diary*, 1294. Marcus C. Levitt believes that Dostoevsky considered Pushkin's ability to "reincarnate" himself in the spirit of other nations literally miraculous, for he understood the nature of Pushkin's genius as Pentecostal: by means of the Holy Spirit, Pushkin—the artist-apostle—is able to "speak in tongues." See *Russian Literary Politics and the Pushkin Celebration of 1889* (Ithaca and London: Cornell University Press, 1989), 134–35.

101 See D., 138-44; also see, for example, the section "Dostoevskii v neizdannoi perepiske sovremennikov" in *F. M. Dostoevskii*.

102 D., 30-1:184.

103 *F. M. Dostoevskii*, 514.

104 Iuliia Fedorovna Abaza, a singer and composer and the wife of the financial minister A. A. Abaza, was a friend of Sofiia Tolstaia and a frequent guest in her salon.

105 *F. M. Dostoevskii*, 509. The edition contains an error: the signature is given as "Sofiia, Iuliia, Vladimir Solov'evy."

106 D., 30-1:187-89; *Letters*, 5:241-43.

107 *F. M. Dostoevskii*, 515.

108 Mochul'skii, *Dostoevskii*, 567.

109 Vl. Solov'ev, *Sochineniia v dvukh tomakh*, 2:288-89.

110 Ibid., 485.

111 S., 3:214.

112 Ibid., 7:316-17.

113 Ibid., 2:401, 412.

114 Mochul'skii, *Vladimir Solov'ev*, 121.

115 Dostoevskaia, *Vospominaniia Dostoevskoi*, 266; *Reminiscences*, 338.

116 Dostoevskaia, *Vospominaniia Dostoevskoi*, 267; *Reminiscences*, 341.

117 See "Materialy k biografii Vl. Solov'eva," 396.

118 Dostoevskaia, *Vospominaniia Dostoevskoi*, 281; *Reminiscences*, 361.

119 Dolinin, *F. M. Dostoevskii v vospominaniiakh sovremennikov*, 2:430. For a detailed description of Dostoevsky's funeral, see *Biografiia, pis'ma i zametki iz zapisnoi knizhki F. M. Dostoevskogo*, 85-101.

120 Vl. Solov'ev, *Stikhotvoreniia, estetika, literaturnaia kritika*, 165.

121 Dostoevskaia, *Vospominaniia Dostoevskoi*, 95; *Reminiscences*, 346n.

122 S., 3:420-21.

123 Vl. Solov'ev, *Pis'ma*, 4:142. Other cultural figures besides Soloviev also spoke out at this time against employing the death penalty on Alexander II's assassins, as well as against the death penalty in general: for example, Leo Tolstoi (see his letter to Alexander III in Tolstoi, *Polnoe sobranie sochinenii*, vol. 63, letter 40).

124 S., 4:149.

125 D., 27:51.

126 Dolinin, *F. M. Dostoevskii, stat'i i materialy*, 2:579.

127 See Sukharev, "K issledovaniiu zhizni i tvorchestva Solov'eva," 147.

128 Mochul'skii, *Vladimir Solov'ev*, 126.

129 S., 3:185.

CHAPTER 3

1 S., 3:221.

2 Trubetskoi, *Mirosozertsanie Solov'eva*, 1:325.

3 S., 3:171.

4 Ibid., 12.

5 Ibid., 36.

6 Ibid., 121.

7 Some critics, for instance, S. Bulgakov, see the idea of "positive unitotality" as "the alpha and omega" of Soloviev's whole philosophy" (see Bulgakov, *Ot marksizma k idealizmu,* 195).

8 S., 3:150.

9 As Robert Jackson observes, "the epilogue, finally, is the transformation of ends into beginnings. . . . On the metaphysical plane of the novel, the prologue, with its act of murder, is really an epilogue, or fall, whereas the formal epilogue serves as a prologue for a new drama and new life" ("Introduction: The Clumsy White Flower," in Jackson, *Twentieth Century Interpretations of Crime and Punishment,* 6).

10 D., 6:322; *Crime and Punishment,* 372.

11 D., 6:322; *Crime and Punishment,* 372.

12 As Edward Wasiolek emphasizes, "the English word 'crime' is exclusively legalistic in connotation and corresponds to the 'human logic'; but the Russian word for crime, *prestuplenie,* carries meanings which point both to human and divine logic. *Prestuplenie* means literally 'overstepping,' and is in form parallel to the English word 'transgression,' although this word no more than 'crime' is adequate to translate *prestuplenie* because of its Biblical connotation" (Wasiolek, *Dostoevsky: The Major Fiction,* 83). In this light it can be said that the semantic spectrum of *prestuplenie* reflects the "progress" of Raskolnikov's "pilgrimage" toward the biblical connotation of his deed during the course of the novel.

13 D., 6:6; *Crime and Punishment,* 8.

14 D., 6:25; *Crime and Punishment,* 30.

15 D., 6:50; *Crime and Punishment,* 60.

16 S., 1:124.

17 D., 7:141.

18 Ibid., 6:322; *Crime and Punishment,* 371-72.

19 D., 6:211; *Crime and Punishment,* 248.

20 It is worth mentioning that Mikolka, a character who misleadingly confesses to the crime committed by Raskolnikov, is a *raskol'nik.* He and Raskolnikov, as Harriet Murav notes, can be seen as doubles, with "Mikolka as true sectarian and Raskolnikov as the false one." See Murav, *Holy Foolishness* (Stanford: Stanford University Press, 1992), 63.

21 D., 6:321; *Crime and Punishment,* 371.

22 D., 6:54; *Crime and Punishment,* 66. Essentially, this devotion to the "service of humanity" is a reflection, even if in extremely groteque form, of the cult humanity (the *Grand Être*) proclaimed by August Comte (though, of course, the positivist philosopher could not have forseen the potential extremism of his sociology).

23 D., 6:116; *Crime and Punishment,* 140.

24 D., 6:378; *Crime and Punishment,* 434.

25 Raskolnikov's aspiration to the roles of Messiah and, at the same time, of Napoleon is noted by V. Ia. Kirpotin in *Razocharovanie i krushenie Rodiona Raskol'nikova*; see also the development of the messianic theme in interpreting Raskolnikov's crime in *The Experience of Time in "Crime and Punishment"* by Leslie A. Johnson.

26 S., 3:196. Soloviev's definition has even deeper meaning if we consider it in the perspective drawn by Jaroslav Pelikan, who points out that for Dostoevsky the sense of sin was "a religious fact. . . . The murder of the old pawnbroker was a sin, but not merely because it was a breach of conventional morality. This made it a crime, not a sin. Raskolnikov's sin was brought on by his egocentricity, his assumption that his position in the universe was so important that he could suspend the existence of another person to advance his own ends" (Pelikan, *Fools for Christ*, 73–74).

27 S., 3:19–20.

28 D., 10:93–94; *The Possessed (The Devils)*, 96–97.

29 D., 10:94; *The Possessed (The Devils)*, 97.

30 D., 24:51; *A Writer's Diary*, 738.

31 D., 11:303.

32 D., 293.

33 D., 308.

34 D., 10:188–89; *The Possessed (The Devils)*, 201–2.

35 S., 1:122.

36 As Gibson comments, Dostoevsky "took over Feuerbach in the warmer Russian style which Belinsky had provided for him. That meant systematically treating statements about God as statements about men" (*The Religion of Dostoevsky*, 10).

37 Later, while working on *The Brothers Karamazov*, Dostoevsky indeed appears to have intended a Faustian reinterpretation of the Gospel verse in the devil's monologue. In his drafts of the eleventh book, Dostoevsky mentions "the Word" several times, probably musing on the devil interpretation of the beginning of the Gospel of St. John. See D., 15:442.

38 Wasiolek, *Dostoevsky: The Major Fiction*, 125.

39 D., 10:37; *The Possessed (The Devils)*, 35.

40 D., 10:182; *The Possessed (The Devils)*, 194.

41 D., 10:514; *The Possessed (The Devils)*, 581.

42 A parallel to this aspect of Stavrogin's character is easily found among the works of E. T. A. Hoffmann. Indeed, there is in Stavrogin's entire demeanor an element of parody on Romanticism.

43 D., 10:165; *The Possessed (The Devils)*, 173.

44 Ibid.

45 D., 10:514; *The Possessed (The Devils)*, 581–82.

46 As is well known, the rape of a minor, to which Stavrogin confesses, also became the subject of speculations concerning Dostoevsky himself, which was provoked by a letter from Strakhov to Tolstoi. A. Amfiteatrov reports Soloviev's opinion on the matter: "I do not believe that it happened, though of course it may have. In

the final years of his life he was in precisely that emotional state where a man does not belong to himself, but is possessed either by God or by the Devil. Either seraphic ecstasy or infernal ecstasy. His enemy, from whom we know the whole story, loved to boast and to fabricate—though never such malicious things. I think the great writer did indeed visit him and confess. But this does not mean that he ever actually did what he confessed to. There exist thoughts that acquire for a man the reality, as it were, of accomplished facts. Not for nothing did Christ say that sexual thoughts are as real a sin as sexual deeds. And I think that it is with just such a thought, one that has created a vivid hallucination, that we are dealing in the present instance" (Amfiteatrov, "Vl. S. Solov'ev. Vstrechi," 8). On the factuality of the accusation, see Jackson, *Dialogues with Dostoevsky*, chap. 5.

47 D., 11:17.

48 Ibid., 208.

49 Ibid., 20.

50 Verkhovenskii speaks, as it were, in the language of Pushkin's Mephistopheles: "I brought her [Liza] to you simply to amuse you, and to show you that you wouldn't have a dull time with me" (D., 10:406; *The Possessed*, 455). Cf.: ". . . then out of boredom, / Like a harlequin, from the fire / You finally summoned me. / I cringed like a petty demon, / I tried to cheer you up" (Pushkin, "Stsena iz Fausta," *Polnoe sobranie sochinenii*, 2:434-35).

51 D., 10:189; *The Possessed (The Devils)*, 202.

52 D., 10:191; *The Possessed (The Devils)*, 204.

53 D., 10:191; *The Possessed (The Devils)*, 210.

54 A candle is one of the few descriptive details mentioned by the author, at the end of the dialogue. Dostoevsky's affinity with Rembrandt has been acknowledged by many scholars. For example, Jacques Catteau, referring to the opinion of Leonid Grossman, writes: "The lighting from one source in many scenes of Dostoevsky's stories and novels is strikingly reminiscent of Rembrandt etchings" (Catteau, *Dostoevsky and the Process of Literary Creation*, 26).

55 D., 10:198; *The Possessed (The Devils)* 211.

56 D., 28-1:176.

57 Ibid., 10:197; *The Possessed (The Devils)*, 211.

58 D., 10:197; *The Possessed (The Devils)*, 210.

59 D., 10:202; *The Possessed (The Devils)*, 216.

60 Ibid.

61 Cf. the above-mentioned motif of sacrifice in Raskolnikov and Kirillov, coupled with the fearlessness (or indifference) of Stavrogin.

62 D., 10:324; *The Possessed (The Devils)*, 356–57.

63 D., 10:326; *The Possessed (The Devils)*, 359–60.

64 D., 10:75; *The Possessed (The Devils)*, 77.

65 D., 10:404; *The Possessed (The Devils)*, 454.

66 D., 10:404; *The Possessed (The Devils)*, 453.

67 D., 10:209; *The Possessed (The Devils)*, 223.

68 Incidentally, the literary tradition of Prutkov (the mythical author of the nonsense

poems invented by Aleksei Tolstoi and the Zhemchuzhnikov brothers) links the parodic verses of Dostoevsky's characters to the jocular and ironic poetry of Vladimir Soloviev.

69 D., 10:209; *The Possessed (The Devils)*, 224.

70 D., 10:214; *The Possessed (The Devils)*, 229.

71 D., 10:429; *The Possessed (The Devils)*, 482.

72 D., 10:205; *The Possessed (The Devils)*, 220.

73 D., 10:37; *The Possessed (The Devils)*, 35.

74 D., 10:231; *The Possessed (The Devils)*, 249.

75 D., 10:513; *The Possessed (The Devils)*, 580.

76 D., 10:407; *The Possessed (The Devils)*, 457.

77 S., 10:161.

78 D., 10:514; *The Possessed (The Devils)*, 581.

79 D., 10:514; *The Possessed (The Devils)*, 582.

80 D., 10:228; *The Possessed (The Devils)*, 246.

81 D., 10:514; *The Possessed (The Devils)*, 580.

82 D., 8:25; *The Idiot*, 26.

83 D., 8:25; *The Idiot*, 25.

84 D., 10:43; *The Possessed (The Devils)*, 41.

85 D., 8:450; *The Idiot*, 518.

86 D., 10:197; *The Possessed (The Devils)*, 197.

87 A. S. Dolinin sees another Gospel association in the story of Marie—with Mary Magdalene; see Dostoevskii, *Pis'ma*, 1:13–14.

88 See D., 9:344–45.

89 D., 246, 249, 253.

90 D., 28-2:251.

91 Ibid.

92 D., 21:11.

93 Vl. Solov'ev, *Stikhotvoreniia* (1974), 130–32.

94 D., 8:207; *The Idiot*, 236.

95 Although we have no documented proof that Soloviev told Dostoevsky about his "vision" in Egypt, it is unlikely that he would have kept silent about it: Soloviev did not hide this event even from people who were far less close to him than Dostoevsky; see, for example, Ianzhul, "Vospominaniia," 488.

96 S., 3:112–13. Cf. Dostoevsky's notes to *The Devils*: "But here there is not even any teaching, only occasional words, while the main thing is the image of Christ from which comes all teaching" (D., 11:192).

97 Bakhtin, *Problems of Dostoevsky's Poetics*, 31.

98 D., 28-2:329; *Letters*, 3:114.

99 See, for example, Gessen, "Bor'ba utopii i avtonomii dobra v mirovozzrenii Dostoevskogo i Solov'eva"; Levitskii, "Vl. Solov'ev i Dostoevskii," 199; Lord, "Dostoevsky and Vladimir Solov'yov"; Maceina, *Der Grossinquisitor*, 14; Radlov, "Solov'ev i Dostoevskii," 158–59; Strémooukhoff, *Vladimir Soloviev and His Messianic Work*, 72–74; and Szylkarski, "W. Solowiew und Dostojewskij," 31–32.

100 Levitskii, "Vl. Solov'ev i Dostoevskii," 203.

101 See D., 15:556–57; *The Brothers Karamazov*, 247–48.

102 D., 14:225–26; *The Brothers Karamazov*, 247–48.

103 D., 14:234; *The Brothers Karamazov*, 257.

104 Rozanov, *Nesovmestimye kontrasty zhitiia*, 125.

105 Rozanov defines in an analogous way "the fulcri in religious contemplation," but his line of thought differs from what I have proposed. See ibid., 111.

106 Berdiaev, *Mirosozertsanie Dostoevskogo*, 65, 74.

107 D., 14:230; *The Brothers Karamazov*, 253.

108 Berdiaev, *Mirosozertsanie Dostoevskogo*, 67.

109 D., 14:236; *The Brothers Karamazov*, 259.

110 Ibid.

111 S., 8:58.

112 D., 14:233; *The Brothers Karamazov*, 256.

113 D., 14:236; *The Brothers Karamazov*, 259.

114 D., 14:238; *The Brothers Karamazov*, 261.

115 Ibid.

116 D., 14:236; *The Brothers Karamazov*, 259.

117 S., 10:217 (my italics).

118 D., 14:236; *The Brothers Karamazov*, 259.

119 Ivan's method of composition recalls Dostoevsky's own writing experience. As he remarks about his early "prehistoric" period in St. Petersburg: "I was continually composing in my mind a novel from Venetian life" (D., 22:27; *A Writer's Diary*, 327).

120 Dolinin, *F. M. Dostoevskii, stat'i i materialy*, 1:170.

121 Dolinin, *Dostoevskii v vospominaniiakh sovremennikov*, 2:170.

122 S., 10:220.

123 Ibid., 88–89.

124 Ibid., 3:165. Besides the traditional sources Soloviev employed in creating his "Tale," we should note material recently discovered by Nikolai Kotrelev, which points to Soloviev's use of a retelling of a mystery play about the Antichrist in the first volume of *The History of the German People from the End of the Middle Ages* by J. Janssen, which Soloviev reviewed for *Pravoslavnoe obozrenie* in 1885. See "Eskhatologiia Vl. Solov'eva" in *Materialy Vtorogo Mezhdunarodnogo simpoziuma po tvorchestvu Vl. Solov'eva*.

125 Trubetskoi, *Mirosozertsanie Solov'eva*, 2:290.

126 S., 10:199.

127 Ibid.

128 S., 10:200. The threefold repetition "He never rose, never rose, never rose!" parodies the canonical exclamation during the Easter service. On the question of parody in the "Tale," see Chap. 4, n. 34.

129 Ibid.

130 Prutskov, *Klassicheskoe nasledie i sovremennost'*, 252.

131 D., 14:237; *The Brothers Karamazov*, 260.

132 It is precisely from an ontological point of view that Soloviev values the idea of superman in Nietzsche, whom otherwise he ironically calls a "superphilologist." Soloviev acknowledged Nietzsche's formulation of the question to be correct: the overcoming of the human element. Granting this, it goes without saying that for him there exists only one "superman"—the God-man Christ, who has shown the "superhuman road," at the end of which lies "complete and decisive victory over death" (S., 9:273).

133 Volzhskii, "Religiozno-nravstvennaia problema u Dostoevskogo."

134 Zen'kovskii, *Istoriia russkoi filosofii*, 2:25.

135 S., 11:309.

136 Losev, *Vladimir Solov'ev i ego vremia*, 210.

137 For a detailed investigation of the aspects of Sophia, see ibid.

138 See, for example, Viacheslav Ivanov's works on Dostoevsky, Sergei Bulgakov's *Russkaia tragediia*, and L. Zander's *Taina dobra*; the female figures in Dostoevsky are similarly treated in Guardini, *L'Univers religieux de Dostoievski*.

139 S., 11:310.

CHAPTER 4

1 S., 1:311–12. Soloviev calls free theosophy "the organic synthesis of theology, philosophy, and empirical science." In the teaching of so-called theosophists, the word *theosophy* has, of course, a different meaning.

2 Ibid., 4:343.

3 Ibid., 337–38. Cf. the three basic principles upon which Dostoevsky's Grand Inquisitor constructs his "theocracy": miracle, mystery, and authority.

4 Ibid., 7:232.

5 S., 4:590.

6 See, for example, Strémooukhoff, *Vladimir Soloviev and His Messianic Work*; d'Herbigny, *Vladimir Soloviev, a Russian Newman*; Mochul'skii, *Vladimir Solov'ev*; and Zen'kovskii, *Istoriia russkoi filosofii*, vol. 2.

7 S., 7:225.

8 Ibid., 3:17.

9 Ibid., 382.

10 Vl. Solov'ev, *Sochineniia v dvukh tomakh* (annotated by N. V. Kotrelev and E. B. Rashkovskii), 1:659.

11 S., 4:105.

12 Ibid., 113.

13 Ibid., 470.

14 Ibid., 488.

15 Ibid., 598.

16 Ibid., 592.

17 Mochul'skii, *Vladimir Solov'ev*, 87.

18 See, for example, chap. 23, *Istoriia i budushchnost' teokratii*.

19 S., 2:119.

20 Trubetskoi, *Mirosozertsanie Solov'eva*, 2:30.

21 Ibid., 18.

22 Ibid., 19-24.

23 Ibid., 23. Bori, discussing the tendency of E. Trubetskoi, Georges Florovsky, and others to believe that "disappointments" include within themselves a progressive renunciation of results achieved earlier and that "all this supposedly led Soloviev to an ultimate rejection of his entire system," reasonably remarks: "'Disappointments' do not necessarily include renunciation" (Bori, "Novoe prochtenie *Trekh razgovorov* i povesti ob antikhriste Vl. Solov'eva," 35.

24 Trubetskoi, *Mirosozertsanie Solov'eva*, 2:21.

25 S., 2:189.

26 Losev, *Vladimir Solov'ev i ego vremia*, 305.

27 Vl. Solov'ev, *Pis'ma*, 4:6.

28 Vl. Solov'ev, *Sochineniia v dvukh tomakh*, 2:631.

29 Vl. Solov'ev, *Filosofiia iskusstva i literaturnaia kritika*, 654.

30 S. Solov'ev, *Zhizn' i tvorcheskaia evoliutsiia Vladimira Solov'eva*, 408.

31 Losev, *Vladimir Solov'ev i ego vremia*, 434.

32 Trubetskoi, *Mirosozertsanie Solov'eva*, 2:33.

33 In Linda Hutcheon's words, "there are probably no trans-historical definitions of parody possible" ("Modern Parody and Bakhtin," in *Rethinking Bakhtin*, 91).

34 Bakhtin, *Problems of Dostoevsky's Poetics*, 127.

35 In Bethea's phrase—see *The Shape of Apocalypse in Modern Russian Fiction*, 113.

36 Bakhtin's utterances on parody vary and require thoughtful interpretation; see Hutcheon, "Modern Parody and Bakhtin." Her objection to the view of parody as practically identical with satire, as seeking to discredit the subject, seems relevant in the case of Soloviev's "Tale of the Antichrist." A promising perspective for further research on the question of parody in the *Three Conversations* would be to analyze Soloviev's "Tale" in the parameters of medieval religious parody (*parodia sacra*): a performance in which sacred stories and themes were the subjects of profanation. For instance, the role of the Mother of God was played by a drunken maiden. Cf. Soloviev's description of the mother of the Antichrist: "His mother, a woman of easy virtue, was very well known to both hemispheres, but too many different men had equal claim to be considered his father." (S., 10:203). According to Olga Freidenberg, "parody is the archaic religious concept of showing the 'second aspect' or 'double' while preserving the full identity of form and content. Moreover the purpose of the religious parody was not to ridicule a lofty subject but "to affirm it with the help of the beneficial element of deception and laughter." (Freidenberg, "Proiskhozhdenie parodii," in *Trudy po znakovym sistemam* [Tartu, 1973], 497).

37 Trubetskoi, *Mirosozertsanie Solov'eva*, 2:35.

38 Krugovoi, "O zhiznennoi drame Vladimira Solov'eva," 255.

39 *Sbornik pervyi o Vladimire Solov'eve*, 123.

40 S., 10:91.

41 Krugovoi, "O zhiznennoi drame Vladimira Solov'eva," 255.

42 As is maintained, in accordance with the antitheocratic interpretation of the philosopher's *"sui generis* testament," in the commentary to the latest edition of Soloviev's works: Vl. Solov'ev, *Sochineniia v dvukh tomakh,* 2:783.

43 S., 10:85.

44 D., 14:16; *The Brothers Karamazov,* 16.

45 Krugovoi, "Khristianstvo Dostoevskogo i russkaia religioznost'," 306.

46 D., 14:57; *The Brothers Karamazov,* 61. Certainly, one has to be aware of the deep ambiguity hidden in Ivan's presentation of the theocratic idea. In this connection W. J. Leatherbarrow observes that "as the novel develops it emerges that Ivan's views on the Church and State have been an ironic preparation for the disclosure of his real views in his unwritten 'poem,' 'The Grand Inquisitor'" (Leatherbarrow, *Fyodor Dostoyevsky: "The Brothers Karamazov,"* 64). See also Lord, "Dostoyevsky and Vladimir Solov'yov," 418.

47 D., 14:57; *The Brothers Karamazov,* 61-62.

48 D., 14:57; *The Brothers Karamazov,* 62.

49 S., 1:268, 269. It is interesting to note a characteristic nuance which eloquently points to the difference in the historical and religious views of the two thinkers: Soloviev speaks of the Roman-Byzantine state, whereas Dostoevsky calls the empire merely Roman.

50 See 2 Cor. 6:15.

51 Ibid., 2:164.

52 Ibid.

53 D., 14:58; *The Brothers Karamazov,* 62-63.

54 Levitskii, "Vl. Solov'ev i Dostoevskii," 201.

55 Belknap, *The Genesis of "The Brothers Karamazov,"* 21.

56 Strémooukhoff, *Vladimir Soloviev and His Messianic Work,* 73.

57 S., 3:197.

58 Ibid., 381.

59 Ibid., 4:601.

60 *Skotoprigonevsk* means literally a stockyard, but here the Russian word *skot* should be interpreted rather as a brute or a beast.

61 S., 4:633; see also *Rossiia i vselenskaia Tserkov',* 11:315-16.

62 D., 14:18, 19, 25; *The Brothers Karamazov,* 18, 19, 26.

63 D., 14:29; *The Brothers Karamazov,* 31.

64 D., 14:259; *The Brothers Karamazov,* 285.

65 D., 14:504; *The Brothers Karamazov,* 558.

66 D., 15:189; *The Brothers Karamazov,* 768.

67 D., 14:63; *The Brothers Karamazov,* 68.

68 D., 14:11; *The Brothers Karamazov,* 11.

69 S. Solov'ev, *Istoriia Rossii s drevneishikh vremen,* 3:277.

70 Ibid., 278.

71 S., 11:316.

72 D., 15:83; *The Brothers Karamazov,* 649.

73 D., 14:77; *The Brothers Karamazov,* 83.

74 Ronald Hingley allegorically links Alesha, Dmitrii, and Ivan to the triad of Soul,

Body, and Mind—an analogy which, being founded on the Platonic tradition, can also be easily correlated to Soloviev's theocratic triad; see Hingley, *The Undiscovered Dostoevsky*, chap. 10. Peter Jones suggests the same allegorical analogy in *Philosophy and the Novel*, 125-26. As Robin Feuer Miller critically observes, "it is a commonplace to discover in the three Karamazov brothers an allegory about spirit, mind, and body or heart" (Miller, *"The Brothers Karamazov": Worlds of the Novel*, 29). Yet, this schematic representation may serve as a point of departure for fruitful interpretations. For example, W. J. Leatherbarrow connects the "fragmented" portrait of the brothers with the Slavophile model of "the integral personality" (an ideal, one may add, which is intrinsically close to Soloviev's thought). See Leatherbarrow, *Fyodor Dostoyevsky: "The Brothers Karamazov,"* 33.

75 D., 14:201; *The Brothers Karamazov*, 220.

76 D., 15:210.

77 Ibid., 250.

78 Ibid., 25:402.

79 Mikhail Bakhtin, tracing the essence of the genre of this tale to the menippea, "but to different varieties of it: to the 'dream satire' and to 'fantastic journeys' containing a utopian element," believes that "what dominates *The Dream of a Ridiculous Man* is not the Christian but the ancient spirit." Bakhtin, *Problems of Dostoevsky's Poetics*, 147, 149.

80 Pomerants, *Otkrytost' bezdne*, 184.

81 D., 25:112, 114; *A Writer's Diary*, 952, 955.

82 S., 2:175.

83 D., 25:112, 114; *A Writer's Diary*, 954.

84 S., 2:321.

85 Florovsky, *The Collected Works*, 11:185.

86 D., 11:21; 13:375.

87 S., 4:633.

88 D., 10:312; *The Possessed (The Devils)*, 344.

89 D., 10:312; *The Possessed (The Devils)*, 344, 345.

90 D., 27:19; *A Writer's Diary*, 1351.

91 Ibid., 5:375.

92 Koni, *Ocherki i vospominaniia*, 212-15.

93 Vl. Solov'ev, *Pis'ma*, 2:104.

94 S., 1:238.

95 Ibid., 227-28.

96 Ibid., 237.

97 See ibid., 3:173-78.

98 Ibid., 2:161.

99 Ibid., 162.

100 In an article by Reinhard Lauth, "On the Question of the Genesis of 'The Legend of the Grand Inquisitor,'" the very possibility of Soloviev's spiritual influence on Dostoevsky is disputed. The author makes reference to early texts by Dostoevsky that in one way or another reflect the idea of the transfer of the three temptations of Christ onto the historical path of Western Christianity, an

idea later embodied in the "Legend" and developed by Soloviev in the *Lectures on God-manhood*. On the basis of this chronology, Lauth, the author of *Die Philosophie Dostojewskis*, not only proclaims Dostoevsky's primacy in this question but even takes an ideological lunge at Soloviev: "In his philosophical outlook Dostoevsky is not in any way indebted to Soloviev, nor could he be indebted to Soloviev for anything, because in his 'profound realism' he far surpassed the idealistic speculations of the Schellingian [that is, Soloviev!]." There is no doubt that the study of the prehistory of the plot is of interest for many reasons. However, the whole complex of ideas of elaborated by Dostoevsky in the "Legend" does not lend itself to valuation on the basis of chronological primacy. See Lauth, "K voprosu o genezise 'Legendy o Velikom Inkvizitore'"; see also Levitskii, "Solov'ev i Dostoevskii," 200. Levitskii's position seems to me the more objective.

101 S., 3:174. Compare this with what Alesha says: "Your Inquisitor doesn't believe in God."

102 D., 14:235; *The Brothers Karamazov*, 257.

103 D., 14:233; *The Brothers Karamazov*, 256.

104 D., 14:231; *The Brothers Karamazov*, 253.

105 D., 14:233; *The Brothers Karamazov*, 256.

106 D., 14:234; *The Brothers Karamazov*, 257.

107 S., 3:16.

108 Ibid.

109 Velichko, *Vladimir Solov'ev: Zhizn' i tvoreniia*, 99.

110 Berdiaev, "Problema Vostoka i Zapada v religioznom soznanii Vl. Solov'eva," 110.

111 D., 27:80.

112 Ibid., 14:58; *The Brothers Karamazov*, 63.

113 Cf. the pride of the intellect in Soloviev's interpretation of Protestantism.

114 D., 25:6-9; *A Writer's Diary*, 812-15.

115 D., 25:8; *A Writer's Diary*, 814.

116 Berdiaev, *Russkaia idea*, 70.

117 D., 26:147; *A Writer's Diary*, 1,294. True, addressing this same idea a few years before, Dostoevsky did not limit its application to national or racial boundaries: ". . . our idea, the union of all the nations of this [Japheth's] tribe, and even further, much further, to Shem and Ham." It is interesting, however, that this statement has an allegorical flavor stemming from the appeal to biblical images, which here sound almost like euphemisms.

118 Gibson, *The Religion of Dostoevsky*, 2. In general, an attempt to prove a distinction between Dostoevsky the artist and Dostoevsky the journalist requires a number of qualifications. As Belknap points out, "Dostoevsky wrote no isolated theoretical works, and the opinions in his letters, fiction, and journalism always contain dialogical adjustments to his reader, his literary persona, or his journalistic opponent" (*The Genesis of "The Brothers Karamazov,"* 11).

119 "The land of holy miracles"—a quotation from Khomiakov's poem *The Dream*.

120 D., 14:210; *The Brothers Karamazov*, 230.

121 D., 13:377; *The Raw Youth*, 464.

122 D., 18:69.

123   Karsavin, "Dostoevskii i katolichestvo," 41.
124   D., 10:197; *The Possessed (The Devils)*, 211.
125   D., 8:450; *The Idiot*, 517.
126   D., 26:139; *A Writer's Diary*, 1284.
127   D., 23:103.
128   Berdiaev, *Mirosozertsanie Dostoevskogo*, 164.
129   D., 13:377; *The Raw Youth*, 465.
130   D., 14:210; *The Brothers Karamazov*, 230.
131   S., 3:178.
132   Berdiaev, *Russkaia idea*, 132.
133   D., 10:200; *The Possessed (The Devils)*, 214.
134   D., 10:199; *The Possessed (The Devils)*, 212-13.
135   D., 10:199; *The Possessed (The Devils)*, 214.
136   Berdiaev, *Mirosozertsanie Dostoevskogo*, 190.
137   Pomerants, *Otkrytost' bezdne*, 189.
138   Radlov, "Solov'ev i Dostoevskii," 168.
139   D., 26:91; *A Writer's Diary*, 1217.
140   Berdiaev, *Mirosozertsanie Dostoevskogo*, 192.
141   S., 4:17.
142   Ibid., 19.
143   Ibid., 7:331.
144   Ibid., 4:49.
145   Ibid.
146   Ibid., 3:120.
147   Ibid., 132.
148   Trubetskoi, *Mirosozertsanie Solov'eva*, 1:457.
149   S. Solov'ev, *Zhizn' i tvorcheskaia evoliutsiia Vladimira Solov'eva*, 256.
150   Later Zagreb turned out to be the only city where a street was named for Soloviev, to honor his ecumenical expectations.
151   S., 5:19.
152   Ibid., 7:134.
153   According to one curious piece of testimony, "Soloviev once mentioned that he would have given much to have but a drop of Jewish blood in his veins." See "Materialy k biografii Vl. Solov'eva," 401.
154   S., 4:159.
155   Vl. Solov'ev, *Sochineniia v dvukh tomakh*, 2:289.
156   Ibid.

CHAPTER 5

1   S., 9:91.
2   Ibid., 1:144.
3   Ibid., 8:204.
4   See Trubetskoi, *Mirosozertsanie Solov'eva*, vol. 2, chaps. 18-23; also, Zen'kovskii,

Istoriia russkoi filosofii, 2:64; Mochul'skii, *Vladimir Solov'ev,* 226; Walicki, *Legal Philosophies of Russian Liberalism,* chap. 3. I shall not elaborate on this polemical issue because it requires an analysis of *The Justification of the Good* which exceeds the parameters of this chapter. However, the vulnerability of Soloviev's opponents is convincingly demonstrated by A. Losev in his study of *The Justificat-ion of the Good* (see *Vladimir Solov'ev i ego vremia,* 261–89) and can, moreover, be illustrated with a flat statement by Soloviev himself: "The independence of moral philosophy within its own sphere does not exclude the inner link of this sphere with the subjects of theoretical philosophy—the study of knowledge and metaphysics" (S., 8:516).

5 S., 8:26.
6 See n. 4 above.
7 Indeed, Dmitrii Merezhkovskii raises a "terrible question": if Dostoevsky "believes in two Gods, God and the Devil, who battle within the hearts of men, it is still unclear who will conquer whom" (Merezhkovskii, *L. Tolstoi i Dostoevskii,* in his *Polnoe sobranie sochinenii,* 12:158).
8 Jackson, *Dostoevsky's Quest for Form,* 40–70.
9 Vladimir Ern, in *Sbornik pervyi o Vladimire Solov'eve,* 137.
10 S., 9:326. One may observe that Soloviev's idea here sheds light on, if it does not solve, the "riddle of beauty" posed by Dostoevsky in his comparison of the "ideal of the Madonna" and the "ideal of Sodom" (D., 14:100; *The Brothers Karamazov,* 108).
11 *Sbornik pervyi o Vladimire Solov'eve,* 86.
12 S., 8:46.
13 Zen'kovskii, *Istoriia russkoi filosofii,* 2:65.
14 D., 14:232; *The Brothers Karamazov,* 255.
15 S., 8:45.
16 Ibid., 10:183, 184, 190.
17 D., 24:48.
18 Ibid., 30-1:14,15.
19 Rozanov, *Nesovmestimye kontrasty zhitiia,* 186.
20 D., 15:110; *The Short Novels of Dostoevsky,* 141–42. An indication of Dostoevsky's possible opponents in his polemic with rationalism is given in V. N. Belopol'skii's study *Dostoevskii i filosofskaia mysl' ego epokhi,* 11–18.
21 D., 5:115; *The Short Novels of Dostoevsky,* 147.
22 See Chap. 3 above.
23 S., 2:32.
24 D., 9:270.
25 In Wasiolek's opinion, "Dostoevsky sees the opposed impulses in Raskolnikov's nature as the signs of two kinds of 'logic' that are basic to the human condition. They correspond to the two poles of his moral dialectic. There is God, and there is the self" (*Dostoevsky: The Major Fiction,* 80).
26 Ibid., 6:43; *Crime and Punishment,* 51–52.
27 There is a hidden irony in the fact that the old woman, who is tied to the idea of

percentages in her financial dealings, herself falls into a percentage which supposedly justifies her death in exchange for the well-being of a hundred others. Dostoevsky even employs the same vocabulary: Raskolnikov reasons that such a percentage must "keep the others fresh," while the student, developing "the very same ideas," speaks of the "fresh young lives" for whose sake the old woman must be killed "without the faintest conscience-prick."

28 Harriet Murav presents another example of Raskolnikov's escape from reality to the abstract world: a replacement of a deceived girl by a notion of percent. But in her line of reasoning Raskolnikov is guided by his attachment to "the seeming neutrality of scientific language—a neutrality, he implies, that belies a series of emotional and moral repositionings. Raskolnikov is obsessed with words, with what he calls the 'new word.' His obsession makes him a particularly sensitive reader of another's language, enabling him to see that scientific language is not value-free. Once the word 'percent' is uttered, the poor girl disappears from view, replaced by a statistic" (*Holy Foolishness*, 58).

29 D., 6:25; *Crime and Punishment*, 29.
30 D., 6:21; *Crime and Punishment*, 25-26.
31 D., 6:166; *Crime and Punishment*, 197.
32 D., 6:177; *Crime and Punishment*, 210.
33 D., 6:147; *Crime and Punishment*, 174.
34 D., 6:422; *Crime and Punishment*, 484.

35 In this symbolic context beauty proves to be a morally neutral category. It acquires ethical definition depending on the "gravitational sphere" of good or evil. It is this quality of beauty that allows us to speak of the aesthetics of evil. And it is with the aid of aesthetic conceptions that the destruction of the boundaries between good and evil inherited by the twentieth century occurred. For this reason, Dostoevsky calls beauty "a dreadful and terrible thing," in contrast to those who saw in the neutrality of beauty the authorization for their own neutrality with respect to good and evil.

36 D., 9:285.
37 Ibid., 8:148; *The Idiot*, 165.
38 D., 8:348; *The Idiot*, 399.
39 D., 8:18; *The Idiot*, 17.
40 D., 8:459; *The Idiot*, 527.
41 D., 8:24; *The Idiot.*, 28.
42 D., 8:192; *The Idiot*, 218.
43 D., 8:6; *The Idiot*, 4-5.
44 D., 8:13; *The Idiot*, 12.
45 D., 8:86; *The Idiot*, 94.
46 D., 8:32; *The Idiot*, 33.
47 D., 8:317; *The Idiot*, 363.
48 S., 1:369.
49 D., 8:354; *The Idiot*, 406.
50 Gibson, *The Religion of Dostoevsky*, 58.

51 D., 8:5.

52 Ibid., 11.

53 Ibid., 13.

54 Ibid., 96.

55 Ibid., 172.

56 Ibid., 174.

57 Ibid., 175.

58 Ibid., 177.

59 Ibid.

60 Ibid.

61 Ibid., 180.

62 Ibid., 194; *The Idiot*, 194.

63 D., 8:192; *The Idiot*, 219.

64 D., 8:380; *The Idiot*, 433.

65 D., 8:32; *The Idiot*, 33.

66 D., 8:195; *The Idiot*, 222.

67 As we know, this work had a profoundly staggering effect on Dostoevsky, prompt-ing the religious experience and interpretation of the idea of the painting reflected in *The Idiot*. According to the reminiscences of Anna Dostoevskaia, during their visit to the Basel museum in 1857, Dostoevsky stood before the picture "as if stunned. . . . His agitated face had the same almost frightened expression that I had noticed more than once during the first moments of an epileptic seizure" (Dostoevskaia, *Vospominaniia Dostoevskoi*, 112; *Reminiscences*, 134; see also D., 9:399).

68 D., 8:182; *The Idiot*, 205-6.

69 D., 8:339; *The Idiot*, 388-89.

70 D., 8:340; *The Idiot*, 390.

71 D., 8:465; *The Idiot*, 534.

72 D., 10:199; *The Possessed (The Devils)*, 212.

73 D., 10:33; *The Possessed (The Devils)*, 29.

74 D., 10:59; *The Possessed (The Devils)*, 59.

75 D., 10:238; *The Possessed (The Devils)*, 258.

76 D., 10:33; *The Possessed (The Devils)*, 29.

77 D., 10:372; *The Possessed (The Devils)*, 415.

78 Catteau, *Dostoevsky and the Process of Literary Creation*, 203.

79 D., 10:373; *The Possessed (The Devils)*, 416-17.

80 Jackson, *The Art of Dostoevsky*, 304

81 *Letters*, 3:324.

82 D., 10:497; Rev. 3:14-17.

83 D., 10:499; *The Possessed (The Devils)*, 563.

84 D., 10:505; *The Possessed (The Devils)*, 570-71.

85 D., 10:180; *The Possessed (The Devils)*, 192.

86 D., 10:470; *The Possessed (The Devils)*, 531.

87 Berdiaev, *Mirosozertsanie Dostoevskogo*, 60.

88 Gessen, "Tragediia dobra v *Brat'iakh Karamazovykh* Dostoevskogo," 358.

89 Golosovker, *Dostoevskii i Kant*, 87.

90 Whether Dostoevsky correctly interpreted Kant is an open question. It is related not only to the confused terminology and other inconveniences that have led even professional philosophers such as Schopenhauer astray in their study of Kant, but also to the fact that Dostoevsky was following a tradition of negative criticism of Kant in Russia. Since the framework of the present study does not allow us to delve deeper into this problem, Dostoevsky's view of Kant must be noted without probing its fairness. In this connection, see A. V. Akhutin's "Sofiia i chert (Kant pered litsom russkoi religioznoi metafiziki)," where the author analyzes from a philosophical standpoint "the idiosyncrasy of Russian thought with regards to Kantian philosophy."

91 Losev, *Vladimir Solov'ev i ego vremia*, 188.

92 S., 10:373.

93 D., 14:76; *The Brothers Karamazov*, 81.

94 Stewart Sutherland rightly observes that Ivan's statement "I accept God" in no way means "I believe in God": "The God whom Ivan accepts is a finite God, he is the god who is the invention of a Euclidean mind, and of whom one *can only* think and talk in anthropomorphic terms" (Sutherland, *Atheism and the Rejection of God*, 36).

95 S., 8:186.

96 Leibniz, *Theodicy*, 136.

97 D., 14:223; *The Brothers Karamazov*, 245.

98 D., 14:215; *The Brothers Karamazov*, 236. Cf. Myshkin's pronouncement: "I do not understand how one can talk to a man and not be happy in loving him" (cited in n. 37 above).

99 D., 24:49; *A Writer's Diary*, 736.

100 D., 14:123; *The Brothers Karamazov*, 134.

101 D., 14:216; *The Brothers Karamazov*, 237.

102 This paradox in Ivan's consciousness is vividly described by Arther Trace: "The irony is that this righteous indignation loses much of its meaning except in a religious context, for if these babies were not creatures with immortal souls, created in the image of God, then there is not much more reason to be horrified at the deaths of these babies than there is of drowning kittens and puppies" (Trace, *Furnace of Doubt*, 95).

103 Bulgakov, "Ivan Karamazov kak filosofskii tip."

104 D., 14:149; *The Brothers Karamazov*, 164. In connection with this formula, "all are guilty for all," it is relevant to recall that a similar resolution to the question of the compatibility of evil with the absolute goodness of God was preached by Joseph de Maistre. According to him, the organic solidarity of all beings permits the suffering of some to serve as a substitute sacrifice, redeeming the sins of the others. But this principle of redemption, bearing the imprint of Catholic casuistries, led de Maistre to a justification of the Inquisition and of capital punishment, both of which are absolutely incompatible with Dostoevsky's thought.

Nevertheless, it appears that this parallel is not accidental, just as it is no accident that Ultramontanism is mentioned in the conversation about Church and state early in the novel. The reflection of de Maistre's views in the historical and philosophical conception of *The Brothers Karamazov* did not slip past Dostoevsky's contemporaries. In the newspaper *Golos*, a piece was printed on 30 May 1879 comparing Dostoevsky to the eighteenth-century French thinker and sharply charging both of them with obscurantism. But this article is of a general nature and points out no concrete intersections. (See D., 15:488.)

105 This organic sense of unity is conveyed exactly in another utterance by Zosima: ". . . all flows and connects; touch it in one place and it echoes at the other end of the world" (D., 14:290; *The Brothers Karamazov*, 319).

106 Apparently, Soloviev had a much more profound "feeling of the Numinous" than of his critics, since he was able to speak about the Good not in its identity with the Holy. On this question, see Pelikan, *Fools for Christ*, as well as Otto, *The Idea of the Holy*.

107 S., 8:229.

108 Ibid., 231.

109 D., 15:82; *The Brothers Karamazov*, 648.

CONCLUSION

1 Ivanov, 4: 403–4. Innokentii Annenskii (1856–1909) was a famous Russian poet, playwright, and literary critic.

2 Eliot, *Notes Toward the Definition of Culture*, 49.

3 Thus, for instance, in a recent article P. Gaidenko criticizes Soloviev's concept of unitotality as it applies to mankind and accuses him of both totalitarianism and utopianism. See *Voprosy literatury* 1994, no. 2:92–103.

4 Lotman, 1:11.

5 This term was introduced by Morson. The present quote is from *Mikhail Bakhtin: Creation of Prosaics*, 28.

6 *Filosofskii slovar'*, 112.

7 Welsch, *Unsere postmoderne Moderne*, 39.

8 See MacIntyre, *After Virtue*, 204.

9 Weinberg, *Dreams of a Final Theory*, 18.

10 *Kniga o Vladimire Solov'eve*, 446.

11 S., 3:213.

12 D., 28-1:54; *Letters*, 1:44.

Bibliography

WORKS OF VLADIMIR SOLOVIEV

Sobranie sochinenii Vladimira Solov'eva. 12 vols. Brussels, 1966, 1970. (All citations of Soloviev's works, unless otherwise indicated, refer to this edition as S.)

Pis'ma Vladimira Sergeevicha Solov'eva. Edited by E. L. Radlov. Vols. 1–3, St. Petersburg, 1908–11; vol. 4, Petrograd, 1923.

Rossiia i vselenskaia Tserkov'. Moscow, 1911.

Stikhotvoreniia. Moscow, 1915.

Stikhotvoreniia. Leningrad, 1974.

Sochineniia v dvukh tomakh. Annotated by N. V. Kotrelev and E. B. Rashkovskii. 2 vols. Moscow, 1989.

Stikhotvoreniia, estetika, literaturnaia kritika. Compiled, with an introduction and commentary, by N. V. Kotrelev. Moscow, 1990.

Filosofiia iskusstva i literaturnaia kritika. Compiled and with an introduction by R. Gal'tseva and I. Rodnianskaia; commentary by A. A. Nosov. Moscow, 1991.

WORKS OF FEDOR DOSTOEVSKY

Polnoe sobranie sochinenii v tridtsati tomakh. Edited by G. M. Fridlender et al. 30

vols. Leningrad, 1972-90. (All citations of Dostoevsky's works, unless otherwise indicated, refer to this edition as D.)

Pis'ma. Edited by A. S. Dolinin. 4 vols. Moscow and Leningrad, 1928-59.

English Translations Used (citations from the translations have been amended for precision when needed):

The Brothers Karamazov. Translated and annotated by Richard Pevear and Larissa Volokhonsky. San Francisco, 1990.

Complete Letters. Edited and translated by David A. Lowe. Ann Arbor, 1988-91.

Crime and Punishment. Translated by Constance Garnett. New York, 1963.

The Idiot. Translated by Constance Garnett. New York, 1953.

The Devils. Translated by Constance Garnett as *The Possessed,* with an introduction by Marc Slonim and including the suppressed chapter, "Stavrogin's Confession," translated by Avrahm Yarmolinsky. New York, 1959.

The Raw Youth. Translated by Constance Garnett. London, 1916.

The Short Novels of Dostoevsky. Translated by Constance Garnett. New York, 1951.

A Writer's Diary. Translated and annotated by Kenneth Lantz. Evanston, Ill., 1994.

OTHER WORKS CITED

Akhutin, A. V. "Sofiia i chert (Kant pered litsom russkoi religioznoi metafiziki)." *Voprosy filosofii* 1990, no. 1: 51-69.

Alekseev, M. P. *Rannii drug Dostoevskogo*. Odessa, 1921.

Amfiteatrov, A. V. "Vl. S. Solov'ev. Vstrechi." *Soglasie* 1991, no. 6: 3-12.

Annenkov, P. V. *Literaturnye vospominaniia*. Moscow, 1989.

B., S. "Iz nedavnego proshlogo." *Russkaia starina,* September 1910.

Bakhtin, M. M. *Estetika slovesnogo tvorchestva*. Moscow, 1986.

———. *Problemy poetiki Dostoevskogo*. Moscow, 1979.

———. *Problems of Dostoevsky's Poetics*. Edited and translated by Caryl Emerson. Minneapolis, 1984.

———. *Toward a Reworking of the Dostoevsky Book*. Appendix 2 in *Problems of Dostoevsky's Poetics*.

Belinskii, V. G. *Sobranie sochinenii*. 9 vols. Moscow, 1982.

Belknap, Robert L. *The Genesis of "The Brothers Karamazov."* Evanston, Ill., 1990.

Belopol'skii, V. N. *Dostoevskii i filosofskaia mysl' ego epokhi*. Rostov, 1987.

Belyi, Andrei. *Simvolizm kak miroponimanie*. Moscow, 1994.

Berdiaev, N. A. *Filosofiia tvorchestva, kul'tury i iskusstva*. 2 vols. Moscow, 1994.

———. *Mirosozertsanie Dostoevskogo*. Paris, 1968.

———. "Problema Vostoka i Zapada v religioznom soznanii Vl. Solov'eva." In *Sbornik pervyi o Vladimire Solov'eve*. Moscow, 1911.

———. *Russkaia idea*. Paris, 1971.

———. "Tragediia i obydennost'." *Voprosy zhizni* 1905, no. 2.

Bethea, D. *The Shape of Apocalypse in Modern Russian Fiction*. Princeton, 1989.

Biografiia, pis'ma i zametki iz zapisnoi knizhki F. M. Dostoevskogo. St. Petersburg, 1883.

Blok, Aleksandr. *Sobranie sochinenii*. 8 vols. Moscow, 1960-63.

Bori, P. C. "Novoe prochtenie *Trekh razgovorov* i povesti ob antikhriste Vl. Solov'eva: Konflikt dvukh universalizmov." *Voprosy filosofii* 1990, no. 9: 27-36.

Bulgakov, S. "Ivan Karamazov kak filosofskii tip." In *F. M. Dostoevsky: 1881-1981*. London, 1981.

———. *Ot marksizma k idealizmu*. St. Petersburg, 1903.

———. *Tikhie dumy*. Moscow, 1918.

Cassedy, Steven. *Flight from Eden*, Berkeley, Calif., 1990.

Catteau, Jacques. *Dostoevsky and the Process of Literary Creation*. Cambridge, 1989.

Chaadaev, P. *Philosophical Works of Peter Chaadaev*. Edited by Raymond T. McNally and Richard Tempest. Boston,1991.

———. *Polnoe sobranie sochinenii i izbrannye pis'ma*. 2 vols. Moscow, 1991.

Chereiskii, L. A. *Pushkin i ego okruzhenie*. Leningrad, 1988.

Clark, Katerina, and Michael Holquist. *Mikhail Bakhtin*. Cambridge, Mass., 1984.

Dobroliubov, N. A. *Literaturnaia kritika v dvukh tomakh*. 2 vols. Leningrad, 1984.

Dolinin, A. S., ed. *F. M. Dostoevskii, stat'i i materialy*. Vol. 1, Petrograd, 1922; vol. 2, Leningrad, 1925.

———. *F. M. Dostoevskii v vospominaniiakh sovremennikov*. 2 vols. Moscow, 1964.

Dostoevskaia, A. G. *Dnevnik A. G. Dostoevskoi 1876 g*. Moscow, 1923.

———. *Vospominaniia A. G. Dostoevskoi*. Edited by L. P. Grossman. Moscow and Leningrad, 1925.

———. *Vospominaniia*. Edited by S. V. Belov and V. A. Tunimanov. Moscow, 1971.

———. *Dostoevsky: Reminiscences*. Translated and edited by Beatrice Stillman. New York, 1975.

Eliot, T. S. *Notes Towards the Definition of Culture*. New York, 1949.

Erofeev, V. "Vera i gumanizm Dostoevskogo." In his *V labirinte prokliatykh voprosov*. Moscow, 1990.

F. M. Dostoevskii. Literaturnoe nasledstvo, vol. 86. Moscow, 1973.

Fedorov, N. F. *Sochineniia*. Moscow, 1982.

Filosofskii slovar'. M., 1913.

Florovsky, Georges. *The Collected Works*. 14 vols. Vaduz, 1989.

Gaidenko, P. "Chelovek i chelovechestvo v uchenii V. S. Solov'eva." *Voprosy literatury* 1994, no. 2: 92-105.

Gessen, S. I. "Bor'ba utopii i avtonomii dobra v mirovozzrenii F. M. Dostoevskogo i Vl. Solov'eva." *Sovremennye zapiski* 46 (1931): 319-51.

———."Tragediia dobra v *Brat'iakh Karamazovykh* Dostoevskogo." In *O Dostoevskom: Sbornik statei*. Moscow, 1990.

Gibson, A. Boyce. *The Religion of Dostoevsky*. London, 1973.

Golosovker, Ia. E. *Dostoevskii i Kant*. Moscow, 1963.

Grigorian, M. *Iz istorii russkoi filosofii*. Moscow, 1958.

Grigorovich, D. V. *Literaturnye vospominaniia*. Moscow, 1961.

Guardini, R. *L'Univers religieux de Dostoievski*. Paris, 1947.

Herbigny, Michel d'. *Vladimir Soloviev: A Russian Newman*. Translated by A. M. Buchanan. London, 1918.

Hingley, Ronald. *The Undiscovered Dostoevsky*. London, 1962.

Hutcheon, Linda. "Modern Parody and Bakhtin." in Gary Saul Morson and Caryl Emerson, eds., *Rethinking Bakhtin: Extensions and Challenges*. Evanston, Ill., 1989.

Ianzhul, I. I. "Vospominaniia I. I. Ianzhula." *Russkaia starina* 141 (1910): 133-48, 271-306, 475-507.

Isupov, K. G. "Ob estetike zhizni i estetike istorii (traditsii russkoi filosofii u M. M. Bakhtina)." In *M. M. Bakhtin kak filosof*. Moscow, 1992.

"Iz perepiski N. A. Berdiaeva, S. N. Bulgakova i L. I. Shestova." *Mosty* 1961, no. 8.

Ivanov, Viacheslav. "O znachenii Vl. Solov'eva v sud'bakh nashego religioznogo soznaniia." In *Sbornik pervyi o Vladimire Solov'eve*. Moscow, 1911.

———. *Sobranie sochinenii*. Edited by Olga Deschartes and D. V. Ivanov. 4 vols. Brussels, 1971-87.

Jackson, Robert Louis. *Dialogues with Dostoevsky*. Stanford, 1993.

———. *Dostoevsky's Quest for Form: A Study of His Philosophy of Art*. Bloomington, Ind., 1978.

Jackson, Robert Louis, comp. *Twentieth Century Interpretations of Crime and Punishment: A Collection of Critical Essays*. Englewood Cliffs, N.J., 1974.

Jones, Peter. *Philosophy and the Novel*. Oxford, 1975.

John of Damascus, St. *On the Divine Images*. Translated by David Anderson. Crestwood, N.Y., 1980.

Johnson, Leslie A. *The Experience of Time in "Crime and Punishment."* Columbus, Ohio, 1985.

Karsavin, L. "Dostoevskii i katolichestvo." In *F. M. Dostoevskii, stat'i i materialy*, ed. A. S. Dolinin. Vol. 1. Petrograd, 1922.

Khomiakov, A. S. *Polnoe sobranie sochinenii*. 8 vols. Moscow, 1900-1907.

Kireevskii, I. V. *Polnoe sobranie sochinenii*. 2 vols. Moscow, 1911.

Kirpotin, V. Ia. *Razocharovanie i krushenie Rodiona Raskol'nikova*. Moscow, 1990.

Kniga o Vladimire Solov'eve. Moscow, 1991.

Koni, A. F. *Ocherki i vospominaniia*. St. Petersburg, 1906.

———. *Vospominaniia o pisateliakh*. Moscow, 1989.

Krugovoi, G. "Khristianstvo Dostoevskogo i russkaia religioznost'." *Mosty* 1956, no. 1.

———. "O zhiznennoi drame Vladimira Solov'eva." *Mosty* 1961, no. 9: 244-57.

Lauth, Reinhard. *Die Philosophie Dostojewskis*. Munich, 1950.

———. "K voprosu o genezise 'Legendy o Velikom Inkvizitore.'" *Voprosy filosofii* 1990, no. 1: 70-76.

Leatherbarrow, W. J. *Fyodor Dostoyevsky: "The Brothers Karamazov."* Cambridge, 1992.

Leibniz, G. W. *Theodicy: Essays on the Goodness of God, the Freedom of Man, and the Origin of Evil*. Translated by E. M. Huggard. London, 1952.

Leont'ev, K. N. "O vsemirnoi liubvi, po povodu rechi F. M. Dostoevskogo na Pushkinskom prazdnike." In *O Dostoevskom*. Moscow, 1990.

———. *Pis'ma k Vasiliiu Rozanovu*. London, 1981.

Leskov, N. S. *Sobranie sochinenii*. 11 vols. Moscow, 1956–58.

Levitskii, S. "Vl. Solov'ev i Dostoevskii." *Novyi zhurnal* 41 (1955): 197–209.

Lopatin, L. "Filosofskoe mirosozertsanie V. S. Solov'eva." *Voprosy filosofii i psikhologii* 1901, no. 1: 45–91.

Lord, R. "Dostoyevsky and Vladimir Solov'yov." *Slavonic Review* 42 (1964): 415–26.

Losev, A. F. *Vladimir Solov'ev i ego vremia*. Moscow, 1990.

Lotman, Yu. M. *Izbrannye stat'i v trekh tomakh*. Tallinn, 1992.

Luk'ianov, S. M. *O Vl. S. Solov'eve v ego molodye gody: Materialy k biografii*. 3 vols. Moscow, 1990.

Maceina, Antanas. *Der Grossinquisitor*. Heidelberg, 1952.

MacIntyre, Alasdair. *After Virtue*. Notre Dame, Ind., 1984.

"Materialy k biografii Vl. Solov'eva (Iz arkhiva S.M.Luk'ianova)." *Rossiiskii arkhiv*, vols. 2–3. Moscow, 1992.

Materialy Vtorogo Mezhdunarodnogo simpoziuma po tvorchestvu Vl. Solov'eva. Moscow, 1993.

Merezhkovskii, D. *Polnoe sobranie sochinenii*. 24 vols. Moscow, 1914.

Mikhailovskii, N. K. *Literaturno-kriticheskie stat'i*. Moscow, 1957.

Miller, Robin Feuer. *"The Brothers Karamazov": Worlds of the Novel*. New York, 1992.

Mochul'skii, Konstantin. *Dostoevsky: His Life and Work*. Princeton, 1967.

———. *Vladimir Solov'ev*. Paris, 1936.

Morson, Gary Saul, ed. *Bakhtin: Essays and Dialogues on His Work*. Chicago, 1986.

Morson, Gary Saul, and Caryl Emerson. *Mikhail Bakhtin: Creation of a Prosaics*. Stanford, 1990.

Morson, Gary Saul, and Caryl Emerson, eds. *Rethinking Bakhtin: Extensions and Challenges*. Evanston, Ill., 1989.

Murav, Harriet. *Holy Foolishness*. Stanford, Calif., 1992.

Nechaeva, V. S. *Zhurnal M. M. i F. M. Dostoevskikh "Vremia."* Moscow, 1972.

Neizdannyi Dostoevskii. Literaturnoe nasledstvo, vol. 83. Moscow, 1971.

Novikov, Nikolai. *Izbrannye sochineniia*. Moscow and Leningrad, 1951.

O Dostoevskom: Sbornik statei. Moscow, 1990.

Odoevskii, V. F. *Sochineniia v dvukh tomakh*. 2 vols. Moscow, 1981.

Otto, Rudolf. *The Idea of the Holy*. London, 1957.

Panaev, I. I. *Literaturnye vospominaniia*. Moscow, 1950.

Pelikan, Jaroslav. *Fools for Christ*. Philadelphia, 1955.

Perepiska L. N. Tolstogo so N. N. Strakhovym. St. Petersburg, 1913.

Perlina, Nina. "Ivan Aksakov's and Nikolai Straxov's Correspondence." *Russian Language Journal* 114 (1979): 137–88.

Pisarev, D. I. *Sochineniia v chetyrekh tomakh*. 4 vols. Moscow, 1956.

Pomerants, G. *Otkrytost' bezdne*. Moscow, 1990.

Prutskov, N. I. *Klassicheskoe nasledie i sovremennost'*. Leningrad, 1988.

Pushkin, Aleksandr. *Polnoe sobranie sochinenii*. 17 vols. 1937–59.

Radlov, E. "Solov'ev i Dostoevskii." In *F. M. Dostoevskii, stat'i i materialy*, ed. A. S. Dolinin. Vol. 1. Petrograd, 1922.

———. *Vladimir Solov'ev: Zhizn' i uchenie*. St. Petersburg, 1913.

Raeff, Mark. *Russian Intellectual History*. New York, 1966.

Rozanov, V. V. *Literaturnye ocherki*. St. Petersburg, 1899.

―――. *Nesovmestimye kontrasty zhitiia*. Moscow, 1990.

Seduro, V. *Dostoevsky in Russian Literary Criticism, 1846-1956*. New York, 1957.

Sbornik pervyi o Vladimire Solov'eve. Moscow, 1911.

Shestov, L. *Dostoevskii i Nitsshe*. Paris, 1971.

―――. *Umozrenie i otkrovenie*. Paris, 1964.

Shumaker, W. *The Occult Science in the Renaissance*. Berkeley, Calif., 1979.

Solov'ev, S. M. *Istoriia Rossii s drevneishikh vremen*. 18 vols. Moscow, 1988.

Solov'ev, S. M. "Biografiia Vladimira Sergeevicha Solov'eva." In Vl. S. Solov'ev. *Stikhotvoreniia*. Moscow, 1915.

―――. *Zhizn' i tvorcheskaia evoliutsiia Vladimira Solov'eva*. Brussels, 1977.

Solov'ev, Vs. S. *Dnevnik*. Literaturnoe nasledstvo, vol. 86. Moscow, 1973.

―――. *Vospominaniia o F. M. Dostoevskom*. St. Petersburg, 1881.

Stakheev, D. I. "Gruppy i portrety." *Istoricheskii vestnik,* January 1907.

Strémooukhoff, D. *Vladimir Soloviev and His Messianic Work*. Translated by Elizabeth Meyendorff; edited by Phillip Guilbeau and Heather Elise MacGregor. Belmont, Mass., 1980.

Sukharev, Iu. N. "K issledovaniiu zhizni i tvorchestva Vl. S. Solov'eva." *Voprosy filosofii* 1991, no. 2: 136-50.

Sutherland, Stewart. *Atheism and the Rejection of God: Contemporary Philosophy and "The Brothers Karamazov."* Oxford, 1977.

Todd, William Mills, III. "Vladimir Solov'ev's Pushkin Triptych: Toward a Modern Reading of the Lyrics." In *Cultural Mythologies of Russian Modernism*. Berkeley, Calif., 1992.

Todorov, Tzvetan. *Mikhail Bakhtin: The Dialogical Principle*. Minneapolis, 1984.

Tolstoi, L. N. *Polnoe sobranie sochinenii*. 90 vols. Moscow, 1935-58.

Trace, Arther. *Furnace of Doubt*. Peru, Ill., 1988.

Trubetskoi, E. N. *Mirosozertsanie Vl. S. Solov'eva*. 2 vols. Moscow, 1913.

Velichko, V. L. *Vladimir Solov'ev: Zhizn' i tvoreniia*. St. Petersburg, 1904.

Vladislavlev, M.I. "'Krizis zapadnoi filosofii protiv pozitivistov', Vladimira Solov'eva." *Zhurnal Ministerstva Narodnogo Prosveshcheniia,* January 1875: 247-71.

Volzhskii, A. S. "Religiozno-nravstvennaia problema u Dostoevskogo." *Mir Bozhii* 1905, no. 8: 25-40.

Walicki, Andrzej. *The Slavophile Controversy: History of a Conservative Utopia in Nineteenth-Century Russian Thought*. Oxford, 1975.

―――. *Legal Philosophies of Russian Liberalism*. Oxford, 1987.

Wasiolek, Edward. *Dostoevsky: The Major Fiction*. Cambridge, Mass., 1964.

Weinberg, Steven. *Dreams of a Final Theory*. New York, 1992.

Wellek, René. "Literary Criticism of Ivanov." In *Vyacheslav Ivanov: Poet, Critic and Philosopher*. New Haven, 1986.

Welsch, Wolfgang. *Unsere postmoderne Moderne*. Weinheim, 1987.

West, James. *Russian Symbolism*. London, 1970.

Zen'kovskii, V. V. *Istoriia russkoi filosofii*. 2d ed. 2 vols. Paris, 1989.

Index